Jean-Baptiste Morin

Astrologia Gallica
Book Twenty-Five

The Universal Constitutions
of the Caelum

Translated from the Latin
by
James Herschel Holden, M.A.
Fellow of the American Federation
of Astrologers

Copyright 2008 by James Herschel Holden

No part of this book may be reproduced or transcribed in any form or by any means, electronic or mechanical, including photocopying or recording, or by any information storage and retrieval system without written permission from the author and publisher, except in the case of brief quotations embodied in critical reviews and articles. Requests and inquiries may be mailed to: American Federation of Astrologers, Inc., Tempe, AZ 85283.

First Printing 2008

ISBN-10: 0-86690-584-7
ISBN-13: 978-0-86690-584-8

Published by:
American Federation of Astrologers, Inc.
6535 S. Rural Road
Tempe, AZ 85283

Printed in the United States of America.

This book is dedicated to:

Kris Brandt Riske

Table of Contents

Translator's Preface	ix

Book Twenty-Five
Part I.

Chapter 1. What is the Doctrine of the Universal Constitutions of the *Caelum*	1
Chapter 2. The Universal Mode of Action of the Celestial Bodies	14
Chapter 3. The Subordination and Dependency of Universal Constitutions	20
Chapter 4. How the Annual Revolution of the World should be erected for any Place on Earth, as well as the figures of the Quarters of that Year	30
Chapter 5. The Radical and Synodic Revolutions of the Planets and their Syzygies	37
Chapter 6. How Should the Figures of the Synods of the Sun and the Moon be erected	49
Chapter 7. The Eclipses of the Lights and what should be particularly observed about them	53
Chapter 8. The Grand Conjunctions of Saturn, Mars, and Jupiter	61
Chapter 9. How the Rulers of Universal Constitutions should generally be chosen	65
Chapter 10. The Application of what was just said, and the Election of Rulers in the Figures shown above	75
Chapter 11. Which Places on Earth a Universal Constitution may be acting upon	80
Chapter 12. The Times of the Events that will occur from the Universal Constitutions	85
Chapter 13. The Quantity of Effects emanating from Universal Constitutions	100
Chapter 14. The Quality of the Effects of Universal Constitutions in general	101

Chapter 15. Some particular things that should be noted   105
 about the Nature and the Actions of the Planets
 in Universal and Particular Constitutions

Part II.

Chapter 1. In which some important things are mentioned   108
 first about the kinds of Effects emanating from
 Universal Constitutions, or are taught about the
 kinds of Prediction

Chapter 2. The Difference between the Periodical and   121
 Synodic Revolutions of the Planets as regards their
 Efficiency

Chapter 3. The Kinds or Types of Effects emanating   123
 from Universal Constitutions. And first, the Effects
 of the Mundane Revolution of the Sun

Chapter 4. The special Effects of the Planets that are   126
 Rulers of the Year, resulting from their Nature

Chapter 5. The special Effects of the Rulers of the Year   137
 [that result] from their own Celestial State. And first,
 by reason of the Sign in which they are posited

Chapter 6. The special Effects of the Planets that are   144
 Rulers of the Year by reason of their Connection
 with other Planets or Fixed Stars

Table of the Mansions of the Moon   154

Chapter 7. The special Effects of the Planets that are   155
 Rulers of the Year, from their Position in relation
 to the Sun and the Moon

Chapter 8. The Special effects of the Planets that are   164
 Rulers of the Year from the Mode of their Motion

Chapter 9. The special Effects of the Planets that are   168
 Rulers of the Year due to their Terrestrial State,
 or their Position with respect to the Horizon

Chapter 10. The Effects of the Quarters of the Mundane   171
 Revolution of the Sun

Chapter 11. The Effects of the Synodic Revolution of the   175
 Sun and the Moon and its Quarters

Chapter 12. The Synodic Revolutions of the Planets, 184
 both among Themselves and with the Lights, their
 Quarters, and their Effects
Chapter 13. The Order of Subordination of the Universal 191
 Constitutions of the *Caelum* and the Mixture of their
 Effects
Chapter 14. The Dependence of the particular Constitutions 194
 of Nativities on the Universal Constitutions already
 discussed; and how they act upon individual Natives
 during their Lifetime.
Chapter 15. The general and particular Significations 203
 of Comets
Chapter 16. How the daily Effects of the Stars on these 207
 Sublunar Things should be predicted
Appendix 1. The Method of Offusius as revised by Morin 217
Appendix 2. World War II Charts 221
Appendix 3. Aries Ingresses for 1914 227
Appendix 4. Table of the Equation of Time 229
Appendix 5. The Mansions of the Moon for the Year 2000 231
Index of Persons 233
Bibliography 237

Translator's Preface

J. B. Morin, M.D. (1583-1656) worked for 30 years on his massive *Astrologia Gallica* [French Astrology] but did not live to see it in print. Its posthumous publication at The Hague in 1661 was subsidized by Queen Marie Louise of Poland (1611-1667), a grateful former client. The main text of the *Astrologia Gallica* fills 784 double-columned folio pages. It has approximately 548,000 Latin words, which translated into English would amount to approximately 995,000 words—a truly massive book! By way of comparison, the English Bible, contains about 775,000 words. The *Astrologia Gallica* is divided into 26 books. The first 12 are mainly concerned with philosophical and religious considerations. Books 13-26 cover the several branches of astrology in great detail.

Since the *Astrologia Gallica* is so extensive, it has never been fully translated into any modern language. After 240 years, Book 21 on Determinations was translated into French[1] by the French revival astrologer Henri Selva (1861-1952). This was the book that first called the modern astrological public's attention to the Morin method. In effect, it launched the modern study of the Morin method of interpretation. Nothing more appeared until 1941, when Jean Hieroz (b. 1889) published a manual on the Morin method of horoscope interpretation,[2] and in that same year he published a translation of the latter half of Book 26 on Horary Astrology and Elections, followed in 1943 by a compilation of short biographical passages from the AG under the title *Ma vie devant les astres* (My Life before the Stars), and in 1946 he published what he called a

---

[1] *La Théorie des Déterminations Astrologiques de Morin De Villefranche*, trans. by Henri Selva (Paris, 1897; repr. by Bodin, 1902) and repr. in facsimile (Paris: Éditions Traditionelles, 1976 ; repr. 1991).

[2] *L'Astrologie selon J-B Morin de Villefranche*. 'Astrology According to J.B. Morin of Villefranche' (Paris: Payot, 1941.).

complete French translation of Book 25. Hieroz was a well-known French astrologer who had studied with Selva.

The first English translations from the *Astrologia Gallica* were published in 1974, when two independent translations of Book 21 appeared.[1] Then, after another 20 years, more English translations began to appear. First, Book 22 on Primary Directions (with excerpts from Books 2, 13, 15, 17, 18, 20, 23, and 24),[2] followed by Book 23 on Revolutions,[3] Book 18 on the Strengths of the Planets,[4] Book 24 on Progressions and Transits,[5] Books 13-15 and Book 19,[6] Book 16 on Rays and Aspects, and Book 17 on the Astrological Houses.[7] So far as I am aware, no other parts of the *Astrologia Gallica* have been published in English.

The French translations of Books 21 on Determinations, Book 25 on Mundane Astrology, and the latter portion of Book 26 dealing with Elections may still be available in reprints.[8]

---

[1] *Astrosynthesis/ The Rational System of Horoscope Interpretation/ according to Morin de Villefranche*, translated from Selva's French version by Lucy Little (New York: Zoltan Mason, 1974); and *The Morinus System of Horoscope Interpretation*, trans. from the original Latin by Richard S. Baldwin (Washington: A.F.A., Inc., 1974).

[2] *Astrologia Gallica/Book Twenty-Two/Directions*, translated by James Herschel Holden (Tempe, Az.: A.F.A., Inc., 1994).

[3] *Astrologia Gallica/ Book Twenty-Three/ Revolutions*, translated by James Herschel Holden (Tempe, Az.: A.F.A., Inc., 2002; reprinted with revisions 2004).

[4] *Astrologia Gallica/ Book Eighteen The Strengths of the Planets*, translated from the Spanish version of Pepita Sanchís Llacer by Anthony Louis LaBruzza (Tempe, Az.: A.F.A., Inc. 2004)

[5] *Astrologia Gallica/ Book Twenty-Four/Progressions and Transits*, translated by James Herschel Holden (Tempe, Az.: A.F.A., Inc., 2005).

[6] Published in an omnibus edition, translated by James Herschel Holden (Tempe, Az.: A.F.A., Inc., 2006).

[7] Published in individual volumes, translated by James Herschel Holden (Tempe, Az.: A.F.A. Inc., 2008).

[8] *L'astrologie mondiale et météorologique de Morin de Villefranche, traduction intégrale du XXVe Livre de L'Astrologie Gallica* trans. by Jean Hieroz (Paris: Les Éditions Leymarie,1946) and *La doctrine des élections* de Morin, trans. by Jean Hieroz (Nice: Les Cahiers Astrologiques, 1941).

Despite Hieroz's assertion, his translation of Book 25 is not complete,[1] and it often resorts to paraphrase and to his own explanations interpolated into the translation. However, I have sometimes benefited from his rendering of the Latin. At the end of his translation he has added a Summary of Morin's rules, his account of Offusius's rules, examples of the application of Morin's rules to predicting the outbreak of World War II, and Morin's Tables for calculating Solar returns.

At the end of my translation, I have added translations of Hieroz's statement of Offusius's rules, and his discussion of the World War II charts. I have also added a few Mundane charts for the year 1914 as a convenience to students, an appendix containing a Table of the Equation of Time, an Index of Persons, and a Bibliography.

In 1996, having temporarily mislaid my photocopy of the *Astrologia Gallica*, I translated Hieroz's French version of Book 25 and its appendices, and at the request of Kris Brandt Riske, Librarian of the American Federation of Astrologers, I later supplied some excerpts from my translation. These dealt mainly with the prediction of the weather. I had originally intended to publish my English version of Hieroz's French translation, but a decade later on comparing it with the Latin text, and noticing the numerous discrepancies mentioned above, I decided to translate Book 25 directly from the Latin original, and that is what you have here.

Some Remarks about Book 25

It might be helpful to the reader who is not familiar with the *Astrologia Gallica* to mention that Morin makes frequent use of some of his own technical terms, in particular the term *determinations*. This term describes his theory of the facets of a person's life

---

[1]It is in fact an abbreviated translation. For example, he begins by omitting Morin's Preface to Book 25 and continues by skipping more than half of Chapter 1. Throughout the remainder of the translation there are frequent omissions of passages that Hieroz evidently thought were unimportant—I estimate that he has omitted 20% of the text of Book 25.

xi

or the field of activity in which a Planet will be active in a particular horoscope or mundane chart. The main criterion is the house position of the planet, e.g. a planet in the 2nd house is primarily *determined* to money matters, but its house rulerships, and its aspects to other Planets also have an influence.

Two other distinctive terms are *celestial state* and *terrestrial state*. *Celestial state* describes the universal influences arising from a Planet's sign position and its aspects; these influences are viewed as being descriptive of the planet's potential influence at a given moment. *Terrestrial state* refers to a Planet's house position in a particular chart, which establishes the *determination* and also the strength of the planet, which depends on the house's relationship to the angles—angular houses being strong, succedent houses middling, and cadent houses weak.

Morin also consistently uses the older term *revolution* where we would speak of *ingresses* or solar or lunar or planetary *returns*, and he uses the word *universal* where we would use *mundane*. In this book he very frequently uses the term *universal constitution*, which means what we would call a *mundane* chart, i.e. a chart drawn to make predictions for a region rather than for an individual—the commonest example is the annual Aries Ingress chart, but the chart of a Mars-Saturn conjunction would be another example. And occasionally he uses the term *constitution* to refer to a natal chart.

He also frequently speaks of *synods*, i.e. conjunctions, and *syzygies*, which can be either conjunctions or oppositions (and sometimes squares or even trines). I have usually retained these terms. And I have also kept the Latin word *Caelum* to refer to the configuration of the celestial sphere at a given moment, rather than translate it as *sky* or *heaven*.

It is perhaps worth mentioning that while Morin's theory of interpreting Aries Ingress charts seems sound, his own experience with such charts is now known to have been misleading. The

Rudolphine Tables that became available in 1627 had a cyclic error in the Sun's longitude that amounted to about 0°07'30" at the equinoxes (but only about 0°00'20" at the solstices). This caused the tabular time of an Aries Ingress to be about 3 hours early and the tabular time of the Libra Ingress to be about 3 hours late, while the times of the Cancer and Capricorn Ingresses were only off by 10 or 15 minutes.

Hence, every single Aries Ingress chart that Morin (or any other astrologer of his day) ever drew and considered was 3 hours off and consequently had the wrong ASC and MC (as well as the wrong house positions)!

In Part I, Chapter 2, Morin gives a table of the times of the Solar Ingresses for the year 1600 as calculated from the *Rudolphine Tables*.[1] They are shown in the following table with the times reduced to Greenwich, the solar longitudes calculated for those times from modern theory, and the error of the older tables in the time of the Ingress in hours and minutes.

	Uraniborg LMT	Greenwich UT	Longitude	Time Error
♈ Ingress	20 Mar 1600 06:31:50 AM	05:41:02	359°52.5	-3:03
♋ Ingress	21 Jun 1600 10:31:16 AM	09:40:28	89°59.6	-0:11
♎ Ingress	23 Sep 1600 0:53:32 AM	00:02:44	180°07.0	+2:49
♑ Ingress	21 Dec 1600 11:26:20 AM	10:35:32	269°59.5	-0:14

Prior to 1617, when Kepler began to publish ephemerides that probably anticipated the positions (at least for the Sun) that could later be calculated from his *Rudolphine Tables*, the available ephemerides were even more in error. The sad truth is that no Aries

---

[1] They seem to have been calculated fairly accurately. If we calculate the Sun's position from the *Rudolphine Tables* for the times given by Morin, we find 0°00.7, 90°00.0, 179°59.4, and 269°59.9 respectively.

xiii

Ingress calculated by any astrologer anywhere before that time was accurate, because the astronomers had been unable to produce ephemerides of the Sun that were accurate to within 1 minute of arc.[1] Astrologers had almost universally trusted the tables and ephemerides prepared by astronomers, and the astronomers had let them down with their faulty solar theories!

James Herschel Holden
August 15, 2007

---

[1] The ephemerides published by the French government achieved this accuracy from about 1710 onward. By the end of the 18th century the French, German, and English government ephemerides gave solar positions that had a maximum error of about 10 seconds of arc. This amounted to 4 minutes of time, so Aries Ingress charts calculated from them would have had an error in the house cusps of 1 or 2 degrees at most. Twentieth century tables and computer programs are generally accurate to within 1 or 2 seconds of arc, so the error in the house cusps of a Solar Ingress chart is now negligible.

ASTROLOGIA GALLICA
BOOK TWENTY-FIVE

THE UNIVERSAL CONSTITUTIONS
OF THE CAELUM

Preface

Since the previous books on particular constitutions of the Caelum, i.e. natal charts, have been sufficiently treated, it follows now that we should also open our mind to the other part of astrology, which is concerned with universal constitutions. Moreover, that part embraces a very beautiful doctrine, one very broad and of maximum importance; about which the old astrologers wrote in various ways but confusedly, imperfectly, and erroneously from the lack of a true understanding of this very noble science, so that it was by no means a little difficult for us, having read their voluminous treatises, to recast that doctrine into some method worthy of this science. And yet, from the principles previously stated by us, and with GOD favoring, we have done it, with the errors of the old astrologers overthrown and cast out, so that in what follows it will be plain to the learned Reader, and not without the greatest pleasure to his mind, when he will contemplate the true and marvelous modes of action of the celestial bodies in this book, illumined with the light that was hitherto hidden.

Section I.

Chapter 1. *What the Doctrine of the Universal Constitutions of the* Caelum *is.*

A *particular* Constitution[1] of the *Caelum* is that which is determined for some particular [thing], as for the man being born or the

---

[1] The phrase 'particular constitution' refers to a *natal* chart, while the phrase 'universal constitution' refers to a *mundane* chart drawn for a particular place and time, such as an Aries Ingress (or Revolution, as Morin calls it), the chart of an eclipse, the chart of a conjunction of the Major Planets, etc.

horse to which it refers. Whence it follows that a constitution of the *Caelum* should be called *universal* that has not been determined for any particular [thing], but rather one that affects and refers to many [things] universally, such as a total region or a city.

And Ptolemy[1] sets forth this doctrine in *Quadripartite* Book 2,[2] but briefly; since, however, Cardan,[3] in the beginning of his *Commentary* on Chapter 1 [says] "it is more difficult and more of a major work than the doctrine relating to an individual man." and Cardan himself offers the reason, "that we have by far a lesser understanding of general constitutions than we do of individual ones." but exactly why we should be unacquainted with this, he does not remark.

However, he will hold the understanding of general things to be more necessary than the understanding of particular things, since from Ptolemy, Book 1, Chapter 2,[4] "many things happen to men on account of a general constitution, not from the proper quality of a particular nature; such as when great conversions or changes of the atmosphere, which can [only] be guarded against with difficulty, kill whole nations, or things such as disease or floods [that damage] trees, since always the inferior cause was submitted to the greater and stronger cause." This [from] Ptolemy.

---

[1]Claudius Ptolemy (2nd cent.), the famous writer on astronomy, astrology and geography.

[2]The Latin translation of Ptolemy's *Tetrabiblos* was called *Quadripartite*. For the convenience of the reader, in what follows I will give the correspodning Book and Chapter numbers of Robbins's translation of the *Tetrabiblos*, which differ slightly from the numbeirng of the chapters in the *Quadripartite*.

[3]Girolamo Cardano, M.D. (1501-1576), usually called Jerome Cardan in English. Very famous physican, mathematician, astrologer, and miscellaneous writer. Amongst other things, he wrote a very detailed *Commentary* on Ptolemy's *Quadripartite*, and it is to this *Commentary* that Morin repeatedly refers.

[4]The reference numbers are reversed. It is actually in Book 2, Chapter 1, that Ptolemy says "the first and more universal [part of astrology] is that which relates to whole races, countries, and cities, which is called general, and the second and more specific is that which relates to individual men, which is called genethlialogical, we believe it is fitting to treat first of the general division, because such matters are naturally swayed by greater and more powerful causes than are particular events . . . since weaker natures always yield to the stronger . . ." (Robbins's translation.)

Besides, the old astrologers begin the doctrine of Universal Constitutions from the motion of the apsides of the planets, the change of the eccentricity of the Sun, and the variation of the Obliquity of the Ecliptic; and to these universal causes, as if they are primary causes in Nature, they attribute the most considerable forces of changing kingdoms, empires, religions, etc.—but absurdly!

For **First**, there is no change in the eccentricity of the Sun or in that of the other planets[1]; and no variation of the Obliquity of the Ecliptic[2]; as we have stated in our *Theories of the Planets* in agreement with Kepler in his *Epitome of the Astronomy of Copernicus* and in the *Rudolphine Tables*.[3] And such fictions were introduced into astronomy by a lack of understanding of the fundamental principles of astronomy that are stated by us in our *Astronomy Restored*.[4]

For how could it have been known hitherto whether the eccentricity of the Sun would have changed, since until now that eccentricity of the Sun was unknown, because until now the parallax of the Sun was unknown, without which the true Obliquity of the Ecliptic, and the true place of the Sun, and its eccentricity, without which the maximum and the minimum distance from the Earth can be known? Therefore, it is plain that the eccentricity of the Sun and the Obliquity of the Ecliptic are varied rather by astronomers [stating] those differences than by Nature herself.[5]

---

[1] Wrong! The eccentricities of the Sun and the Planets do vary slowly, although this was unknown in Morin's time.

[2] This is also wrong, for Kepler has tables in the *Rudolphine Tables*, Part 4, pp. 103-104, for calculating the long term variation of the Obliquity of the Ecliptic, although he expressed some doubt as to whether the variation was real or whether the value $23°\ 30'\ 30''$ that he had determined for his own time was actually fixed. Morin chose to think it was fixed. But in fact, it is now known that the Obliquity slowly decreases at about $49''$ per century.

[3] *Tabulae Rudolphinae . . . (Ulm: J. Saurius, 1627).*

[4] *Astronomia jam a fundamentis integre et exacte...* 'Astronomy, now wholly and completely restored from its Fundamentals . . . ,' (Paris: The Author, 1640.) 4to 361 pp.

[5] But Nature, that is the force of gravity, slowly alters the Obliquity and all of these orbital elements.

Second. Is it not ridiculous to ascribe no smaller virtue to causes that are altogether fictitious or at least uncertain—certainly to the revolution of the orbital center of the Sun in a little circle around the center of the World—rather than to raising up, expanding, suppressing, and destroying the greatest monarchies of the World? And this without experiences, unless perhaps frivolous ones, such as Joachim Rheticus did,[1] to which Origanus[2] subscribed, speaking of the Roman and Turkish Empires, as if the revolution itself would be determined to these rather than to other monarchies of the Chinese, Persians, Tartars, Mexicans, Peruvians, and others?

Third. Every influential virtue is inherent only primarily and per se in each celestial body—either a Planet, or a fixed star, or the *Caelum* itself. But the aforesaid Astronomers locate such a force in a point or in its imaginary revolution; even if it is made under the signs of the zodiac, with a concourse of those conceived to be universal, which however is absolutely alien to true philosophy. Therefore, of the three aforesaid universal causes, two of them are already rejected by us—that is, the variations of the eccentricity of the Sun and the Obliquity of the Ecliptic, one of which supposes the other to be scarcely proven.

But that which pertains to the motion of the apsides[3] is a given certainty, and in the case of the Moon is most evident; that is, be-

---

[1] Georg Joachim Rheticus (1514-1576), German astronomer and mathematician. He was a pupil of Copernicus and the person responsible for having Copernicus's book, *De revolutionibus orbium celestium* printed (Nürnberg, 1543). Morin's reference is probably to Rheticus's book *Narratio Prima* [The First Narration], an account of the Copernican theory that was published at Danzig in 1540.

[2] David Origanus (1558-1628), professor of mathematics and Greek. The reference is probably to his book, *Astrologia Naturalis* 'Natural Astrology' published at Marseilles in 1645.

[3] The apside is the point in the Planet's orbit where it is the farthest from the Sun. It is equal to the perihelion (the closest point of the orbit) + 180°. Following Ptolemy's lead for 1,500 years, astronomers reckoned a Planet's anomalistic or mean motion from its apside. But once they began to calculate parabolic and hyperbolic orbits for comets, they reversed the origin of the mean motion and began to reckon it from the perihelion (since those cometary orbits have a perihelion but no aphelion).

cause its apogee is moved forward almost 41 degrees per year in the zodiac; but it is more obscure in the other Planets, of which the swiftest aphelion is that of Mercury, which is moved forward not even two minutes [of arc] annually. And a yet slower aphelion is that of Jupiter, which is moved forward 13°06′ every thousand years according to the Rudolphine Tables. Which surely is sufficiently convincing that the apsides of all the Planets revolve, for [otherwise] so great an error of the Tables could scarcely agree with observations.[1]

Moreover, nothing in universal Nature seems to be more worthy of admiration than those apsides and their motion in the zodiac. For certainly it is a primary [fact], because the Sun and the Moon seem, at some times nearer to the Earth., and at other times more remote; and consequently, the Earth is not at the center of the orbits of the Sun and the Moon.

But a line connecting the center of the Earth with the center of the orbit of the Sun or the Moon, continued in both cases to the periphery of the orbit and the sphere of the fixed stars or the *Primum Mobile* is called the line of apsides of the Sun or the Moon, in the extremities of which, when the Sun or the Moon is there, they are said to be in the highest or lowest apside or in their apogee or perigee; and the reasoning is the same for Saturn, Jupiter, Mars, Venus, and Mercury with respect to the Sun.

Secondly, it is certain that the lines of the apsides cut themselves at the center of the Earth. which is consequently the node of the orbits of the Sun and the Moon, as if the Sun and the Moon belong to the Earth's system.[2] Moreover, the lines of the apsides of Sat-

---

[1] The *Rudolphine Tables* have for the centennial motion of the apsides 1°19′ for Jupiter and 2°55′ for Mercury, while modern tables have 1°37′ for Jupiter and 1°33′ for Mercury. We must remember that precise planetary elements were not known in the 17th century. Those in the *Rudolphine Tables* were derived from observation and speculation, since the theory of gravity had not yet been postulated.

[2] Here, and elsewhere, Morin is disagreeing with Kepler's theory (which was correct) that the Sun was the center of the Solar System, not the Earth. But the dogma of the Catholic Church stated that the Earth was the center of the Universe, and Morin accepted that.

urn, Jupiter, Mars, Venus, and Mercury, the satellites of the Sun, cut themselves mutually in the center of the Sun itself, which is also the node of the orbits of those same satellites that belong to the system of the Sun, as the astronomical observations confirm. And similarly, it can be said that the lines of the apsides of the satellites of Jupiter are intersected in the center of Jupiter.

But from this, Kepler concludes in his *Epitome of the Copernican Astronomy* that the Sun is the source of the motion of the Planets for their own revolution around their own axis, which opinion we have however refuted in our *Theories of the Planets*, in our Solution of the *Famous Problem of the Motion and the Stillness of the Earth*. But by what force and how the apsides are moved, he has not said, nor can the motion of the Sun be explained by him, since the apside of Saturn according to him is moved more quickly than the apsides of Jupiter and the Sun, which are closer than that of Saturn.

Since therefore we have hitherto seen no astronomer or philosopher who can satisfy us in this matter, and I do not have anything of certainty about this matter, I think it to be better for the divine wisdom to be venerated in this matter with a modest silence, than to set forth false or dubious [explanations]. For even if it is conceded that God, who is the power and wisdom without end, has made the machine of the World to be naturally internally mobile from the beginning, and in the case of the Earth, the Sun, and Jupiter, the sources of the motions for the above said orbits are established; nevertheless, how from this to explain how the Planets and their apsides revolve, surpasses man's own understanding.[1]

But if we keep [the idea that] the Heavens and Planets are moved from an external beginning, namely by the understandings of Aristotle, [and] Theologians, and by a more probable opinion, it

---

[1] This was true in Morin's time, but after the publication in the 18th century of Sir Isaac Newton's laws of motion and gravity, it became possible for mathematicians to calculate the variations of the orbits from the mutual gravitational attractions of the Planets.

always remains obscure, by what way that motion is distributed to the heavens, Planets, and their apsides; and it seems to be denied to the omnipotent wisdom of God, because just as an artisan constructs a machine that is artificially mobile; so God could have naturally constructed the mobile machine of the World. But I do not at all deny it, I who believe in and adore the omnipotent wisdom of God.

But because neither the *Caelum* nor the stars are moved by the grace of their own goodness, but for the grace of man, for the benefit of whom this whole World was founded, as we have already stated elsewhere; and the motion of the celestial bodies will cease at the moment in which God imposes an end to the generation of men; it seems more probable that just as each one of us according to the theologians and sacred scripture has a personal Guardian Angel; and so do Bishops and Kings, then the provinces and kingdoms of this Earth, have other general rector angels, it seems that no valid reason can be offered for not concluding that this universal World and its individual globes are ruled by angels that are movers,[1] since in the way of an efficient moving cause locally, nothing can be done by a corporeal spirit, which cannot be done by understanding, unless we have said that the spiritual nature is inferior or weaker than the corporeal.

And it does not matter that we cannot explain the means by which the understandings perform that, since the ways of acting of understandings or Demons are unknown to us, and the work of understanding may not seem to be material reins for ruling the course of the Sun and its satellites, just as for them the charioteer has the work to rule the horses of his chariot, and as an ant by an elephant, so one understanding can differ from [another] understanding in strength and also in knowledge.

---

[1] The motion of the Planets was a mystery to Kepler (who thought it might have something to do with magnetism) and everyone else. People were used to the fact that something had to pull a wagon, so it seemed logical that something must be pulling the Moon and the Planets around in their orbits. Here Morin supposes it might be angels.

But actually the difficulty cannot be resolved about the motion of the apsides, for it is not sufficient that angels are in charge of the globes of the Planets that move them regularly (which can be done by immovable apsides), but in addition it is sought how and by whom the apsides are moved. For the motion of these cannot be conceived otherwise than if the center of the ellipse described by the Planet in its own motion is moved circularly and equally around the other focus of that ellipse.

Just as, with the Earth placed in the other focus of the ellipse of the Moon arranged in circular motion around the Earth, and placed at an invariable distance from the center of the ellipse of the Moon from the center of the Earth (which connecting center line, is called the line of the apsides) from the motion of the center of that ellipse around the center of the Earth there will arise the motion of the line of apsides of the Moon—indeed the motion of the line of apsides of every ellipse—and perhaps that includes the motion of the Ether, always having preserved the same elliptic figure. But although I know from the phenomena that this can certainly be done; nevertheless, how and by whom it can be done, I freely confess that I don't know, and I do not envy him who will satisfy everyone in this matter.[1]

The same difficulty arise about the motion of the nodes of Saturn, Jupiter, Mars, Venus, Mercury, and the Moon, which differ greatly from the motion of the apsides, which are moved more rapidly than the nodes, just as was observed by our predecessors, especially in the case of the Moon; so that consequently the motions of the nodes and the apsides cannot be [caused] by the same principle.[2]

Therefore, having conceded the motion of the apsides, it remains to define whether universal effects may be produced in the

---

[1] It was Sir Isaac Newton (1642-1727), who deduced the true reasons for all the celestial motions.

[2] But, unknown to Morin and his contemporaries in the 17th century, both of these motions are caused by the force of gravity.

lands [of the Earth] by that same motion. Cardan, in Book 1, Aphorism 37, says "The mutations of the apsides change kingdoms, regions, and religions." But in the case of change from the apside of the Sun, he says in Book 5, Aphorism 129, "The apside of the Sun being in the arc from Aries to Cancer renders the southern part [of the World] uninhabitable, but it makes the northern part habitable. From Cancer to Libra, the northern part is very habitable, and it will dominate the southern part. From Libra to Capricorn, the southern part will be habitable, but it will scarcely rule the northern part. From Capricorn to Aries, the southern parts will rule the northern parts as if they were abandoned."[1]

These [remarks] of Cardan, who inserted here not the least of his own fictions—not only fictions devoid of all reason, but also contrary to experience—when he makes the southern part of the World inhabitable only when the apogee of the Sun is moved from Libra to Capricorn, that is after 5044 years have elapsed from the present[2]; and yet from all the centuries that have already passed it has already been inhabited in both hemispheres. And in addition, he extends the duration of the World to more than 20,000 years, which is absolutely absurd.[3]

Besides, the influential force inherent only and per se in some celestial body, but not in a point or line, as was already said above; "therefore..., etc." And it must not be said that the influential force of the upper or lower apside is in a point of the *Caelum* at which the continued line of the aspsides leaves off. For if it is sought from

---

[1]Modern figures for the motion of the solar apogee show that it would require about 5234 years to move through ¼ of the zodiac

[2]If Morin was measuring from 1646, this would be the year 6690. However, modern figures put the motion of the solar apogee at $1.71953°$ per century, so it will reach a longitude of $270°$ in about 752 years or in the year 2752.

[3]Morin was a devout Catholic, and in his day the religious faithful (Catholic as well as Protestant) believed that God had created the Universe about 5,600 years previously. Consequently, Morin could not accept Cardan's implied hypothesis of 20,000 years or more for the age of the world. Cardan was estimating that the solar apogee would make a complete $360°$ revolution in somewhat more than 20,000 years. His estimate was good—modern figures indicate that about 20,900 years would be required!

11

what that point has such a force, it will have to be said from the apside, in which however it is not present; but no one gives what he doesn't have.

Besides, the point of the *Caelum* at which the continued line of the apsides leaves off is absolutely indivisible; but no active virtue, especially a physical one, can be in an indivisible point. Otherwise, the thing would have itself in the places of the Planets and in their aspects in the *Primum Mobile*, and in the cusps of the houses. For the place of a Planet is a part of the *Caelum*, which the planet conceals from us by its own body; still, with the orb of virtue amplified, to which an equal amount is determined in the *Caelum* for the individual aspects by that same Planet for whom the virtue formally exists.

And the cusp is the beginning of a celestial house, for which the virtue also exists by determination. But the line of the apsides only and simply leaves off at a mere point, for which no virtue can exist—neither formally nor by determination.

Therefore, no active virtue must be attributed to the apsides or to their places in the *Caelum* [that can act] upon these sublunar things, at least per se, nor consequently to their motion; for the celestial motion is not active per se, but only by accident, as far as being mobile it spreads its force; moreover, there is no force in the mobile apside, as was already made plain.

You will object. Having conceded a motion to the line of apsides of the Moon, it is certain that the site of the ellipse of the Moon with respect to the *Primum Mobile* or the signs[1] and the Earth, so that the maximum and minimum distances of the Moon from the Earth runs through the whole zodiac in 9 years, or it is done in the individual signs of the zodiac. But this is done in vain and without any notable effect of its own with respect to the Earth,

---

[1]Morin has used the word *duodecatemoria* 'twelfths', i.e. twelfths of the zodiac, for 'signs'. I usually translate the longer word by 'signs', but sometimes by 'true signs'.

on account of which we have many times said that the motion of the Planets is not conjectural. And the same logic applies to the rest of the apsides.

I reply. If any particular effect can come forth from the motion of the apside, it must not be ascribed to the apside per se or to its motion, on account of the reasons set forth above, but only the maximum or minimum distance of the Planet from the Earth in this or that sign; namely because with the Planet not acting at an indefinite distance, it would act more strongly both elementally and influentially at a closer distance than at one more remote. But of these effects, no observations have hitherto been made in the case of the Moon[1]; and much less can they be done in the case of the other Planets, since the line of the Solar apsides, from the foundation of the World has down to now traversed only three signs and six degrees.

Therefore, those things about the effects of those apsides that have been handed down up till now by the astrologers are groundless, especially because the greater or lesser distance of a Planet from the Earth cannot vary the kind of effect, for otherwise it would continually vary; and so the judgments of astrology would be utterly overturned. And it must only be conceded that a Planet in its least distance from the Earth may act more effectively upon the Earth itself when it is in the sign that it occupies when it is in its lesser distance from the Earth. And so the virtue of the Planets [acting] on these inferior things is increased or slackened by that distance, when it is now under this sign, and now under that sign.

But as for that which looks to the great orb and its revolution in 360 individual years for the universal and most powerful cause, and for the great mystery of Nature thought up by Albumasar[2] and

---

[1] Curiously enough, the longitude of the lunar apside is now given the name Lilith by modern European astrologers, who suppose that it does have a noticeable astrological influence.

[2] In his book *De magnis coniunctionibus* ' 'The Great Conjunctions' (Augsburg:

accepted by many, I would be ashamed to waste time in refuting nonsense and fictions, by which it is indeed established in futility, so that if the reason of anything is sought from Albumasar or another, it is plainly irrational.

Therefore, it is established from what was said above, that the old astrologers had wrongly imagined the causes hitherto set forth as an active and universal force and allotted their effects on these inferior things; and consequently, the doctrine of universal constitutions is not concerned with such causes. Moreover, we shall show below that it is only concerned with the annual revolutions of the World, the synods of the Sun and the Moon, as well as the conjunctions of the other Planets, both among themselves and with the Lights,[1] about which we shall speak individually in what follows, after we have expressed some things about the universal mode of acting of the celestial bodies.

Chapter 2. *The Universal Mode of Action of the Celestial Bodies.*

This mode of acting is discussed at length in Book 20, Sections 2, 3, & 4, and especially in Section 3, Chapters 2, 3, & 8, for the Planets, concerning which it must be chiefly discussed in this Book, from which we shall take excerpts only cursorily that will be seen to make our instruction.

And so we have said in the same place **First**. That as the *Primum Caelum* pours forth its own eminently universal force throughout this whole World like some spirit, so do the planets also pour forth their own and formal virtue throughout the whole World, both elemental as well as influential, and that by some ray—the Sun by a solar ray, the Moon by a lunar ray, etc., [they act].

Erhard Ratdolt, 1489), Albumasar (9th century), the great Arabian astrologer, speaks of a large number of profections associated with the mean conjunctions of the superior planets, thus postulating various cycles of time. See the Note to Chapter 3 below.

[1]That is, the Sun and the Moon.

Second. The seven Planets are of a diverse nature, and each one acts on sublunar things more effectively in accordance with its own nature, temperament, habits, age, region, dignity, etc.—more akin to its analogy, and to those things that it more easily affects, moves, directs, and produces.[1] Therefore, in these sublunar things the Sun principally affects, moves, directs, produces, and perfects Solar things, the Moon Lunar things, Saturn Saturnian things, etc.; which is plain in the individual kinds of things shown in our Table on the Rulership of the Planets in Book 13, Section 2, Chapter 3; but those that are contrary, either moderate or destroy, especially if the Planets are strong for that effect and [acting upon] subjects that experience weaknesses.

But from this it follows, that when the Sun is badly afflicted in the *Caelum* by the conjunction, opposition, or square from Saturn or Mars, then the solar things or those that are analogous to the Sun in these inferior things are also badly afflicted; but if it is well disposed, those things will also be well. And so with the lunar, Saturnian, and Jovian things, etc.; moreover, the subject experiencing an analogy will be known from the site or the rulership of the Sun in the figure erected at the moment of the conjunction, opposition, or square with the malefic that is badly afflicting. And so with the others.

Third. Generations and corruptions of these inferior things, and also the diversity of effects on each kind of thing are caused not only by the common motion of the Planets around the Earth, but especially by their own motion in the zodiac and by their various mutual syzygies.[2] For when they are combined in various ways by two motions, with the signs of the zodiac and the houses of the figure, then among themselves, they make a mixed virtue by their configurations, and they produce every possible diversity of things generated and of effects.

---

[1] See the translation of *Astrologia Gallica* Book 13 by James Herschel Holden (Tempe, Az.: A.F.A., Inc., 2007).
[2] By *syzygies* he usually means conjunctions, squares, and oppositions.

This is sufficiently discussed in Book 21, Section 2, as far as those figures that are not only particular or genethliacal, but also as pertains to universal figures; for the doctrine is the same for both; namely, because Planets that are well disposed by their celestial state, and especially by their benefic nature, act fortunately on the house of the figure that they occupy; that is, they promote the good things of the good houses, and they temper or hinder the evils of the evil houses. Moreover, Planets that are badly afflicted by their celestial state, and especially those that are malefic by nature, plainly act in a contrary fashion.

Fourth. The Planets never act alone, but perpetually along with the signs of the zodiac. But with these they act elementarily for the whole Earth, by reason of their own nature, and their sign, and their ruler. For the elemental action of the stars is not changed by the houses of the figure; except by more or less, they do not vary the *kind* of effect, as we have said elsewhere.

And a Planet always acts stronger elementally in that place where it is more perpendicular.[1] But what it does can be known universally, as that Saturn in Capricorn freezes and dries the whole Earth, by reason of its own nature and the sign; and therefore cold and frost increase in winter, and especially in the frigid zones, but particularly in the southern part [of the Earth] to which it is then more perpendicular. But on the contrary, it lessens the heat in the summer throughout the whole Earth, but more in the southern part; and therefore, it harms the more frigid natures by freezing, especially in the frigid zones—both plants and animals, for whom heat is necessary for vegetation and life. Moreover, it tempers the hotter things, that an intense heat harms; however, Mars in Leo does the contrary to that. And so with the rest [of the Planets].

But the Planets also act influentially throughout the whole Earth by reason of their own nature and the sign and its ruler, and its celestial state, on account of the causes expounded by us else-

---

[1] That is, where it is elevated in the figure.

where; for the elemental and influential virtues are transmitted to these inferior things by the same ray, although they act in a diverse way.

But why they act can be known in general, as that by Saturn in Capricorn an especially saturnine influx on all sublunar things is produced, so that seen in general rather than specifically and individually, it also benefits some things, but it harms others. From Saturn in Sagittarius a mixed influx of the Saturn and Jupiter nature comes forth, etc.; but why Saturn acts in a particular way, whether it influences life, death, marriage, wars, kingdoms, etc., cannot be determined other than by the erection of a celestial figure, without which looking only at Saturn in the *Caelum*, it must be said to act influentially on everything at the same time, in accordance with its diverse application for individual places on Earth.

Fifth. In universal figures erected for a particular place on earth, such as a region or the city of any kingdom, the individual houses of the figure are allotted a universal meaning of those things that that house signifies by its nature. For they cannot be of one nature in particular figures of nativities and of another nature in universal figures, since that same division of that same mundane space is [the same] to both, in which the rising of sublunar things, their vigor, their decline and their death are seen—the former particularly, but the latter universally.

Wherefore, the 1st house in universal figures will in fact be especially [the House] of the Life and temperament of the plants, of the animals, and of the men in that region, arising or being born under the universal constitution or during its [effectiveness]; but besides those natives who inhabit that region, or who will pass through it during the [time of the] effects of that constitution. If indeed it is established that those who only pass through a region afflicted by plague, war, famine, or an immoderate inclemency of the air, are made to be exposed to those evils, and are participants in them.

The 12th [house] will be about the illnesses, secret enemies, prisons, and bodily miseries common to that region, according to the nature and disposition of each individual experiencing them. The 11th [house] about friends and confederates. The 10th about honors, magistracy, kingdom, undertakings, actions, and their success. The 9th about religion, travels, and missions. The 8th about death. The 7th about spouses, lawsuits, and wars; and so with the rest [of the houses]. And constantly, from the particular place of the universal constitution in the figure, from its rulers, and their celestial and terrestrial state, judgment is made about the things signified by those houses.

Sixth. The older astrologers formerly handed down many aphorisms on universal mutations in the air, the land, peoples, kingdoms, etc. for the Planets in Aries, Taurus, Gemini, etc., which were perhaps then true from the concourse of the signs and the constellations that they were occupying, and then from the unknown motion of the fixed stars. But because the constellations are moved from Aries into Taurus, Gemini, etc., and the constellation that in the time of Ptolemy and the older astrologers was in Aries, is now found in Taurus, and so with the others, there is nothing indeed marvelous if such aphorisms are now apprehended to be false, inasmuch as they are not corresponding either to the constellations alone or to the signs alone, but to both at the same time, which concourse will never return.

Therefore, first the effects of the Planets in the simple signs must be defined from the proper nature of the Planets and the signs; and then the powers of the fixed stars and the constellations must be observed added to them, so that from the concourse of these three, the [joint] effect may be conjectured. But thus the effects of the Planets in the signs will always be the same and immutable per se, and they will only be varied by the access of new fixed stars or constellations into those same signs, or by the syzygies of those same Planets among themselves.

Furthermore, the proper elemental and influential forces of the fixed stars and constellations are becoming known from diligent observations, when in individual months and years the Sun and the Moon and also the other Planets will apply to them and be conjoined to them, or they will rise with them, culminate with them, or set with them; for having known in advance the nature of the Planets or the signs, it will have to be noted what fixed star or constellation increases or decreases [its effect] by its concourse, for that was from the mixture of its own proper virtue, which thus may become known.

In fact, Cardan in his *Comment* in Book 8, Chapter 3, which is on the forces of the fixed stars, must be corrected here, for he thought with Haly[1] that

> "the powers of the fixed stars are not brought down to the Earth, because they are very remote from it, but the light of the Sun reflects them to us, which light imbued with the powers of a star, especially when that star rises by night, not at all hindered for the natives (that is, for us directly) by the rays of the Sun, produces the greatest, sudden, and swift effects on these inferior things."

For it is false that the Sun's light extends to the fixed stars, as we have demonstrated in Book 9, Section 4, Chapter 8. And therefore it is false that it is reflected by the fixed stars, which would thus not shine by their own light, since indeed from that demonstration the opposite [conclusion] would follow. And finally it is false that the fixed stars transmit their own force by the light of the Sun or by other Planets; for from what was said before they shine with their own light; if they can launch their own light onto these inferior things, much more can they launch their influential force, which is still more subtle than that light and which penetrates the whole globe of the Earth.

---

[1] Haly is the Western name of several Arabic astrologers. The two best known are Haly Abenragel (ʿAlî ibn abî al-Rijâl, 11th century) and Haly Abenrudian (ʿAlî ibn Riḍwân, 11th century). Probably the former is meant here.

Chapter 3. *The Subordination and Dependency of Universal Constitutions.*

It is not unreasonably done that, contrary to Ptolemy's method, particular constitutions of nativities are by us put ahead of universal constitutions. For as Aristotle said in the first of his *Physics*, "particulars are more preferable and more noticeable for us than universals; and [yet] the latter are more preferable and more noticeable in themselves than particulars." That is to say, this [particular] man is easily recognized by the senses by anyone, even by a rustic or a boy; but as a universal man, not except by a philosopher and by an intellectual abstraction. Moreover, in discovering the sciences progress must be made from things that are more known to us [personally] with regard to things that are inherently known; for the universals are known from the particulars.

As, therefore, in the particular constitutions of men, a subordination and a dependency of the signs or of the celestial constitutions is given; and the primary one of all of these is the radical figure, on which they depend, and to which are subordinated the revolutions of the Sun and also the revolutions of the Moon during the whole life of the Native, who is commonly termed the *microcosm*.

Just so, in the universal constitutions of the World, there is given a dependency and a subordination. And the primary elemental universal constitution of the World is the state of the *Caelum* at that moment of time for individual places on Earth when the elemental World itself was [first] exposed to the forces of the celestial bodies, both elemental and influential. But that moment and that constitution is unknown, although some have wanted to define it by plainly chimerical concepts,[1] even as Julius Firmicus Maternus has handed down his own fictitious genethliacal figures for Alexander the Great, Achilles, Homer, Thersites, etc.—a venture not

---

[1] Probably a reference to the chart of the World given by Firmicus in Book III of the *Mathesis*. It is ascribed to the early Alexandrian writers and has the Sun in Leo and the Moon rising in Cancer, with each of the planets in its own sign.

only ridiculous but also stupid, since he knew for certain neither the natal hour, nor the month, nor the year.[1]

Similarly, moreover, it is not precisely known how many years ago this world was founded, since the Chronologists disagree among themselves about this—not only as to the number of centuries, but even the number of millennia. And much less do they agree on the time of day at various locations on Earth. And then on what the location of the Planets in the *Caelum* was, at least with the exception of the Sun, which we have shown by valid reasons in Book 2, Chapter 4, to have been posited at the beginning of Aries.[2]

Moreover, with these things unknown, it is the premier or radical constitution of the *Caelum* with respect to any particular place on Earth, on which the proper fate of that place principally and primarily depends while this World lasts (just as the fate of a Native depends upon his radical figure while he lives) and to which all the other constitutions erected for that place are subordinated—namely, the revolutions of the Sun, the conjunctions of the Lights, etc.—which explain and dispense the fates of that radical constitution that pertain to that place with respect to the dependency on that radical constitution, as is done in particular nativities; for astrological science ought to be uniform, both in universal [constitutions] as well as in particular ones; otherwise, particulars could not

---

[1]This is mostly wrong! In Book VI of the *Mathesis*, Firmicus cites horoscopes for Homer and several other ancient persons, but not for Achilles nor for Alexander the Great. (There is a chart for Paris Alexander, Prince of Troy. Morin must have supposed that that was Alexander the Great. It wasn't!) Firmicus states that some of these persons *are said to have had such a chart*, which shows that he himself was skeptical of them. They are in fact schematic charts that he found in some Greek astrological treatise that has not come down to us, and they were obviously intended to present a horoscopic pattern that was thought to resemble the character and life of the famous person, not an actual horoscope. Morin was right to disregard them.

[2]But here Morin is simply making just such a speculation, as did the old astrologers whom he criticizes. It seems likely that he has taken this idea from Albumasar, who, following a Hindu speculation, proposed a grand conjunction of the mean longitudes of all the Planets at 0° Aries at some remote epoch. Morin rejected the part of the idea that dealt with the conjunction of all the Planets, but he kept the part that put the Sun at the beginning of Aries.

21

be concluded or deduced from universals, nor could universals be inferred from particulars.

Therefore, just as in the figures of Natives, the radical figure, its directions, revolutions, and transits are given, so the same things are given in universal figures. And in the radical figure of the World with respect to any place on Earth, directions must be made, just as in the figures of nativities, with the same measure of 59' 08", etc. for each year. For if Adam and his sons and grandsons would have lived to the end of the World, then the measure for directions would have been the same as it is now; and every 360 years the significators would have returned to their own radical beginnings with a completed revolution to begin a new revolution; because there must not be any doubt that it happened to the first men who surpassed 800 and 900 years of life.[1]

So, therefore, the directions of the radical figure of the World with respect to each place on Earth return to their own radical places every 360 years. And that is perhaps that true Great Cycle[2] of 360 years, about which Albumasar, Omar, and the other old [astrologers] handed down many fictions on account of their ignorance, asserting that it had begun from the conjunction of Saturn and Jupiter that preceded the Flood by 279 years, and was its natural cause, which is mere nonsense, as we have shown in Book 2, Chapter 32.

Besides, even so among Adam and the other first men, with the first or second circuit of directions completed, not the same accidents at all could have recurred, as those that happened in the first circuit, on account of the different state of the *Caelum* that was

---

[1] Morin is referring to the exaggerated life spans assigned to some of the early figures in the Old Testament.

[2] As mentioned in a footnote to Chapter 1 above, Albumasar in his book *De Magnis Coniunctionibus* 'The Great Conjunctions' sets forth a detailed scheme of world history based on Jupiter-Saturn conjunctions with very elaborate sets of profections measured from them. One of the profection cycles is called in English the Great Fardâr or Great Cycle, and it has a period of 360 years. This is probably the one to which Morin refers.

current in the second circuit, and also different revolutions for the Native; although some similar things would have happened on account of the identity of the directions; so at any place on Earth it must be judged with respect to its own radical figure of the World, by which that great cycle is allotted some effects on the individual places on earth.

But because that radical figure of the World is lacking to us for any particular place on Earth; and it is only just permitted to us to erect a figure of the Revolution of the Year of the World for that same place; hence it is [the case] that for predicting the fates for individual places, regions, and kingdoms on Earth, we are no less in the dark than a person who, from the known true place of the Sun in the figure of some Native, but with the year and the day of the nativity unknown, and therefore the radical figure and its revolutions, would like to set up forecasts for the fates of that Native in individual years, and to put them out for true fates. But the situation is otherwise in the nativities of men, in which the radical figure *is* given, which is the certain foundation of judgments for the following revolutions of the Native. And therefore, it can be judged much more certainly than about the effects of universal constitutions.

Nevertheless, since every revolution always acts according as and as much as it can on that subject with respect to whom it is erected, to the extent that the figure is particularly plain for that and determined to that; nevertheless, it does not act on it simply and absolutely, as we have said in Book 23, but with respect to the radical figure, which we suppose to be unknown in the case of universal constitutions; and there is generally available to us no foundation more certain for predicting future things for any year at any place on Earth.

Therefore, we say that the annual Revolution of the Year of the World for any place on Earth is the more substantial foundation that remains to us for predicting those things that are going to be at that place on Earth from the [indications of] the *Caelum*. And all those other universal constitutions, namely both those of the Lights and those of the other Planets with the Lights, and those constitutions that are subordinated among them by conjunctions, oppositions, squares, and the rest of the syzygies, all of which are certainly nothing other than an explanation and a dispensation of the fates of that place on Earth from the radical and annual constitution. For even thought the Lights and the other Planets with the Lights and the mutual conjunctions may be some special universal causes and principles of the actions of the *Caelum* on these inferior things, yet they are not simply and absolutely causes, but [only] with respect to the *radical* (which is not known) or *annual* mundane constitution of the place.

Moreover, this is plain from the practice of all astrologers, who do not pronounce simply and absolutely from the new Moon or the full Moon, but [rather] with respect to the annual Revolution; whose effects, since without doubt they last until the next Revolution, do not permit the pronouncement [to be made] simply and absolutely from some [individual] new Moon, and without such respect.

But this is much more evidently plain in genethliacal particulars, where each lunar Revolution takes into account the quality and state of the [preceding] Revolution of the Sun. For if that was very evil, there will certainly happen something of evil signification in that year, although even if the radical figure does not agree it will be less than if it did agree. And the same thing must also be said about a very good Revolution.

Therefore, if a Revolution of the Moon agrees with a Revolution of the Sun, the effects of the Revolution of the Sun will still more certainly occur in that same Revolution of the Moon, and the more so when the Revolution of the Sun agrees with the radical figure. Therefore, it must be said that there is some force per se to that same Revolution of the Moon, but with respect primarily indeed to the radical figure, but secondarily to the figure of the Revolution of the Sun, so that consequently the latter can be said to be subordinate to the former.

The same thing must be judged in the case of universal constitutions about the radical figure of a region and the Mundane Revolution of the Sun and the lunations. In fact, other universal constitutions—certainly mundane Revolutions or radical ones of the Moon, Saturn, Jupiter, Mars, Venus, and Mercury, are not known any more than the moments of the true conjunctions of Saturn, Jupiter, and Mars. But the time of the Revolution of the Sun is known, which among all the other constitutions lays claim for itself to primacy of virtue and efficacy. Namely because the Sun surpasses all the other Planets in magnitude and virtue, and Saturn, Jupiter, Mars, Venus, and Mercury are only its satellites and therefore inferior. But the Moon with respect to the Sun is only like a woman with respect to a man in the generation of offspring.

You will object first. Ptolemy, in *Quadripartite*, Book 2, Chapter 9,[1] Cardan in his *Commentary*, and the rest of the astrologers, judge from the annual Revolution of the World or its quarters with respect to the closest preceding new Moon or full Moon, on which they will have that Revolution to depend; therefore, that Revolution is subordinated to those syzygies of the Lights, not the opposite.

I reply. A Revolution of the Sun does not depend on the preceding new Moon, as [if it were] a superior or prior cause, by order of its virtue or dignity, but only on the cause initially disposing it. For, because it was said above that the conjunction of the Lights and the other Planets are the particular principles of the actions of the *Caelum* on these inferior things, and that the force of one conjunction lasts until the next following conjunction; from this it happens that when judgment is made from the annual Revolution of the World, in the prognosis there would be had the signification of the immediately preceding new Moon, to the extent that it is the cause that is initially disposing and preparing the sublunar nature to the effects of the annual Revolution of the World that is following it, which is the primary one of all the universal constitutions.

---

[1] *Tetrabiblos* (ed. Robbins), Book 2, Chapter 10.

But if a few days of the preceding new Moon would have passed, say 4 or 5, it will not have that force in a future Revolution of the Sun; namely because its force would be exhausted. Moreover, we think that only the new Moons ought to be looked at, and not the full Moons; because the quarters of the Sun and Moon would also have to be looked at, since the figures of those are also erected by astrologers, and there would not be a greater consideration of the former than of the latter, which was still never used by the old [astrologers].

And there is no need to pay attention at the individual quarters of the year to the new Moons next preceding them, but only to [the one at] the beginning of the year, because of course the quarters are only used for the transits with respect to the annual Revolution of the World, as was already stated elsewhere, and they would not be primary constitutions. And yet, whoever at the beginning of the year and the beginnings of the individual quarters will look not only at the immediately preceding new Moons but in addition at the oppositions and squares of the Sun and the Moon that will occur between the new Moon itself and the Ingress of the Sun into the cardinal point, that one will perhaps judge more accurately, namely because the oppositions and squares pertain to the new Moon itself.

And it must not be thought that the new Moon preceding the Sun's Ingress into Aries would have force over the whole year, or even its first quarter, since the active force of that new Moon would only last for a synodic month; but it would have force on the beginning of the year as a dispositive cause for the sublunar effects of the Revolution of the Sun. And thereby the proper effects of both charts must be distinguished among themselves, and their affinity or contrariety must be noted for their combination at the beginning of the year. But if between the Ingress of the Sun into Aries and the new Moon most closely preceding it, there occurs a synod of the Sun with another Planet, especially Saturn, Jupiter, or Mars, that will be of great virtue for the whole year, because the period of these synods exceeds a year.

Moreover, if anyone argues about this—that having accepted the subordination of the universal constitutions—if the Ingress of the Sun is dependent in any way upon the preceding new Moon, and that [in turn] upon the preceding Ingress of the Sun into Aries as the monthly constitution of the year, it will give a progression into infinity. It will have to be said that the last new Moon of the year defines the force of the annual Revolution; and consequently the latter must be seen to be no greater than the former—if not perhaps much weaker—which suffices to setting up a progress into infinity.

But that which pertains to the preceding synods of the Sun with Saturn, Jupiter, or Mars, since those last more than a year, their signification and that of the annual Revolution in which they began must be taken into account, so that a more correct judgment about the current annual Revolution may be made by combining the significations of both years; which certainly demands a notable skill in astrology and the greatest prudence.

You will object secondly. Ptolemy, in *Quadripartite*, Book 2, Chapter 1, calls those constitutions to be universal causes that are more powerful for moving more things, as for a whole region; acting on which according to their own force, they are said to produce a universal effect, of course by affecting each individual region with its own disposition. Moreover, in Chapter 4, Ptolemy says that the first and most effective cause of universal effects is the eclipses of the Sun and Moon. And finally in Chapter 10, discussing the annual Revolution of the Sun and its quarters, he thinks that these causes are less universal than the eclipses are; and consequently, from the above said Chapter 1, they are subject and subordinated to the eclipses.

I reply. From Book 7, chapter 8, a universal cause per se is said to be that which produces an effect along with the principal cause of the nature or the dignity inferior to itself. As when the Sun causes a man to generate [another] man, the Sun is the universal cause per se, because a sublunar body is by its nature inferior to a celestial body; and the Sun acting with Saturn is the cause per se of universal dignity. For the Sun is the primary Planet, not dependent upon Saturn; but the latter is its satellite, dependent upon it also in its own motion, and in its rulership of signs of the zodiac, as was stated elsewhere.

But a cause is said to be universal *by accident* that produces many [different] effects at the same time; as the Sun at the same time liquefying wax and hardening clay by the same heat; or that during its own time there is comprised the times of many other causes of the same kind or nature, such as the annual Revolution of the Sun, which includes the times of many Revolutions of the Moon, both periodical and synodical,[1] as well as a synodical Revolution of Saturn and Mars.[2] But from those two causes compared among themselves, the one that is accidentally more universal is the one that extends to more, as a cause that is affecting a whole region is said to be more universal than one that affects an individual man of that region; and the one that lasts for a longer time is also considered to be more universal.

But now, an *eclipse* is nothing else than a new Moon or a full Moon, but [taking place] in the ecliptic, and therefore of greater virtue than one happening beyond the ecliptic. Moreover, any figure of a new Moon erected for any particular region is equally widely extended to other regions; and it lasts in its virtue until the following new Moon, as will be said in more detail below.

Therefore, an eclipse of the Sun is not a more universal cause than any other synod of the Lights, neither by nature, nor by dignity, nor by duration, nor by its extension on the face of the Earth.[3] Or if sometimes an ecliptic synod should last longer or should be

---

[1] A *periodical* Revolution of the Moon is a return to the same place in the zodiac, which takes place in 27.322 days. A *synodical* Revolution of the Moon is a return to conjunction with the Sun—that is, the lunar month—which takes place in 29.531 days. (Both of these times are average times.)

[2] The synodical period of Mars-Saturn conjunctions is 2.0092 years on the average, so that on the average the conjunctions occur every other year.

[3] Apparently a reference to the shadow path of a total solar eclipse.

extended more widely than a common synod, that one will be ebbing. That is, any common synod will last longer and will be extended more widely than an ecliptical synod, as will be explained further below. But a Mundane Revolution of the Sun includes twelve time-periods of synods of the Sun and Moon, in which also many eclipses occur in individual years.

Therefore, the annual Revolution of the Sun is at least by its duration a more universal cause than any eclipse; for an eclipse is only a part of the Mundane Revolution of the Sun, and the whole is more universal than a part. I said "at least by its duration," since a Mundane Revolution of the Sun erected for any particular region is not even extended more widely across the face of the Earth than a synod of the Sun and Moon. Therefore Ptolemy does wrongly prefer eclipses to the annual Revolutions of the World or to their quarters, insofar as the universality of the cause, and the Revolutions are wrongly said to be subordinated to eclipses.

You will object thirdly. At least the synodic Revolution of Saturn and Jupiter is a more universal cause than the annual Revolution of the Sun and the synods of the Lights. For a single synodic Revolution of Saturn and Jupiter or Saturn and Mars includes in its duration many revolutions of the Sun and [even] more synods of the Sun and Moon.

I reply. A synodic Revolution of Saturn and Jupiter or of Saturn and Mars. with respect to the annual Revolution of the Sun, is indeed by accident a more universal cause by reason of its duration. But the Revolution of the Sun is per se a universal cause by reason of its duration; and the Revolution of the Sun is [also] a more universal cause by reason of its virtue and dignity. For the Sun is the primary and principal, and the prime planetary cause, of all the sublunar effects, to whose primary and universal state those of Saturn, Jupiter, Mars, Venus, and Mercury belong, which are companions of the Sun that he perpetually carries them around,[1] just as a King does his satellites and ministers.

---
[1] This refers to the fact that those Planets revolve about the Sun.

Therefore, their motions, Revolutions, and conjunctions should only be thought to be parts of the Revolutions of the Sun. Nevertheless, that Revolution of the Sun in which the conjunction of Saturn and Jupiter occurs produces great effects more so than the rest of the Revolutions, because among the Planets these are secondary Planets especially of virtue and authority, in whose sign there are also followers[1]; but that conjunction will be dependent on that particular Mundane Revolution of the Sun.

Therefore, having set forth these things in advance, we should now discuss the individual universal causes separately, having taken a beginning from the annual Revolution of the World.

Chapter 4. *How the Annual Revolution of the World should be erected for any Place on Earth, as well as the figures of the Quarters of that Year.*

Of how great moment it is to restore astronomy [based] on its own true fundamentals, which previously unknown, we have set forth in our *Asronomy Restored*,[2] will be plainly evident here. For, since the radical figure of the World is unknown to us, with respect to any particular place on Earth; therefore, all of the universal constitutions for which we have certitude chiefly depend upon the annual Revolution of the Sun to the beginning of Aries, which was its radical place at the beginning of the World.

But the true moment of time of the Ingress of the Sun into that point at individual places on Earth in individual years, has hitherto been so in doubt, that although by the Very Noble Tycho Brahe the gross error of the old [astronomers] was corrected by his outstanding care, still the proper *Tables of the Sun* of Tycho and the *Rudolphine Tables*[3] constructed for the same meridian of Uraniborg

---

[1] Morin refers to the fact that both Saturn and Jupiter have satellites of their own and thus resemble the Sun.

[2] *Astronomia jam a fundamentis integre et exacte restituta...* 'Astronomy now wholly and exactly Restored from its Fundamentals...' (Paris: The Author, 1640.

[3] Johann Kepler, *Tabulae Rudolphinae...* 'The Rudolphine Tables' (Ulm: Jonas Sauk, 1627).

from the same hypotheses, still differ among themselves by some minutes of an hour; namely because Kepler still [further] refined Tycho's hypotheses. And yet the *Lansbergian Tables*[1] and the rest [of the astronomical tables] differ still more. And this error is common to [both] the mundane and genethliacal Revolutions of the Sun. And there will not be had any true and certain remedy, until the true parallax of the Sun and the true Obliquity of the Ecliptic are discovered by the methods set forth in our *Astronomy*.

In the mean time, since it can be said that not the whole difference but only its part is in excess or in default of the true moment of time of the Ingress of the Sun (which error would at least appear to be small in the erection of the figure as is seen by its force and directions), so the time of the Ingress of the Sun into the beginning of Aries will be found with perfection from the *Perpetual Table of the Revolutions of the Sun* appended to Book 23, Chapter 5,[2] which I consider to be preferable to all other [such Tables].

From Tycho's fundamentals as refined by Kepler, the mean length of the tropical year is 365 days 5 hours 48 minutes 57 seconds and 36 thirds, as is set forth in Chapter 2 of the Precepts in the *Rudolphine Tables*.[3] And therefore according to calculation and that Perpetual Table, the Sun in the year 1600 entered the 4 cardinal points of the zodiac at Uraniburg at these mean times:

The Beginning of	♈	March	19	18: 31: 50
	♋	June	20	22: 31: 16
	♎	September	22	12: 53: 32
	♑	December	20	23: 26: 20

---

[1]Philip van Lansberge (1561-1632), *Tabulae motuum coelestium perpetuae* 'Perpetual Tables of the Celestial Motions' (Middelburg,1632) . His tables were based to some extent on Kepler's theories of the planetary motions, but he introduced some variations, which, according to reports were generally less successful than those incorporated in the *Rudolphine Tables*.

[2]See my translation, *Astrologia Gallica Book Twenty-Three Revolutions* (Tempe, Az.: A.F.A., 2004) 2nd ed. revised.

[3]The latest modern figures are 365 days 5 hours 48 minutes 45 seconds and 18 thirds.

Now, for example, the true time of the Vernal Equinox at Paris in this year 1646 is sought.

From Book 23, Chapter 5, the motion of the Apogee of the Sun for 1600 is taken from the first Table, which is 3 signs 5 degrees 44 minutes (95° 44′). And this is subtracted from the true place of the Sun located in the beginning of Aries, which is 0 signs 0 degrees 0 minutes. and there remains 264 degrees 16 minutes for the true anomaly of the Sun at that time—namely, at the Vernal Equinox of the year 1600, which you look for on the left side of the Table of the Revolutions of the Sun in that same chapter; moreover, for 46 years elapsed from the year 1600; in breadth, with the doubled ingress, as is taught in that same place for nativities, and in the common angle (not having omitted the proportional part) there is found 3 hours 37 minutes 46 seconds, which added to the time of the Ingress of the Sun into Aries given above, [viz.] 19 March 18 hours 31 minutes 50 seconds, it makes 22 hours 9 minutes 36 seconds for the mean time in which the Sun is in the beginning of Aries at Uraniburg, for which are taken the places of the Moon and the other Planets from the ephemerides, or the *Rudolphine Tables*, and from which, having subtracted 8 minutes for the Equation of Time, according to our Table of the true Equation of Time put in Book 17, Section 2, Chapter 5, there remains 22 hours 2 minutes for the true time, and having again subtracted from that 45 minutes for the difference of meridians between Uraniburg and Paris (which Kepler wrongly put at 40 minutes),[1] there will remain 21 hours 17 minutes for the true time at Paris, for which the figure is erected, as is the custom for nativities, and this figure will emerge.

---

[1] But Kepler's difference (40 minutes) was closer to the truth (41 minutes 27 seconds) than Morin's (45 minutes). Tycho's Observatory that he called Uraniburg is located on the (now) Swedish Island of Ven (Hven) in the Oresund at 55N54 12E42.

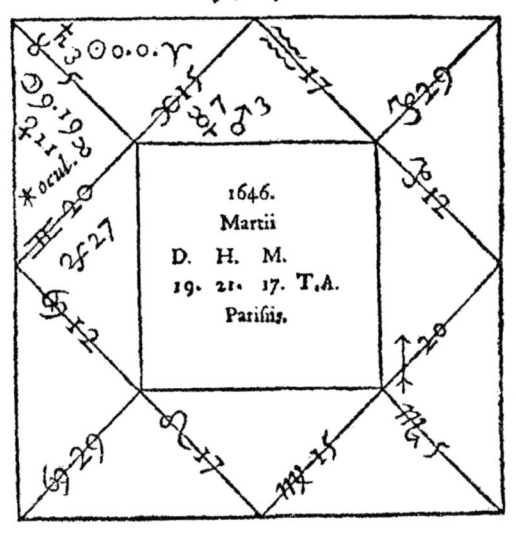

**Aries Ingress
Paris, France
20 March 1646 9:17 AM LAT**

If you want to test the precision of this time, [do this]: At the above said mean time at Uraniburg namely on 19 March 1646 at 22 hours 9 minutes 36 seconds, the mean motions of the [Sun's] longitude and apogee are taken; and having subtracted the place of the apogee from the place of the longitude, for the remainder, which is the mean anomaly, the Equation of the Center of the Sun is taken from the tables of the Equations of the Sun according to Tycho's hypothesis, reported by Magini in the supplement to his *Ephemerides*[1]; and the Sun's place is found precisely at the beginning of Aries, which can be done with no other Tables. Besides, it must be known that the Perpetual Table of the revolutions is founded on the length of the tropical year placed above, Kepler's mean motions of the Sun, and the Tables of the Equations of the

---

[1]*Ephemerides*... (Venice: D. Zenarius, 1582.), but probably a later edition is referred to. See the note to Section II, Chapter 6, below.

Center of the Sun reported by Magini from Tycho's fundamental [motions].

But as for that which pertains to the figures of the quarters that Ptolemy thinks should be erected for the more accurate understanding of the state of the whole year, in [*Quadripartite*] Book 2, Chapter 9,[1] when the Sun enters the signs Cancer, Libra, and Capricorn, we have said in Book 23, Chapter 11, that in the genethliacal Revolutions of the Sun and the Moon we should not reject [this] in the subdivision of these into quarters. For even if the force of these should be principally attributed to the transit of the Sun and Moon through the squares and opposition of their own radical places, for which the inherent force is greater than the rest [of the aspects]; yet it is established by experience that a notable virtue is inherent in these figures of the quarters—that is, they exhibit the state of the *Caelum* at the moment of that transit; by reason of the state of that *Caelum*, which state is stronger or weaker, more fortunate or more unfortunate, and it operates in a varied manner, both elementarily and influentially. Wherefore, in universal constitutions, namely in the annual Revolutions of the World, and in the synods of the Lights, we think that the figures of the quarters should also be erected—at least as secondary charts dependent on the primary charts.

Moreover, the figure of the entrance of the Sun into the beginning of Cancer, Libra, or Capricorn is erected in absolutely the same manner as the figure of the Ingress into the beginning of Aries explained above. And so, for those three quarters there will be had the following figures for the mean time of Uraniburg, having collected the mean motions of the longitude and apogee of the Sun, and having taken the Equation of the Center of the Sun as was done above, there will also be found very exactly those [times of the] beginnings of Cancer, Libra, and Capricorn.

---

[1] *Tetrabiblos* (ed. Robbins), Book 2, Chapter 10.

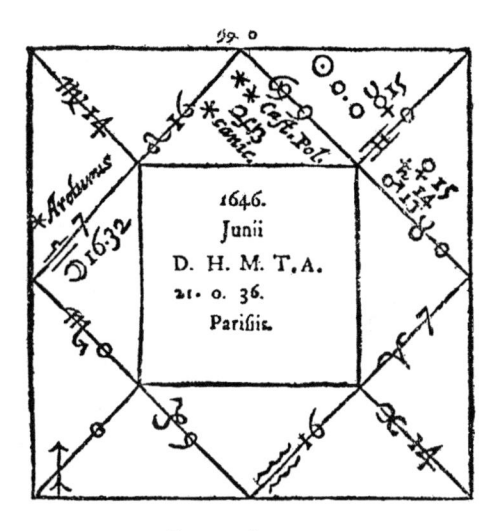

**Cancer Ingress
Paris, France
June 1646 0:36 PM LAT**

**Libra Ingress
Paris, France
23 September 1646 3:45 AM LAT**

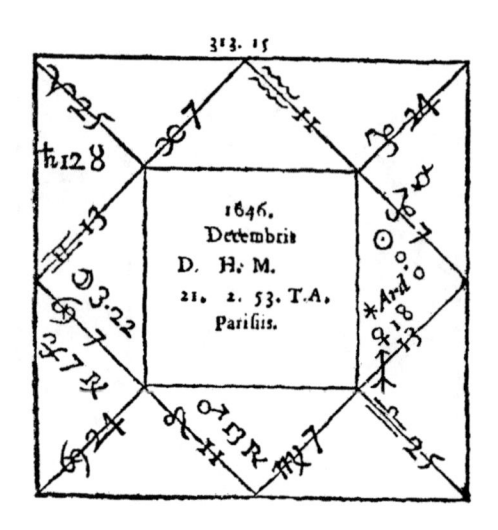

Capricorn Ingress[1]
Paris, France
21 December 1646 2:53 PM LAT

But here it should be warned incidentally that Cardan in his *Commentary* on [*Quadripartite*] Book 2, Chapter 10, thinks that the figures of the Solar Ingress into the cardinal points cannot be erected because the hour of that Ingress cannot be known; and therefore, one can only judge about those Ingresses from the celestial state of the planets and from the figure of the conjunction or opposition of the Lights immediately preceding [the Ingresses].

In all of which Cardan himself errs. **First** because it is false that the hour cannot be sufficiently [well] known for erecting the figure of the Ingress.[2] **Secondly**, because a judgment on an Ingress of the

---

[1] There are several errors in this chart: (1) Saturn should be shown Retrograde; (2) the Moon should be shown as 19 Gemini, not 4 Cancer; (3) Jupiter should be in 8 Leo, not in 7 Cancer; and (4) Mercury's degree number is missing – it should be 13 Capricorn.

[2] But alas, Cardan was right, since the true times of the Aries Ingress and the Libra Ingress calculated by Morin were off by about 3 hours, and only the Cancer Ingress and the Capricorn Ingress were within an hour of the truth. Calculated from modern figures, the true times of the Ingresses were: Aries 0:31 PM, Cancer 0:02

36

Sun from the celestial state of the Planets is common to the whole Earth. **Thirdly**, because the force and efficacy of any new Moon or full Moon only extends down to the next following new Moon, as will be shown below. **Fourthly**, because the conjunction and opposition of the Lights is subordinated; and they depend for their own effects on the Ingress of the Sun into Aries, Cancer, Libra, or Capricorn. **Therefore**, with these unknown, the effects of the conjunction and the opposition of the Lights is [also] unknown.

Chapter 5. *The Revolutions of the Planets, both to their own Radical Places at the Beginning of the World, and to their Synods and Syzygies among themselves, as well as their general Effects.*

In this chapter we approach a doctrine hitherto neglected, and yet one without which astrology—both universal and particular—can only be understood confusedly and very imperfectly; and it cannot be known by what means the seven Planets would govern these inferior things by their own motions and by their syzygies among themselves.

Moreover, the truth of this compelled the old astrologers to observe the synodical Revolutions of the Sun and Moon, and then those of the superior planets, Saturn, Jupiter, and Mars. For they discovered that these Revolutions are especially causes of changes that are happening in this inferior World. And indeed they erected figures for the synods of the Sun and Moon because the motions of those Planets would have been better known than the motions of the rest of the Planets; but they did not erect them for the synods of Saturn, Jupiter, and Mars, because their slower motion would deny the hour of their true synod with respect to us to human understanding—at least for the Saturn and Jupiter synods.

But both about the latter and also the former conjunctions, by a

---

PM, Libra 0:58 AM, and Capricorn 3:49 PM. So, the errors of Morin's times were -3:14 for Aries, +0:34 for Cancer, +2:47 for Libra, and -0:56 for Capricorn. But he was not aware of this, since he believed that Tycho's and Kepler's theory of the Sun's motion was exact. Unfortunately it was not.

very confused, indeed, by a false tradition, so that in the knowledge of the celestial Lights handed down by them, the understanding only comes upon obscurities. But from those things that became known to the old [astrologers] by experience and that are deduced by the natural light from the principles of astrology propounded by me, the doctrine that follows is drawn, by which medium that knowledge of the celestial Lights may at least illuminate the human intellect.

Therefore, **I say first**. The seven Planets, the Sun, the Moon, Saturn, Jupiter, Mars, Venus, and Mercury, by their own motions in the signs of the zodiac, their returns to their radical places at the beginning of the World, then their synodic revolutions and their syzygies among themselves, are the causes of all the sublunar changes. For, with the Planets removed, no changes would occur in the sublunar World. That is, the *Caelum* would always be the same every day, or affected in the same manner for the same [place] on earth. *But the same remaining the same, always does the same to the same.*[1]

For what change would occur from the very slow motion of the fixed stars?—even during the longest interval of years it would be insensible. Moreover, the Sun by its own revolution through the zodiac makes Spring, Summer, Autumn, and Winter during [the course of] the year; and this [space of] time is given to it by the Divine Wisdom for an individual period [to have] its own effects upon the Earth. But the Moon revolves around the zodiac in the space of a month; and it is also given this [space of] time for renewing its own effects periodically upon the Earth. And so with the rest [of the Planets], Saturn, Jupiter, Mars, Venus, and Mercury.

For the individual Planets, by their own Revolutions in the zodiac to the same radical point in which they were placed at the beginning of the World, can do only the same thing per se, namely that because [all those Revolutions] are per se the same. But when

---

[1] Morin italicized this statement.

they are combined among themselves in various ways, they produce various effects. Just as from the combination of 23 letters all the words and all the discourses are constructed; and from different combinations of the four elemental qualities, different temperaments are also produced. Moreover, that the revolutions of the Planets to their own radical places at the beginning of the World are very effective, having taken into account the diversity of the combinations among the Planets, is proved both by the Mundane Revolution of the Sun, which is the norm for the rest, and by the annual Revolution of the Sun itself in nativities.

And the reason is because in that radical place the radical force of the Planet is renewed; and from it begins the revolution not only of the motion, but also of the proper effects of a Planet on the Earth, which are not distributed without [some] order. Moreover, in every order there is given something that is first, which [in this case] is the radical place of the Planet at the beginning of the World. And the same thing must be said similarly about the Revolutions of Nativities. Finally, that the synodic Revolutions of the Planets and their syzygies are of the greatest virtue [in their action] upon these inferior things is plainly proved, both by the synods and syzygies of the Sun and the Moon, whose effects are also visible to the rustics, and by the conjunctions of Saturn, Jupiter, and Mars to which all antiquity ascribed the greatest effects.

I say secondly. That in universal astrology—or what is involved in universal constitutions—the radical places of the Planets at the beginning of the World are unknown (except the place of the Sun); and therefore, their periodic Revolutions to those same places are also unknown—to the great detriment of astrology itself as well as to us. Certainly no more solid fundamentals of universal judgments remain, after the Mundane Revolution of the Sun that is at least known to us, than the mutual synodic Revolutions of the Planets among themselves and their syzygies, which were stated above to be of notable virtue [in their action] on these inferior things, which is proved by experience.

I say thirdly. The synodic Revolution of any two Planets has its own force and its own effects that are mixed from the natures of both Planets and of the sign in which the synod is located. For Saturn with Jupiter does one thing, and Saturn with Mars does another thing; and their conjunction does one thing in Aries and another thing in Taurus, etc., according to the Book of Principles. And that force and its efficacy lasts until the next following synod of those same Planets, although their effect and impression, if it is at least a strong one, can last not only through that whole time, but even beyond it. And that is plainly evident in the case of the synods of the Sun and the Moon, whose forces and effects are renewed in each new Moon on account of the change of sign and ruler in which the following new Moon occurs; but if the Sun experiences an eclipse, not only are more intense effects produced, but also effects lasting longer than a month, on account of the magnitude of the cause and its extraordinary force.

I say fourthly. The synodic revolutions of the Sun and the Moon and their syzygies are the most effective of all with regard to the Earth, because the Sun and the Moon are primary Planets arranged primarily around the Earth, but the other Planets are only satellites of the Sun. Therefore, the Moon's configurations with them are of less virtue, at least per se, than those with the Sun itself. Then, because the Sun is the greatest and most powerful of the Planets; but the Moon on account of its closeness is of the same apparent size as the Sun. Whence both Planets are more active on the Earth than the rest of the Planets.

I say fifthly. Among the syzygies of two Planets (among which we hold their conjunction), there is some order and dependency; and consequently, some one of them is primary, to which the rest of them refer. But that one is the conjunction itself, or the synod, for that one is independent, but the rest of them depend upon it, as from their own beginning, from which when both Planets are being separated, the rest of the syzygies occur, as is plain per se.

I say sixthly. From what has already been said, it follows that the synod, i.e. the celestial chart of the synod, has an effect that continues in power from that synod until the next one following it. And those things arising can be explained both from the synod itself and from the rest of the syzygies of both of the Planets—the sextile, square, trine, and opposition—among themselves according as they are subordinated to the synod or conjunction, from which those effects start, as they are returned to their own beginning, as the synodic Revolution reduces its own force to action.

I say seventhly. During a synodic Revolution of two Planets, such as the Sun and the Moon between themselves, their syzygies both between themselves and with the other Planets, especially with those having power in the chart of the synod, pertain per se to the effects of the Revolution itself. But not the syzygies of two other Planets, such as Saturn and Jupiter between themselves, unless perhaps by accident, as when there is a syzygy of Saturn and Jupiter, those syzygies also do something with the Sun or with the Moon, or some other [Planet], or when both of them have power or rulership in a synod of the Sun and Moon.

I say eighthly. From that, it follows that the same Planet with several others produces at the same time many different effects; at one time, because the same syzygy of two Planets can pertain at the same time to the effects of many Revolutions; at another time, because both Saturn, the slowest of all [the Planets], and the Moon, the swiftest of all [the Planets], revolve synodically and are configured with several others. Moreover, the effect of Saturn and Jupiter is of one kind, and the effect of Saturn with Mars or the Sun is of another kind.

And because there are only 7 Planets, namely the Sun, the Moon, Saturn, Jupiter, Mars, Sun, Venus, and Mercury, hence it results that anyone of them in 6 Revolutions is exposed at the same time to Revolutions of a diverse nature and virtue, such as the synodic Revolutions of the Moon with the other 6 Planets, and so with the rest of the [Planets]. And consequently there may always be seen in the *Caelum* 42 synodic revolutions of the Planets.[1] Moreover, some of the planets revolve swifter, like the Moon, and others slower, like Jupiter with Saturn; therefore, not only in a year from the Sun, but also in a month from the Moon, many synodic Revolutions with the other Planets occur and [also] their syzygies of diverse forces.

Nevertheless, it must be known that the swifter Planets are properly said to revolve with the slower ones, and not the other way around; and Saturn will be properly said to revolve with the fixed stars, and those with fixed points in the *Primum Mobile*[2]; and the mobile points of the diurnal motion with the fixed points of the *Empyrean Caelum*, which is absolutely immobile, and beyond which there is no motion.

I say ninthly. The multiplicity of the virtues [resulting] from the synodic Revolutions of all the Planets and from their syzygies, and the mixture of so many diverse virtues is entirely incomprehensible by human understanding; and it would be sufficient if we discern the greater and more evident ones. And the individual synods do not produce the same effect on each horizon on Earth, but one effect in one place, and another [different] effect in another place, according to their diverse applications to the individual horizons of the whole Earth, and according to the diverse particular rulers of the synods.

For although a conjunction of the Sun and the Moon and their syzygies may be common to all horizons on Earth; nevertheless, throughout the whole circuit of the Earth there is not the same ruler of the new Moon, as will be stated hereafter, from which however the effects of the new Moon are varied in accordance with the [ruler's] proper nature and its state; therefore, that multiplicity of

---

[1] Morin got 42 by multiplying 7 by 6, which would be the proper number of combinations if either planet could come first; but as Hieroz noted, when Morin says that only the faster planet can combine with a slower one, that reduces the number of possible combinations to 6+5+4+3+2+1, which equals 21.

[2] That is, the signs of the zodiac.

virtues allots its own effect—not only a particular effect in all horizons, but also a particular effect in each individual horizon.

I say tenthly. For instance, in individual celestial charts, a constitution is presented for judging—either a universal one, or a particular one—but so far it has only been judged insofar as its present condition occurs, and without respect to its current synodic Revolutions. But since there may be much to notice in the [current] Mundane Revolution of the Sun—namely, what Planet the Sun was last conjoined to and in what sign—that is what was then in fact in its last synodic Revolution that is currently running, and whether it is a Revolution with Saturn or with Jupiter, etc.—for these are the most effective of those currently running, especially if Saturn or Jupiter should be allotted the rulership in that Revolution of the Sun.

And for that reason, in the case of the annual Revolution of the Sun, the old [astrologers] were accustomed to observe the new Moon, or the full Moon most closely preceding it. And similarly, in the case of a new Moon there may be much to notice—to what Planet the Moon was conjoined immediately before the new Moon, and in what sign; and the same thing should be observed about the Planets that are individual significators in nativities; e.g. if Saturn is ruler of the ASC and therefore the significator of those things that are attributed to the ASC, and the Moon was last conjoined to it, but she was the ruler of Saturn in the genethliacal figure, the force of the Moon in connection with those things signified by the ASC will be greater than if it was only the ruler of Saturn, which ruled the ASC. And so with the rest.

I say in the eleventh place. That having added in the case of the Planets the determined force of the degrees of the *Primum Caelum*, which are the true places and aspects of the Planets themselves, each force in the figures of nativities and in others erected for the annual Mundane Revolution of the Sun, the new Moons, the beginnings of illnesses, etc., is most evident; and it is adequately proved by us in Book 21, Section 1, Chapter 4, that it cannot be denied that in the conjunction of two Planets, the places in the *Primum Caelum* in which those conjunctions fall, and their squares and oppositions, are most effectively determined to the nature of the conjunctions of the Planets; and those same places are the most notable in virtue, because they are determined not by a single Planet but by two at the same time.

And Ptolemy himself favors this doctrine at the end of [*Tetrabiblos*], Book 2, Chapter 5, even though the *arcanum* of the determination was unknown to him. For he says, "the increases and decreases of the effects of an eclipse are to be judged from the conjunctions that are in that place where the eclipse was, or in those aspecting that place." Which is to ascribe the virtue to the places determined by both of the Lights.

I say in the twelfth place. That the squares and oppositions of the syzygies of the Lights put in the ephemerides do not have any force by reason of the determination of the parts of the *Primum Caelum* by the preceding conjunction of the Lights. For the Moon shown in the ephemerides in the first square (which can be said to be the quarter of the light), around 6 or 7 degrees has gone past the sinister square of the preceding conjunction of the Moon and the Sun; and in the opposition by around 12 or 13 degrees it has gone past the true opposition preceding the conjunction; and it has gone past the true dexter square of that conjunction by around 21 degrees; which are very noteworthy differences.

And yet because they intercept the elemental and influential force they have on these sublunar things, all astrologers are accustomed to erect figures for their times to predict the future from them; and it cannot be said that that force is reflected upon these inferior things [more] from the light of the Sun than from the light of the Moon, namely because the sole source of the light is for illuminating, but not for doing anything else per se, as was shown by us in Book 11, Chapter 13; [so that] it must necessarily be said that the force itself is from the partile aspect of the square or opposition of the Lights between themselves, which is of itself effective on these sublunar things, even as the syzygies of the rest of the Planets, both with the Sun and the Moon, and among themselves, which we have stated in Chapter 3 to be particular universal causes, and the beginnings of actions on these inferior things.

I say in the thirteenth place. Both of the above said oppositions in the synodic Revolution of the Sun and the Moon have one determination,[1] and another of the simple syzygy, so then both of the squares[2] must be observed as being effective in their own effects of the synodic Revolution. Nevertheless, the greater force is inherent in those that are by determination; for the syzygies of the Lights among themselves certainly operate in nativities according to their determination in the Native's radical figure, and according to the houses of the figure in which the syzygies occur, as is plain from the observation of their daily effects; but the transits of the Lights through the places of the squares and the opposition to their radical places are more effective and more frequent, as experience teaches. And therefore, the force inherent in the square and opposition aspects is greater by determination than the squares and opposition of the simply syzygy.

Moreover, that which we say for genethliacal figures must similarly be judged to be valid for new Moons and the other primary universal constitutions, which are the synodical Revolutions of the Sun, Moon, Saturn, Jupiter, and Mars among themselves with respect to their own square and opposition syzygies. For the conjunctions of the Planets are the first or radical principles, with respect to which the rest of those syzygies are related, as was already said above. Moreover, the force inherent in the radical principles is the principal one for effectively determining the *Caelum*, as is plain from nativities.

---

[1] Here and in what follows, when he speaks of the *determination*, he is referring to the actual chart of the lunation, and to the position of the Sun and Moon in that chart.
[2] That is, the squares to the radical position of the lunation (i.e. to the *determination*) and the subsequent squares of the syzygies, which occur later in the lunar month.

Therefore, the transits of either of the Planets of a conjunction through the place determined by the conjunction are effective, and they reduce the force of the synodic Revolution from potentiality to action by reason of their transit. And that is proved in the Mundane Revolution of the Sun, for the transit of the Sun through the beginnings of Cancer, Libra, and Capricorn, places that are square and opposed to the place of the Revolution of the Sun itself for the remaining three quarters of the year—Summer, Autumn, and Winter. And the effects of the constitution of the Mundane Revolution of the Sun are not suppressed by the constitutions of the quarters, the new Moons, and the rest of the synodic Revolutions of the Lights with the other Planets, but they are only explained, increased, diminished, and moderated in accordance with the agreement or the disagreement of the figures, or of the subordinate constitutions, with the primary ones and among themselves, as much as it can be conceded to the primary itself—that is to the solitary Mundane Revolution of the Sun, that is apart from the radical figure of the World.[1]

Similarly, the transits of the Moon through the squares and opposition to the place of the [preceding] new Moon do not suppress the effects of the constitution of the new Moon, but they explain, increase, or diminish, and moderate them in accordance with the agreement or disagreement of the figures. To which the rest of the syzygies of the Sun and the Moon concur. And the reasoning is the same for the synodic revolutions of the other Planets. But the principal universal causes are the Mundane Revolution of the Sun and the synods of the Sun and the Moon, because these are the primary Planets.

But as for that which pertains to the synodic Revolutions of the Sun and Venus, they cannot be deployed to the other syzygies of the sextile, square, trine, or opposition because the maximum elongation from the Sun of Venus and Mercury does not extend to a partile sextile, nor does the maximum mutual distance of Venus

---

[1]Which, as was explained above, is unknown.

and Mercury in the zodiac with respect to us extend to a partile square.[1] But nevertheless, in the case of their conjunctions, the places of the conjunction, square, and opposition are effectively determined in the *Caelum*, not otherwise than in the case of the other Planets, which is proved from their transits and those of the other Planets through those same places in genethliacal figures. And this still confirms that the efficacy in the aspects from their determination is greater than in the aspects of a simple syzygy, seeing that a synodic Revolution can be lacking to the latter, but not to the former.

I say in the fourteenth place. That since in the case of the synods of the Sun and the Moon, the Sun can in only three months reach the sinister square of the place of the new Moon; but then the virtue of that new Moon will have lapsed; therefore, not the transits of the Sun through those places determined by the new Moon should be looked at, but only those of the Moon during the synodic Revolution of the Moon. And the same thing should similarly be considered about any swifter Planet with respect to a slower one, unless it should happen that some powerful planets in that synod should transit by body or by aspect through those places.

I say in the fifteenth place. That both the opposition and the squares from the determination and from the simple syzygies of the synodic Revolution of the Sun and the Moon, pertain to the effects of the synodic revolution itself. And in the case of the opposition and the squares of the determination, that is evidently plain because they formally depend upon the very place of that new Moon, as they are referred to it. And in the case of the opposition and squares of the simple syzygy, that is also proved because otherwise there would be no primary syzygy, and no subordination between the syzygies; and no effects of one new Moon would last until another one, but only until the next following syzygy that is acting independently of the chart of the new Moon. And as for the

---

[1]The maximum elongation of Venus from the Sun is about 48 degrres, and the maximum elongation of Mercury from the Sun is about 28 degrees. Therefore, their maximum distance from each other is the sum of these or about 76 degrees.

rest, they would all be confounded; that is, because in the case of the squares, there are given two places, namely of the Sun and the Moon that are mutually independent of each other; moreover, the beginning of every quality ought to be some unity to avoid confusion, that is the place of the synodic Revolution. And the reasoning is the same for the rest. Moreover, a judgment should be rendered both on the transits through the aspects of the determination, and by the simple syzygies of the figures erected for those same moments, giving primacy to the transits unless the syzygies of the Sun and the Moon and their opposition are in the ecliptic.[1]

I say in the sixteenth place. The aspects from the determination, and the simple syzygies, act universally upon the whole Earth, and particularly with respect to each place, and they are such that transits through the aspects of their determination initiate or dispose the effects, but the syzygies perfect them; or the transits may effect them, but the syzygies confirm or destroy them in accordance with the different virtue of the latter as well as the former. And this must be especially understood about the transits and the similar syzygies of the synodic revolution of the Moon with the Sun, in which the transits and syzygies are similar on the same day, and they cannot differ by [more than] two days.

But in other synodic revolutions, such as that of the Sun and Mars, in which the Sun or Mars, in which the Sun or Mars transits through the sinister square of the place of the conjunction within 3 or 4 months, but the dexter square is scarcely completed in [less than] 9 or 10 months; and although the effects of the transits and the syzygies pertain to the same synodic Revolution, yet very often they differ among themselves, but are not connected, so that the later one is sometimes the perfection or confirmation of the former one, but sometimes the other way around. And especially when the ruler of the place in which the synod occurred, or the ruler of that synodic constitution, has no power in the places of the

---

[1] This exception is for the Sun-Moon conjunctions and oppositions that occur in the ecliptic, which, as he mentioned above, occur in the case of solar and lunar eclipses.

syzygies, or no power of rulership or of exaltation in the constitution of the syzygy. Therefore, the aspects of the determination, and the syzygies must be attended to in the same synodic revolution of the two Planets.

Chapter 6. *How the Figure of any Synod of the Sun and the Moon, as well as the Figures of the Monthly Quarters should be erected.*

After what was said about the synodic revolutions of the planets in Chapter 5, now it follows that we should discuss the synodic Revolutions of the Moon with the Sun, both because they are [more] important than the rest, and because only the true times of these are known,[1] at least closely, and finally because the effects of the annual Revolution of the World, which was discussed in Chapter 4, or its quarters may depend upon the immediately preceding new Moon or full Moon as we observed in Chapters 4 and 5.

However, it is not our purpose here to show the method from the fundamental tables by which the moment of mean time in which the true synod of the Lights may be exactly found, both because those tables would have to be put here beyond our purpose, and because they have not yet attained the desired precision. And so, until the most accurate tables may be constructed in accordance with the fundamentals given by us in our *Astronomy Restored*, it will be sufficient to warn the Reader that from the most accurate ephemerides that are available for the motion of the Sun and the Moon, he should see at what mean time the new Moon occurs whose figure he desires to erect, for that time is put on the page of syzygies.[2]

Then in those same ephemerides on the left side of the page, having taken the true places of the Planets for the degree of the true

---
[1] Morin recognized that the exact times of the planetary synods could be determined with less accuracy than those of the Sun and the Moon.
[2] Many ephemerides both then and now have a table showing the times of the lunar phases.

place of the Sun, he should reduce that mean time into apparent time according to our Table of the Equation of Days,[1] and thus there will be had the true time[2] of the new Moon for the meridian of the ephemerides; and after that he should reduce that [time] to the meridian of the place for which the figure is to be erected, as is usually done; and finally, for that time last reduced, he should erect the figure of the new Moon, as is customary for every sort of figure for the latitude of the place.

For example. The mean time of the new Moon immediately preceding the Ingress of the Sun into the beginning of Aries in this year 1646 is put by Origanus from Tycho's [solar theory] on the day of 16 March at 20:21 on the meridian of Frankfurt an der Oder, for which Origanus's ephemerides are constructed. Therefore,[3] for that time, let the true places of the Sun and Moon be taken from those ephemerides [made] according to Tycho's calculations, and the Sun will be found to be in 26°57'19" ♓, and the Moon in 26°57'43" ♓; and consequently, that is the [place of] the new Moon, not however in the ecliptic, because at that time the Moon's latitude is more than 3° South,[4] and therefore more than three times greater than both the semi-diameters of the Sun and the Moon taken together.[5]

And because the Sun is in the 27th degree of [Pisces, and] the

---

[1] Now called, The Equation of Time.

[2] That is, the Local Apparent Time (LAT).

[3] Probably his *Novae Motuum Caelestium Ephemerides Brandenburgicae Annorum LX incipientes ab anno 1595 et desinentes in annum 1655*... 'The New Brandenburg Ephemerides of the Celestial Motions for 60 years, beginning in 1595 and ending in 1655...' (Frankfurt: Johann Eichorn, 1609).

[4] The LMT (for Frankfurt an der Oder) and the true positions of the Sun and Moon from modern astronomical data are as follows: Time 20:54, Sun 356°50'17", and Moon 356°50'18". The Moon's latitude was 3S48. Note the discrepancy in the Sun's longitude, which is mainly due to the incorrect value of the solar eccentricity deduced by Tycho as 0.01800 instead of the true value for 1646, namely 0.01687.

[5] Actually, nearly seven times as great, since the sum of the mean semi-diameters is nearly 0°32'. But Morin was probably thinking of the sum of the *diameters* rather than the sum of the semi-diameters.

Moon's latitude was 3S48, therefore in our Table of the Equation of Time, shown in our abbreviated *Rudolphine Tables*, 9 minutes must subtracted from that mean time of 20:21, and there will remain 20:12 for the true time at Frankfurt, which, since from Origanus's Table of Places, Paris is East by 0:54, therefore, with that subtracted from 20:12, there will remain 19:18 for the true time at Paris.[1] For which [time] a figure such as that which follows is erected, in which however the other Planets are put according to the opinion of Kepler, who has their places more accurately than Origanus from the *Prutenic Tables*.[2] Moreover, as for the time of the new Moon, Kepler puts it only two minutes later than Tycho.

Plainly, the celestial charts for the squares and the opposition syzygies of the Lights, must be erected in the same manner, the mean times of which are also put in the ephemerides; but the charts of the transits of the Moon through the places of the squares and the opposition of the determination of the new Moon will be erected in exactly the same manner as we have taught in Book 23, Chapter 9, that a figure should be constructed for the Moon, namely taking the places of the squares and the opposition to the place of the new Moon, as if they would be the places of the radical Moon, to which the Moon itself would have revolved.

As in the figure below, the conjunction of the Sun and the Moon was made in 26°57′ ♓, the sinister square of which place is 26°57′ ♊, to which the Moon came on the 23rd day of March; and it must be known at what hour [that occurred] at Paris. And operating as

---

[1] In this calculation, Morin subtracted the Equation of Time, which was +9 minutes, from 20:21 to get 20:12 LAT at Frankfurt an der Oder, then he used Origanus's time difference of 0:54 to get a Paris time of 19:18 LAT (= 7:18 AM LAT on the next morning). The geographic longitude of Paris is 2E20 and the longitude of Frankfurt an der Oder is 14E33, a difference of 12°13′, which is equivalent to 0:49 in time, not 0:54. (The *Rudolphine Tables* put Paris at 0:40 W of Uraniborg and Frankfurt an der Oder at 0:08 E, which is a difference of 0:48, closer to the true difference of 0:49.) From modern figures, the true time of the lunation at Paris was 7:56 AM LAT with ASC 20 ♉. The error in Morin's calculated time was therefore 38 minutes.

[2] Erasmus Reinhold (1511-1553), *Prutenicae tabulae coelestium motuum* 'The Prutenic Tables of the Celestial Motions' (Wittenberg: Matthew Welack, 1585).

instructed in that same chapter according to Tycho's calculation as [given] in Origanus, you will find 6:56 mean time on the meridian of Frankfurt, but 5:55 true apparent time at Paris, namely [by the calculation] made with our Table and with reduction to the meridian of Paris. And the method is the same for the dexter square and the opposition.

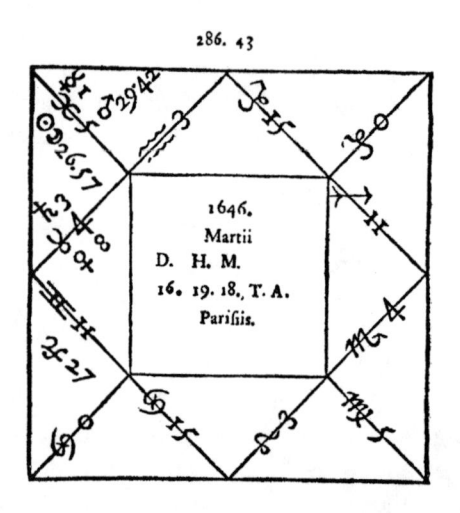

286. 43

[Astrological chart:
1646.
Martii
D. H. M.
16. 19. 18., T. A.
Parisiis.]

The New Moon Preceding the Aries Ingress.
Paris, France
17 March 1646 7:18 AM LAT[1]

The celestial charts for the syzygies of the Lights—the squares, and the opposition—should be erected in the same manner; their mean times are also put in the ephemerides. But that the charts of the transits of the Moon through the places of the squares and the opposition of the determination of the new Moon should be erected in exactly the same manner as the figure of the Revolution of the Moon is constructed, we have taught in Book 23, Chapter 9,

---

[1] In this figure, Mars is incorrectly shown in 30 Aquarius; it was actually in 1 Pisces. Mercury was in 2 Pisces instead of 1 Pisces, and Venus was in 10 Taurus instead of 8 Taurus. The Mars error is significant because it changes the rulership of Mars's dispositor from Saturn to Jupiter.

namely including the places of the squares and the opposition of the new Moon, just as if they were places of the radical Moon to which the Moon itself would be revolved.

As in the figure placed above, the conjunction of the Sun and the Moon was made in 26°57' ♓, the sinister square of which place is in 26°57' ♊, to which the Moon came on the 23rd day of March, and it must be known at which hour [that occurred] at Paris. And operating as instructed in that same chapter according to Tycho's calculation as [given] in Origanus, you will find 6:56 mean time on the meridian of Frankfurt, but 5:55 [P.M.] true apparent time at Paris, namely [by the calculation] made with our Table and with reduction to the meridian of Paris. And the method is the same for the dexter square and the opposition.

Chapter 7. *The Eclipses of the Lights and what should be particularly observed about them.*

Although the eclipses of the Lights are only special parts of the revolution of the Moon with the Sun, certainly an eclipse of the Sun at new Moon and an eclipse of the Moon at full Moon is discussed in Chapter 6. Nevertheless, because in the case of eclipses something peculiar happens that should be noted—not something common—as in the rest of the lunations. And moreover, the whole of antiquity along with Ptolemy himself, and those following Cardan and others, have thought that eclipses are the first and most powerful universal causes [operating] on these inferior things; and therefore, they have labored very studiously in handing down their doctrine.[1]

Before we pass on to other things that must be said by us about universal constitutions, it seems to be opportune to explain our opinion about eclipses briefly here, and to show how much the old [astrologers] were deluded about them, and along with them almost all the modern writers have been deluded still.

---

[1] The Babylonians were convinced of this, and they established definite rules for assaying the effects of eclipses and the duration of those effects.

Therefore, I say that men unskilled in the celestial motions, were not entirely without reason terrified from the beginning to see the light of the Sun to fail by day, and the light of the Moon also to totally fail by night, and the day to become night. Indeed, this portent in Nature incurred no little terror in those ignorant of its causes. And the forest-dwelling Canadians[1] still think so; then, [they assumed that] either the declining light was affected by a notable debility, or a great danger was threatening it, and from that the whole inferior World [was threatened]. And so, if anything notable should happen afterward, such as a plague, a war, famine, a flood, and something similar, men would commonly think it to be such a portent as should be ascribed to it.

But those who undertook the perfection of astronomy from the beginning uncovered the causes of those phenomena by a marvelous sagacity—that is, the interposition of the Moon between the Sun and us in the case of an eclipse of the Sun, and the interposition of the Earth between the Sun and the Moon in the case of an eclipse of the Moon; but about the notable change of sublunar things from eclipses as causes, they retained the commonly received opinion that they were the most powerful of all [causes]—thinking with all the old philosophers, and indeed with the moderns down to my own time, that the Sun, the Moon, and the rest of the Planets and fixed stars accomplish by their own light whatever they do to these sublunar things.

For, having made that hypothesis, it necessarily followed that from a diminution [of light] in partial [eclipses], or from a total interruption [of it] in total [eclipses], i.e. by the action of the declining light, these sublunar things are strongly affected and changed; that is because the Sun and the Moon are the primary celestial causes of sublunar effects. But because in Book 11 it is more clearly shown that the light only *illuminates* and doesn't do anything else, and in Book 12, [it is also shown that] there is inherent in the Sun, besides its light, an actual heat, but that in all the stars

---

[1] The Canadian Indians.

their own individual influences penetrate the body of the Earth, and they scarcely affect it less from subterranean places than from places above the Earth.

We must now philosophize about eclipses in a different way, by having looked at things in Nature, rather than things seen in the books of authors.

But the reader must be warned in advance that they are studiously mistaken who think that astrologers only look at the eclipses of the Lights as a deprivation of their light on these sublunar things, since they only look at those eclipses as conjunctions or oppositions of the Lights, through which the Sun and the Moon pour out their own influences more strongly than through any of their other syzygies.

And so, astronomers and astrologers observe the same moment of time of the middle of the eclipse—the former so that they may see whether their Tables of the Motions are accurate; but the latter so that from a celestial figure erected at that moment they may see what effects on these inferior things the eclipse is going to produce—not by reason of the declining light, about which learned astrologers are uninterested, but by reason of their influence. And so, having noted these things in advance. . . .

I say first. In those eclipses that happen above the earth, we are indeed deprived of the light and heat of the Sun, totally in fact if the eclipse is total, but partially if it is a partial one. And this lasts as long as the eclipse; but we are not at all deprived of the influence of the Sun, or at least no more than when the Sun is under the Earth, which every night makes for us a total eclipse of the Sun with a space of time of many hours. For just as the influence of the subterranean Sun penetrates the Earth, as is established from the figures of those born at night, so the influence of the Sun in eclipse above the Earth penetrates the dense and opaque body of the Moon, which neither the light nor the heat of the Sun is able to penetrate.

For the Moon is discerned by the telescope under the disc of the Sun to be blacker than black, as I have learned to the detriment of my eyes; but in the case of subterranean eclipses of the Sun, at least total ones, the upper hemisphere of the Earth is more affected by the eclipse than by one that occurs above the Earth. The reason is because the influence of the Sun is not of infinite virtue; and therefore, if it can penetrate the globe of the Earth, it cannot except more weakly cross the globes of the Earth and the Moon at the same time. Therefore, in those eclipses, at least the total ones, we experience unchanged the influence of the Sun on us.

And that is perhaps why for about 30 years so many wars and all kinds of evils are taking place in this hemisphere of the Earth that Europe lies in the middle of. For during that time very many total or almost total eclipses of the Sun occurred in the opposite hemisphere, as can be seen in Origanus, who studiously noted and calculated the ones above the Earth and below the Earth, when however scarcely two notable ones occurred in this hemisphere.[1]

I say secondly. In the case of the eclipses of the Moon, we are indeed deprived of the light and heat of the Sun reflected by the Moon—of all of it, if the eclipse is total, but of part of it if the [eclipse] is partial—and only while the eclipse lasts. But we are no more deprived of the influence and elemental powers of the Moon than if we were not experiencing an eclipse; indeed, because between it and us nothing is interposed that would be able to blunt its elemental or influential powers. And this is true (at least for the influences) both for the subterranean eclipses of the Moon and for those above the Earth. Whence it is established that sublunar Nature is more affected by solar eclipses than by lunar eclipses on account of the diminished influence of the former on us. And in all

---

[1] A reference to the widespread devastation caused by the Thirty Years War 1618-1648, which was still in progress at the time when Morin wrote this (1646). A convenient resource for eclipses is Theodor Ritter von Oppolzer's *Canon of Eclipses*, translated by Owen Gingrich (New York: Dover Publications, 1962), which has diagrams of the shadow paths of the eclipses. I note eclipse paths below the equator in 1618, 1619, 1621, 1622, 1625, 1626, 1629, 1636, and 1637; but only two in the northern hemisphere, in 1621 and 1630.

the eclipses, the influx of the Moon prevails over the influx of the Sun, more indeed in the case of lunar eclipses.

I say thirdly. From what has been said, it is plain that the old [astrologers] were much deceived, thinking that in the case of eclipses the Light that is being eclipsed stops its action on these inferior things—namely, because they were thinking that the Lights act by their light alone; and therefore, they were of the wrong opinion; secondly, that from the minor Planets the ability to perform in the world was from the Light being eclipsed.

More so than the others, Cardan erred in his *Commentary [on the Quadripartite]* Book 2, Chapter 5, Text 26, when he concludes that "the force of the eclipse consists of the failure of its light"; but afterwards, considering the failure of its light to be only a removal that cannot be an acting cause, he concludes in another way, but in an equally false one, " In eclipses, the light of the Sun or the Moon is not taken away but changed, and affected in its external quality to impair and change the sublunar things," and he says falsely that, "the Moon of itself is bright and shiny, just as Venus can be seen by itself"; since (as I saw and said above), the Moon in a solar eclipse appears blacker than black,[1] which however the light of the Sun would penetrate much more effectively than the light of Venus.

I say fourthly. Therefore, by the eclipses of the Lights, the Earth and its inhabitants are more strongly affected than by the rest of the synods, or by an opposition of the Sun and the Moon,

---

[1]Cardan actually says this (*op. cit.*, p. 193, col.1): *Ergo dicendum est quod per deliquia luminarum lumen ipsum quod ad nos transit (nam neque vnquam Luna, vt dixi, ex toto priuatur lumine & multo minus Sol, sed in maximis deliquiis quod corpus Lunae perspicuum sit adeo vt Venus per ipsam intueri possit, vt in physicis declarauimus, lumen croceum ad nos deueniat) affectum externa qualitate immutat et concutit partes orbis loco in quo est, addictas.* 'Therefore, it must be said that during eclipses of the Lights, the light that passes along to us (for the Moon is not ever, as I have said, totally deprived of light & much less the Sun, but in the maxima of the eclipses that the body of the Moon is evident rather as Venus can be seen by itself, as we have stated in *Physics*, a yellow light reaches us) affected in its external quality, changes and impairs the affected parts in that place in the World in which it is.'

because a united virtue is stronger. But in eclipses, the rays of the Sun and the Moon are united in the same line (or at least approximately) that is directed by them onto the Earth. And in an eclipse of the Sun, the Earth is found within the cone, which, derived from both of the Lights as a base, grazes the Earth itself in its circumference[1]; moreover, in an eclipse of the Moon it is found within the column whose extremes are the discs of the Sun and the Moon.

Add that in every eclipse, both Lights are in the ecliptic, where the virtue of the zodiac flourishes the most. But from that it follows that the greater and longer in duration an eclipse is, the greater the effects that it produces—that is, because in the major eclipses, the central rays of the Sun and the Moon are more united into the same line that penetrates the Earth, and they are united for a longer time.

I say fifthly. Ptolemy and the other old astrologers down to our time were again greatly deluded about these things in two ways. **First**, in defining the places on Earth to which the effects of any particular eclipse pertain. For they would have them pertain to those regions and provinces that are ruled by the sign in which the eclipse occurred, or to others of the same triplicity, according to the distribution made by Ptolemy of the [places] on Earth to the twelve signs of the zodiac.

However, since we have shown in Book 20, Section 1, Chapter 2, that that distribution is a mere fiction, it is plain that they erred in assigning the places on Earth in which the effects of eclipses occur. Which is more fully confirmed, because an eclipse, just as any other lunation, is a universal cause, universally active for the whole circle of the Earth; but particularly active in any place on Earth according to the particular position of the eclipse, and of the whole *Caelum* with respect to that place on Earth. But [this may be] in a place where very frequently the eclipse would not be allotted any effect according to the old [astrologers], because that place would not be ruled by the sign in which the eclipse is, nor by others

---

[1] Here Morin is talking about the shadow cone that is cast by the Moon onto the Earth.

that are of its triplicity. However, that illusion is intolerable, and most alien to the principles of astrology.

You will say that Ptolemy [also] calls attention to the places of the Lights and the angles of the celestial figure under which cities themselves were founded, or to the MC of the nativities of the Princes who rule those cities. And if those have any familiarity or agreement with the places of the Lights and the angles in the figure of the eclipse, the effects pertain to those cities.

But I reply. The celestial bodies do not influence artifacts, at least per se, as we have proved in Book 20, Section 4, Chapter 8. And consequently, that doctrine about cities collapses from the fundamentals, although it would hold for the radical figures of cities, but scarcely any one of them is known. But as for what looks at the MC's of Princes, indeed given the above said familiarity, namely what may happen from an eclipse falling in the MC of the natal figure of a Prince, or what [when it falls] in both the natal figure and the ecliptical figure; and the same thing in the case of the MC—the eclipse will signify [something] about the actions and the particular fate of the Prince. But what things will happen to the citizens of that city, as well as to the land, the water, and the air, such as plagues, sterilities, etc., will not be foreseen from that, unless perchance by accident, in so far as the Prince is passively or actively determined to war; and from the similarity of the figures, plagues, sterilities arising from those wars may be sought. But those things confer nothing on the constitution of the air—at least, on its heat, cold, moistness, and dryness.

The second thing in which the old [astrologers] erred was in defining those things on which an eclipse might act most strongly from the form and nature of the *constellation* in which the eclipse might be. Saying that if the constellation was human, such as Gemini, Virgo, or Aquarius, men would be affected; but if it was bestial, such as Aries, Taurus, Cancer, Leo, etc., beasts called by similar names would be affected. For these names do not properly suit the signs, which should properly only be called by the names of the

Planets that rule them, whose natures they refer to. But the starry constellations, in so far as their name, form, and nature are concordant with the name are only mere fictions and the subjects of fables, from which true astrology must be purged, not only in the case of eclipses, but also in the case of other universal constitutions, in which similar fictions are assumed to be real causes by the unskilled.[1]

And these [considerations] about the eclipses of the Sun and the Moon can also be applied to the eclipses of the other Planets, when they are sometimes occulted by the Moon. Moreover, about the rest of the things that are accustomed to be inquired about eclipses, such as how should its ruler be chosen, when do they begin, and how long will their effects last, and similar things; since these [questions] are common to the rest of the universal constitutions, we shall discuss these in general below in their own proper place.

And because in the year 1646, taken by us for an example of things that must be said, a total eclipse of the Moon [occurred] with a [lengthy] duration, and therefore of notable virtue. It preceded the Ingress of the Sun into the beginning of Aries; and it occurred namely on the 30th day of January at 18:05 apparent time at Paris according to the observation of Gassendi,[2] the Regius Professor of Mathematics and my colleague; and so I have been led to put its celestial chart here.[3]

---

[1] Here Morin disagrees with most astrologers, both ancient and modern, who apply the natures of the constellations to the signs that have the same names, regardless of the fact that most of the stars of a constellation may today be in an adjacent sign. And yet, the common practice seems to work.

[2] Pierre Gassendi (1592-1655). He became Regius Professor of Mathematics at the Collège Royale in Paris in 1645, and thus held a post similar to that held by Morin, who from 1630 was the Regius Professor of Mathematics at the Collège de France.

[3] The time and the chart are correct—a tribute to Gassendi's skill in calculation.

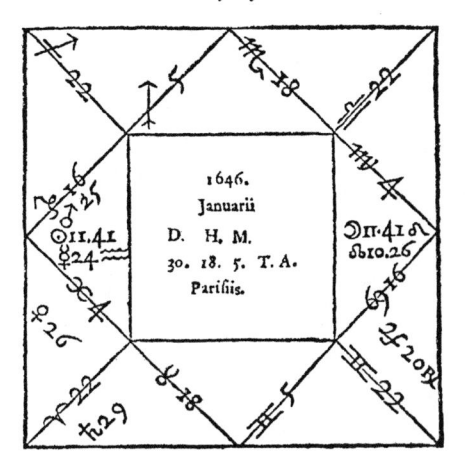

**Total Eclipse of the Moon.
Paris, France
31 January 1646 6:05 AM LAT**

Chapter 8. *The Grand Conjunctions of Saturn, Jupiter, and Mars and their Intervals.*

The conjunctions of these Planets among themselves, are called Grand Conjunctions on account of two most powerful reasons—namely, because they occur more rarely than the conjunctions of the other Planets, and because they produce greater effects on these sublunar things. The first reason is certain to be sure, as is established by the *Tables of Motions*. But the second, some astrologers try to prove from the histories of principal events of the World, which they strive to apply to these conjunctions. And indeed, if we were to consider that Saturn and Jupiter also have their own systems, or satellites, like the Sun, it cannot be denied that, at least after the Sun, Saturn and Jupiter are more so than the rest of [the Planets] of great virtue and authority in the World; and consequently, their conjunctions, squares, and oppositions can arouse great and also universal changes in sublunar things.

Therefore, since the conjunctions among themselves of these three, Saturn, Jupiter, and Mars, are famous among astrologers, even though we cannot erect celestial charts for the moments of these, on account of their slow diurnal motion,[1] especially when they are located around their stations[2]; nevertheless, we shall propose some things here that must be noted about those conjunctions, which will also lead to establishing a more certain forecast from them.

Therefore, of those mutual conjunctions, one is said to be a Grand Conjunction in which those three planets are conjoined with themselves, which very rarely happens.[3] A Great Conjunction is one in which only Saturn and Jupiter [are conjoined]. A Medium Conjunction is one in which only Mars and Jupiter [are conjoined].[4] But a Minimal Conjunction is one in which only Mars and Saturn come together, for these are the most frequent of all.[5]

But according to others, the Grand Conjunction is called the one in which Saturn and Jupiter are conjoined in a sign of absolutely

---

[1] Morin was aware that with a motion of only a few minutes of arc per day, it was impossible to determine the exact moment of the conjunction. And the uncertainty of the moment was even greater than he realized because in his day the calculated longitudes were inexact by several minutes of longitude. Consequently, the true time of a Jupiter-Saturn conjunction might be uncertain by a whole day or more. But with the high precision positions available today, the true time can now be accurately calculated.

[2] That is, when they are nearly SRx or SD and their daily motion is close to zero. At those times, the very date of the conjunction might have been in doubt by a week.

[3] These occur at irregular intervals of 20 or 40 years. The most recent occurrence of the triple conjunction was in April 2000, when on the 11th Mars at 15 ♉ was half-way between Jupiter at 12 ♉ and Saturn at 17 ♉. This was two months before the partile Jupiter-Saturn conjunction on 28 May 2000 in 23 ♉. Before that, in June of 1980 the three planets were in Virgo. Before that, in January 1940 they were in Aries. Before that they were in Libra in November and December of 1921. And there was a close triple conjunction of Mars, Jupiter, and Saturn on 15 December 1901 with Saturn, Mars and Jupiter at 16, 17, and 18 ♉ respectively. Also, in Chapter 12 below Morin mentions the close triple conjunction that occurred in February 1524.

[4] These occur at intervals of a little more than 2 years.

[5] They occur every other year, a little more often than the Mars-Jupiter conjunctions.

contrary nature to the one in which the last preceding conjunction [occurred]. As, if their preceding conjunction was in a water sign, and the [conjunction] immediately following was in a fire sign, that is said to be a Grand Conjunction.[1] The Medium [Conjunction] is one in which Saturn and Jupiter are conjoined in a sign partly of the same nature and partly of a nature contrary to the one in which their last preceding conjunction occurred. As if the preceding conjunction of Saturn and Jupiter was in an air sign, and immediately following the conjunction was made in a fire sign. Finally, the Minimal conjunction is one in which these same Planets are conjoined in a sign of the same nature as the one in which there last preceding conjunction occurred. As, if the preceding conjunction was in Sagittarius, and the one immediately following was in Leo, which signs are of the same fiery nature.

Whence it is plain that those astrologers only look at Saturn and Jupiter for the Grand Conjunctions. However, their Minimal Conjunctions occur [on the average] in 19 years and around 319 days according to the mean motions of those Planets, as Origanus chose from the *Prutenic Tables*.[2] The Medium Conjunctions in 198 years and around 265 days.[3] But the [very] Greatest Conjunction in 794 years and around 331 days.[4] But even if both appellations should be lacking in their own reasons; nevertheless, the previous one seems to me to be more natural and truer. Both because in the latter only Saturn and Jupiter are taken into account, with Mars excluded, for the greatest effects are with Jupiter or Saturn, or both of them, very powerful. And because the first conjunction of Saturn and Jupiter that occurred, either at the creation of the World or after that, could not be said to be the Greatest, the Medium, or the Minimal by reason of the signs, since it was the first conjunction,

---

[1]Nowadays, that change of elements is called a Mutation. But it does not begin definitively until a conjunction in the next element is followed by subsequent conjunctions in that element.
[2]Modern figures would put the cycle at 19 years 313.7 days.
[3]Modern figures would put the cycle at 198 years and 215 days.
[4]Modern figures would put this great cycle at 794 years and 130 days. This is sometimes called a Grand Mutation.

and since no other one preceded the first conjunction. And only those that follow can be so called, by comparison with the one next preceding.

Besides, about these Great Conjunctions, three things must be noted from the outset. **First**, because the effects attributed to those conjunctions are not produced by the mean conjunctions of those Planets—that is by those calculated according to their mean motions—but only from their true conjunctions—that is those that are completed according to their true motions.[1] And because, as we have already said elsewhere, the mean motions and the mean places of the Planets are only fictitious things, and therefore of no real and active virtue, but only one contrived by astronomers for finding the true motions and the true places of the Planets in the *Primum Mobile* with respect to us, whence they are perceived to act upon us, and not from their mean [places] where they are not [located] with respect to us.

And finally, not only in other universal constitutions but also in the nativities of men, the mean places of the Planets are not noticed for the causes of effects, but only the true places—both in directions and also in transits. For the mean places of the Planets are only related to the center of the orbit of the Planet, in which the Earth is not [located]. And hence no light error can happen—certainly, because the conjunction [calculated] according to the mean motions is in one sign, and that according to the true motions may be in another sign and under the rulership of another Planet. And in this, many astrologers who attach the history of things done in the World to those conjunctions were able to be deceived by having only taken into account the mean [conjunctions], and not the true ones.

Second. The conjunctions of Saturn, Jupiter, and Mars among themselves act on sublunar things in two ways: certainly, elemen-

---

[1]This and what follows is a slap at Albumasar (9th century), whose book, *De magnis conjunctionibus* 'The Great Conjunctions' (Augsburg: Erhard Ratdolt, 1485) is based entirely on the *mean conjunctions* of the Planets.

tally, having taken into account the proper elemental natures of the Planets that are conjoined and the sign in which the conjunction is located; and influentially, having taken into account the proper influences of those Planets and the sign; and both of those natures must be noted with regard to the elements, and any mixture, both imperfect, such as meteors, and perfect—namely minerals, vegetables, and animals.

Third. The conjunctions of Saturn and Jupiter, the Planets with satellites, are more effective nd produce greater effects, than the conjunctions of Saturn and Mars, or Jupiter and Mars, especially when they are made in signs of an absolutely contrary nature to those in which the immediately preceding conjunctions of those Planets were made.

Chapter 9. *How the rulers of Universal Constitutions should generally be chosen.*

Since the effects of universal constitutions mainly depend upon their rulers, that is upon the Planets ruling those constitutions or powerful in them, it is evidently plain that in the prediction of their effects, the greatest error will occur if some Planets are falsely assigned to the rulership of the constitution; and consequently, the selection of the true ruler of a constitution is of great moment in this doctrine. But before we unfold its method, it seems to us that some things should be stated in advance.

First. In every universal constitution there is some principal point of that constitution that should be noted before the rest. And that is indeed easily distinguished if the constitution is the periodic Return of a Planet to its radical place of creation, or the synodical Revolution of two Planets. For in the latter there is given a single such point that ought to be particularly looked at—namely, the Planet that is making the Revolution and its place in the zodiac. Also in syzygies, namely the opposition, squares, trines, etc. of the two Planets, or in the transits through the determined places in the universal constitution.

But it can be doubted whether both of the Planets or the place should be noticed—[or] whether only one of them, and [if so] which? For many will have, in the case of the syzygial opposition of the Sun and Moon, that Planet to be especially looked at that is under the Earth or in the ASC, and also that is square to that Planet that is above the Earth. But if both of them should be above the Earth, or both of them under the Earth, [it should be] the one that occupies the most important house or an angle. Moreover, the ASC is preferred to the MC, and that to the DSC, and that to the IMC. Moreover, in the case where many Planets are contending equally for the rulership, they prefer the one that rules in the Moon's place, however, as another ally to it, and as less than the principal rulership.

Moreover, I think that in the case of the syzygies, the lighter Planet is the one that mainly should be looked at, whether it is above the Earth or below the Earth, at least for influential effects; and in transits, the transiting Planet. For both the lighter one, and the transiting one—that is the one that is revolving, either periodically or synodically—and the effects of that one's revolution are required. Therefore, that one must particularly be looked at, not however with neglect of the other Planet with which it is making a sygygy, or through whose place, determined by body or by aspect, a transit is being made. Taking note of the fact that a Planet transiting in a synodic revolution transits through the places determined by both of the Planets that made the synod, and therefore that transit is more powerful.

Second. In the charts of universal constitutions, the four angles must always be looked at, just as the rising, vigor, decline, and death of sublunar things. But among those angles, the ones that must be principally looked at are the ASC and the MC, but most of all the ASC, for that is the one that gives the essence of the effects emanating from that constitution, or it shoots out their seeds into the womb of Nature, and more so than the rest, it rules the temperament of the air.

Third. All of the ancients will have it, that besides the primary point in the constitution about which [we spoke] above, the angle following according to the sequence of signs should be principally noticed among the four angles of the figure. But since that primary point is always a Planet, if it is direct, the angle following would be looked at, unless it would be joined at least platically to a preceding Planet. The reason is that "angle" must not be understood [to mean] the "space" of the angular house or of its cusp, but it must be understood [to mean] "the degree occupying that cusp" to which the Planet is moving, and to which it can come by direct motion, but not the degree of the preceding cusp.

If however that Planet should also be joined platically to that degree by separation, that angle would be prepollent over the one following, on account of the presence of the conjoined Planet. But [in the case of] a Planet in its retrograde state, as can happen in the synods or periodical revolutions of Saturn, Jupiter, Mars, Venus, or Mercury, the preceding angle would be more powerful than the following angle on account of the same reason, unless the Planet would be at least joined platically to the following angle. And not only the degree of the cusp must be looked at, but also the part of the *Caelum* occupying that angle and the Planets in it.

Fourth. The Planet that is the primary point of the constitution, such as the Sun in its Mundane Revolution, the Sun and the Moon in their synod, the Moon in its square syzygies with the Sun, or in its transits through the determined places in the synod, must be looked at considering its proper nature, the sign that it occupies, the ruler to which it is subject, and both their celestial and terrestrial states. But the angles of the figure, in so as far as they are such a sign of such a Planet, and in such a state, both celestial and terrestrial, should also be looked at, so that a judgment may be extracted from all of these.

Fifth. A universal constitution is not distinguished by a signification or effect for the whole circuit of the Earth by reason of the primary point, its ruler, and both its celestial and terrestrial state, but only by reason of the angles of the figure, or the position of the primary point, and the position of the whole *Caelum* with respect to the horizon, and by reason of the terrestrial state of the rulers of the constitution. For the force and the effects of this are valid through the whole circumference of the Earth; and therefore, for each horizon those things must be especially looked at. For the primary point, its ruler, and its celestial state signify only universally and without distinction for the whole Earth. But the rest determine the universal constitution for the kinds of effects pertaining to the houses of each horizon, and they produce differing effects according to the diversity of the ASC's, in which the individual places on Earth differ among themselves, even places under the same meridian.

Having put [these thing] down, it must now be stated by what reason any particular Planet may be allotted rulership. First, according to Ptolemy, Cardan, and the old astrologers, but second according to our own opinion. And so, from Ptolemy, *Tetrabiblos*, Book 2, Chapter 7, with Cardan in his *Commentary*, the reason for the rulership of a Planet over a universal constitution, such as an eclipse, is taken from the conjunction of that Planet with the primary point of the constitution, or from an aspect to that point, or from [having] power in that point by domicile, triplicity, exaltation, and terms, and this is set forth in the order of [the strength of] virtue, so that the conjunction is more powerful than an aspect, and the aspect more powerful than a dignity.

Moreover, in the case of a conjunction and an aspect, the [Planet] applying is preferred to the one separating; and among the aspects, the opposition is stronger, then the square among the inimical aspects, and the trine among the friendly ones, and finally the sextile and the antiscion. But among the powers, the domicile claims primacy for itself, then the triplicity, then the exaltation; moreover, the terms are inferior to the rest, [since] they also have been shown elsewhere to be mere fictions.[1]

---

[1] See Book 15, Chapter 13.

And [all of] this was the opinion of the ancients about [choosing] the ruler of the primary point of the constitution, which besides that point is the Sun in its annual Revolution or an eclipse, the Moon in its syzygies or in an eclipse, etc. They attributed no force to the effects of the constitution, but the whole force to the rulers of the constitution, which in eclipses they imagined to perform the functions of the eclipsed Light, and to receive its virtue, especially by conjunction or aspect, and to pour it out upon sublunar things, as if the Moon declining in light would also decline in influence; and this would be nothing other than that light accidentally received from the Sun, either such from an eclipse, or from the subtraction of light, the influence of the Moon might move into the body of the ruler of the constitution. But they said that a combust Planet or one beneath the Earth is incapable of rulership on account of its debility, as well as if it was in exile, dejected, or in a bad house of the figure, or in a cadent house.

And they would have only the stronger Planets in the figure to be taking the rulership, which is however alien to reason. For in a Revolution of the Sun, or in a synod of the Sun and the Moon, the Sun and the Moon act in accordance with the nature and state of their own rulers, whether good or evil; and no other Planet can be substituted for this, but another Planet that is the strongest in the constitution does not prevent this, even though it may produce notable effects as a less important part of its constitution.

And as for the angles, Ptolemy takes the Planet that was in the angle following the primary point, or the one ruling it, and a bright fixed star that is adjacent to the preceding angle, and from those he judges. But Cardan in his *Commentary* gives a reason for that choice—[namely], that the Planets are moved from their setting to their rising, that is into the following [places]; but a fixed star in the preceding angle is oriental to the Sun, which is no reason! For a fixed star also moves from its setting to its rising, but a Planet in the preceding angle is oriental to the Sun in its annual revolution or in its eclipse. Therefore, the reasoning about those angles that we have put above seems to be more credible.

But from the principles of astrology that we have put down, we may judge that it ought to be determined in quite another way. For we ascribe the cause of the effects to the primary point of the constitution, and not to the Light that is losing its light and also its virtue in those eclipses and its effect on these inferior things; and [rather than that] we have asserted that another [Planet] performs its function on account of the reasons expounded in Chapter 7, but principally in Book 16, Section 3, where the discussion is about combust Planets.

Besides, although according to Book 20, Section 2, Chapter 2, Planets endow themselves elementally, at least with heat or cold; and the Moon heated by the Sun reflects upon us at the time of full Moon something of the heat of the Sun, and yet this is not noticeable; therefore, how much less will it be noticeable in the case of the other planets heated by the Sun, as we have said in Chapter 3 of that same Section? But the Planets do not act influentially on themselves in turn according to the first Chapter of that same Section; and consequently one of them does not receive influential force from another, so that it can pour it out upon these sublunar things; and in consequence, one does not take on the function of another, either influentially, or elementally. And if one Planet was able to perform the function of another elementally, that would especially be the Moon, the closest of all to us; which therefore in all the Revolutions of the other Planets, it would have to be declared to be the ruler—but wrongly, on account of what was said above about the heat of the Sun reflected by the Moon.

And so, that Planet will be said to be the principal ruler of the constitution, that in the place of the primary point and following it, or in the preceding angle (just as was explained previously), will be the one more powerful by domicile, by connection by body or aspect, by exaltation and by triplicity. Moreover, among the connections, those that are by body or conjunction will be preferred to those that are by aspect, and those applying will be preferred to those separating. And among the aspects, the stronger one is the opposition, then the square in maleficent constitutions, and the trine in beneficent ones.

Moreover, a Planet powerful by domicile is preferred by us over one powerful by connection, against Cardan's opinion. Then, because his reason is false, "that rays are more according to Nature, than power," which [power] seems to be in his opinion something fictitious; then, because the diversity of effects emanating from the same kind of universal constitutions, such as the synod of the Sun and the Moon, is sought first and per se from the diversity of the signs in which they occur, and from the signs of the Planets ruling them and from their state. For can there not be a synod that is in another sign and under another rulership? But there can be one without connection with any other Planets by body and by aspects; therefore, as far as specifying or determining [power] from a part of the *Caelum*, it will depend primarily upon the sign and its ruler.

Therefore, the Sun and the Moon coming together in Pisces, act indeed from themselves according to their proper nature, but they act with the sign Pisces, but it acts only according to the nature and state of its ruler Jupiter, as was shown in detail elsewhere. And consequently, to say that the Sun and the Moon act with Pisces is the same thing as to say that they act according to the intrinsic nature and state of Jupiter, or with Jupiter viewed thus, which thus specifies and determines the proper effects of the coming together of the Sun and the Moon. But if another Planet, such as Mars, is conjoined to the Lights in Pisces, that one will indeed combine its own forces with the forces proper to the Sun and the Moon, but as the Sun and the Moon would act with Pisces—that is, in accordance with the nature and state of Jupiter; and so, Jupiter would always be the Planet in that synod that should principally be looked at for primarily determining the effects of that part of the *Caelum*. If, however, the conjoined Planet would occupy another sign, its ruler would become a partner in the rulership of the constitution, but a weaker one than if it would be in Pisces, or in its own domicile.[1] And in addition, if it was not in the same house of the figure with the primary point, its determination on the effects of the

---

[1]Morin is speaking of a case in which Mars is within orbs of the synod in Pisces but is either in the latter part of Aquarius or in the first part of Aries.

synod would be still weaker and more obscure. Therefore, the diversity of the effects of the synod arising from the part of the *Caelum* is primarily sought from the sign in which the synod is, and from its ruler and its celestial state, and only secondarily from the Planets connected with the principal point.

And the objection here will not be valid, because the presence of a Planet is stronger than the rulership of an absent one. For this is indeed true about a Planet looked at for the effects to which they are determined by reason of their house, as was shown in Book 22, Section 2, Chapter 4, but not in the case of a Planet with respect to the primary point of a universal constitution, as its effect should primarily be seen from the part of the *Caelum*. And in fact, the effects of the Planets are specified or determined in two ways: Certainly, from the part of the *Caelum*, and from the part of the Earth [that they occupy].

By the first way, they are determined to accidents of the kind that agree with the signs in which those planets are placed, and with their rulers and their celestial state. As if [for example] the Sun was in Sagittarius, the proper celestial effects of the Sun will be determined to Sagittarius and Jupiter along with its celestial state. By the second way, they are determined to accidents of the kind that pertain to the houses of the figure in which those Planets are found, or which they rule. As if the Sun was in Sagittarius and in the 10th house, the force of the Sun will be primarily determined to acting in a Jupiterean manner, or with Jupiter, and secondarily to acting on actions, profession and honors, or dignities, and so with the rest [of the combinations].

Moreover, because in the first category, that is the celestial one, the effects of the universal constitution will be primarily specified by the sign and its ruler, but not by the conjoined Planets. This may also be proved thus—For if in a synod of the Sun and the Moon in Gemini, the effects of that synod will not be specified celestially by the Sun rather than by the Moon; indeed, if Mars is also attached partilely to them, the effects of that synod will not even be specified more by Mars than by the Sun of the Moon, for both ways are equal.

Therefore, the effects of the conjunction of the Sun and the Moon will be primarily specified celestially—only from the sign and its ruler—but they will be *qualified* by the conjoined Mars, with the nature and celestial state of Mars, especially if the Moon applies immediately to Mars or to another conjoined Planet. And it does not follow from this, that in the Mundane Revolutions of the Sun they will always be of the same kind from the part of the *Caelum*, because they are always in Aries under the rulership of Mars, for in each individual year the celestial state of Mars with which Mars acts is not the same.

And the rest of the Planets are not in the same celestial state among themselves as is the case with the primary point of the constitution. And the same thing must be thought about the Revolutions of Nativities. Because if this logic is persuading about a conjunct Planet, it will be much more persuasive about its aspects; however, although Cardan will have it above from Ptolemy that a Planet by its sextile to the primary point of the synod can have more effects of the synod than by its rulership, that is manifestly contrary to experience in nativities; namely, because if the ASC is in Taurus and sextile Saturn, the native would be more Venerean in his character than Saturnian; and because his character of the Venerean kind would only be colored and qualified by some influx of Saturn.

But also from this, the opinion of those should be rejected who will have the primary ruler of a constitution, such as the conjunctions of the Sun and Moon, to be the [Planet] to which the Moon first applies. Add that for the whole circuit of the Earth the ruler of such a constitution would be the same, and consequently universal, but at the same time some particular [ruler] would be sought for every place on Earth.

Furthermore, if the same Planet is the ruler of the primary point and the following one, or the preceding angle, it will be very powerful; but if in addition it is connected by body or by a strong ray to that primary point or angle, it will be still more powerful. But it will be most powerful if it is still in an angle with that primary point, especially in the ASC or in the MC, which two angles are always powerful in every constitution.

But if the same Planet is not more powerful than the rest in both places; namely, in the place of the primary point or in an angle, the more powerful one will in fact be preferred in the primary point, that is the ruler of the sign, but that Planet will be associated with it that in both places is at the same time more powerful than the rest, always having taken into account the rulers of the ASC and the MC, which always have great power.

But with many Planets assuming the rulership for themselves equally, on account of an equal regard to both places, either the one that is more angular will be preferred, or the one with the stronger celestial state, or the one that has the most suitable condition—either matutine to the Sun or vespertine to the Moon—in their Revolutions or syzygies; but, with all of them being equal, the one above the Earth will always be preferred to the one below the Earth, because the force of the one below the Earth is hindered by the interposition of the Earth.

In the case where two Planets would be rulers at the same time, and would be in mutual dignities, or would be aspecting each other with a strong ray, and at the same time aspecting the primary point, or the principal angle, they would act strongly. See what we have said about a similar situation in Book 23, *The Revolutions of Nativities*, Chapter 17.

Finally, aside from the Planets, two at least of the brighter fixed stars will also take the rulership of the constitution, of which one attends the preceding angle, but the other one the following principal point, not very distant from those angles, and which are together with the primary point in the MC, or together on the horizon; or one of them is on the meridian and the other on the horizon; otherwise, they will be weaker. And if the Planet that is ruler of the constitution is also ruler of the fixed star by reason of its sign, and if it aspects it with a strong ray according to its longitude, latitude, or otherwise, it will be much stronger, especially if it is of the nature of that ruling Planet. Moreover, whether they should be chosen only in the zodiac, or whether they are also far distant [by latitude], I do not see that it was definitely stated by the astrologers.

Moreover, even if I should think—speaking absolutely—that those close to the ecliptic are more effective than the more distant ones, especially if they were conjoined to Planets; nevertheless, having taken into account the places that are vertical to the place of the chart, or close, it does not seem to me that they should be put behind the rest. For not without necessity God sowed the whole *Caelum* with fixed stars; indeed, He placed brighter fixed stars around the poles (where the force of the Planets acts more weakly), so that these would in some way supply the functions of the Planets, especially when all of them are hidden under the horizon. But if those fixed stars should be looked at in angles, therefore much more should the Planets be looked at in the angles.

Chapter 10. *The Application of what was just said, and the Election of Rulers in the Figures shown above.*

Although the figures placed above are particular to the place for which they were erected, namely Paris, they are nevertheless universal, or common to all those living around the city itself to a distance that would retain the same signs on the angles of the figures and the same rulers of the figures. For thus, that whole space of the kingdom or the region would be subject to the same virtue of the constitution; and the only diversity of effects in that space can arise from the diverse proper constitution of the parts of that space.[1]

---

[1] In what follows, Morin explains how to choose the rulers of a universal constitution. Some of the charts that he discusses have errors in them; however, he is not *interpreting* the charts, but only showing how to *choose the rulers* of the charts drawn *as you see them*, so the errors in the charts (which are mentioned in the notes below) do not invalidate his explanations.

And so, in the figure placed above of the annual Revolution of the World, or the Ingress of the Sun into the beginning of Aries, the Sun of a fiery nature enters a fire sign and its own exaltation and triplicity in the 11th house of the figure; but Mars is the ruler of the primary point, or the Sun, and it is in its own triplicity, oriental to the Sun, and angular in the 10th. Mercury, however, is the ruler of the following angle, namely the ASC, in its triplicity powerful in the MC, also oriental and angular in the 10th; and they are both conjoined in Pisces, a water sign; and their ruler Jupiter is in the following angle; and in mutual reception by domicile with Mercury, applying by square to the Sun and by trine to Mars and Mercury[1]; therefore, Mars, Mercury, and Jupiter are strongly powerful in this chart, but Mars claims the primacy for itself; and Mercury prevails over Jupiter on account of its conjunction with Mars. For if Mercury in Pisces is under the dominion of Jupiter and acts in dependence on Jupiter, the latter in turn is under the dominion of Mercury. But since Mars applies immediately and partilely to the sextile of Saturn, which is powerful in the MC and the ASC that is in its own triplicity, Saturn therefore will also exercise something of power in this constitution. Finally, the Eye of Taurus, a bright fixed star of the nature of Mars, partilely located on the ASC on account of its latitude, alone among the fixed stars will exercise rulership.[2]

In the figure of the Sun's Ingress into 0 ♋ 00, the Sun near the MC is entering into a water sign, which the Moon rules by domicile and Jupiter rules by exaltation and triplicity, being above the Earth by day; and it therefore rules both the Sun and the following angle; and both [Jupiter and the Moon] are angular—namely, Jupiter in the MC, the following angle, and the Moon in the ASC—and they are also in square; and then both of them are with bright fixed stars[3]; and finally, the Moon is in trine to Mercury, ruler of its

---

[1] Here Morin is describing the aspects that Jupiter will make after it has left Gemini and moved into early Cancer.

[2] The star Aldebaran or α Tauri, which in 1646 was at 4 ♊ 51 and 5 S 30, rose at Paris with 14 ♊ 54, which was within 5° of the ASC in 20 ♊.

[3] The stars are *Cast. Pol.* and *canic*, which I take to be Castor or α Geminorum,

triplicity; moreover, Jupiter is in sextile to Mars, Saturn, and Venus.

Both of them are therefore very strong in this figure; however, Jupiter prevails in Cancer, because it is in its own exaltation, which increases the powers of an exalted Planet, and in its own triplicity, above the Earth by day. But that does not hinder its acting with Cancer, and Cancer with the nature and state of the Moon; and therefore much more does the Sun in Cancer act with the Moon according to her nature and state. But Mercury and Arcturus in the ASC by their own nature and state concur with the effects of the Moon; but Mars [concurs] with Saturn and Venus and the stars in the 10th with the virtue of Jupiter, which in this association prevails over the Moon.

In the figure of the Sun's Ingress into 0 ♎ 00, the Sun in the 2nd house is entering into an air sign that Venus rules by domicile and triplicity, by night under the Earth, and in the exaltation of Saturn retrograde in Taurus in his own triplicity. Moreover, the Sun is in mutual reception by domicile with Venus, applying by sextile to Jupiter, which is powerful in the places of the Moon and Mars.[1] But Mars in the domicile of the Moon rules the following angle, and the Moon, from [her place in] the DSC in Pisces the domicile of Jupiter, applies to Mars by trine.

Moreover, both Mars and the Moon in their own triplicity, by night above the Earth, are applying by mutual sextile to the retrograde Saturn, which, separating from a square to Venus, immediately applies to a sextile to Mars; and Saturn and Mars are elevated above the rest of the Planets. And so, from many considerations, Saturn in this figure is superior to Venus, which is peregrine in Leo and in the 12th house without any aspect to the Sun or to other Planets, with the exception of Saturn, from whom she is separating

---

and Pollux or α Geminorum, and Sirius or α Canis Majoris. In 1646, Sirius was at 9 ♋ 13, Castor at 15 ♋ 19, Pollux at 18 ♋ 20 and Arcturus at 19 ♎ 18.

[1] The Moon is in Jupiter's domicile Pisces, and Mars is in Jupiter's exaltation Cancer.

by square; [and so] she must be thought to be of little virtue in this constitution; and consequently, Saturn and Mars applying to themselves mutually will prevail, along with the Heart of Hydra[1] of the nature of Saturn in the ASC, and the Pleiades[2] with the MC and Saturn.

In the figure of the Sun's Ingress into 0 ♑ 00, the Sun is entering an earth sign in the 7th house; and Saturn rules the place of the Sun and the following angle; then also the ASC[3] with Mercury, which Saturn also rules, and in addition it is also found in trine to the Sun and Mercury and sextile the Moon, and to Jupiter, to which it mutually applies[4]; but first and immediately Saturn squares Mars. Moreover, the Sun immediately applies to the opposition of the Moon in Cancer, and she is mutually conjoined to Jupiter.[5]

And Saturn, Jupiter, and Mars are retrograde. And Saturn is elevated above all the Planets, if you make exception for Mercury. And so Saturn is the principal ruler in this figure without any dispute. Moreover, the Moon, to whom the Sun applies by opposition,[6] will be allotted no small force in the effects, along with Mercury, the diurnal ruler of the Sun's triplicity, and being above the Earth in its own triplicity.

In the figure of the new Moon in Chapter 6 [above], Jupiter rules the domicile and the triplicity by day of the place of the synod, but it is in exile under the Earth. Moreover, Venus rules the place of the synod by exaltation, and it also rules the following an-

---

[1] Alphard or α Hydrae was in 22 ♌ 22.

[2] The brightest star of the Pleiades is Alcyone or η Tauri, which was in 25 ♉ 03.

[3] Presumably, Morin means that Saturn rules the triplicity of the ASC itself, which it rules by domicile and triplicity.

[4] As noted above, the Moon was not in 4 Cancer (where it would have been in sextile to Saturn), but rather in 19 Gemini (without any aspect to Saturn); and Jupiter was not in 7 Cancer but in 8 Leo, so Saturn was square Jupiter.

[5] Again, both of these statements are wrong, because the Moon was in Gemini not in Cancer, and Jupiter was in Leo conjunct Mars, not in Cancer and conjunct the Moon.

[6] Not so, as explained in the preceding notes.

gle, which is the ASC itself, by domicile and triplicity. And Venus is angular, joined to the ASC, in its own domicile. Therefore, Jupiter and Venus rule this new Moon, with some participation by Saturn, which is in the ASC. And the Moon applies partilely by square to Jupiter her own ruler; so that consequently, Jupiter and Venus are seen to compete with equal powers for the predominance; but it seems to me that Venus prevails.

In the figure of the eclipse of the Moon in Chapter 7 [above], the Sun is the ruler of the place of the Moon, with Mars the ruler of the triplicity,[1] and Saturn is ruler of the place of the Sun and the ASC with the triplicity ruler Mercury; however, Mars rules the domicile and the triplicity of the following angle, i.e. the MC; then it rules the ASC by its exaltation in which it is found, applying by square to its ruler Saturn. Therefore, Mars and Saturn rule this eclipse. Being in mutual reception by domicile, and [in aspect] by square, but Mars prevails.

But as for that which pertains to the Great Conjunctions, the latest of which is the conjunction of Saturn and Jupiter that was made on 24 February 1643 in the 25th degree of Pisces according to the *Rudolphine Tables*; the one that immediately preceded was in the 7th degree of Leo in the month of July in the year 1623[2]; and therefore it is called a Grand Conjunction.[3] The [exact] moment of the conjunction being unknown, for which a figure could be erected

---

[1] Morin is referring to the fire triplicity in which the Moon is located. In his scheme of triplicity rulers (see Book 15), Mars is the night ruler of the fire triplicity.

[2] Calculations from modern figures show that the 1643 conjunction occurred on 24 February at about 11:25 pm LMT at Paris in 25 ♓ 07; and the previous conjunction occurred at Paris on 16 July 1623 at about 10:52 PM LMT in 6 ♌ 36. The Rudolphine Tables would have put the 1643 eclipse on 26 February at about 3 PM LMT at Paris in 25 ♓ 26 and the previous eclipse in 1623 on 17 July at about 2 PM LMT at Paris in 6 ♌ 41.

[3] The 1623 conjunction in Leo was not a Grand Conjunction, i.e. what is now called a Mutation, because the next conjunction in 1643 was in Pisces. The definitive change from water signs to fire signs occurred subsequently at Paris on 17 October 1663 at about 0:00 AM LMT with the conjunction in 12 ♐ 58. The next Mutation (to the earth triplicity) occurred subsequently in 1842 with a conjunction in Capricorn.

determining its force for particular horizons, it can only be said that Jupiter is its universal ruler for the whole circuit of the Earth, and the most powerful [Planet] of all—that is, because that conjunction occurs in a domicile of Jupiter in sextile to the Moon in Taurus and to Mars in the beginning of Gemini; and Mars and the Moon should be more powerful by triplicity in the place of the conjunction.

Similarly, moreover, we must proceed in all other universal constitutions to define their rulers. Besides, these things must be understood about simple constitutions. For in connection with composite constitutions, which are the Solar Ingresses into the four cardinal points; for which Ptolemy, not unjustly will have it that the new Moon or the full Moon immediately preceding the Sun's Ingress should be considered; therefore, two figures are to be noted for each quarter of the year.

It will have to be seen which Planet is more powerful in both figures; or, if there were more than one, how they were related among themselves in the individual figures, especially when the new Moon or the full Moon is in the ecliptic, and therefore of greater virtue, so that at least more properly the judgment may be made on the principal [character] of the effects of that Ingress, as was already said in Chapter 3. But if the Sun's Revolution or its quarter has begun at the same time as the new Moon or the full Moon, then it will be independent and very strong. And the procedure is the same with the other universal constitutions.

Chapter 11. *Which Places on Earth a Universal Constitution may be acting upon.*

Ptolemy, in [*Tetrabiblos*], Book 2, Chapter 4, says of universal constitutions that nothing is more important and more effective on sublunar things than eclipses of the Sun and the Moon, and the state of the other Planets, especially Saturn, Jupiter, and Mars, at the time of the eclipse, with their stations or aspects and rulerships over the place of the eclipse. Moreover, four things are inquired into about those eclipses. **First.** What region or city does the eclipse portend for. **Second.** When would its effects begin and how long will they last. **Third.** Which effects of a [particular] kind would it produce—namely, whether it would be famine, or war, etc. **Fourth.** What will be the manner of the events—as in the signification of war, who would be the victor.

Therefore, with respect to these four things, it will be shown below that Ptolemy's doctrine is erroneous. Even though Cardan in the beginning of his *Commentary* on Chapter 4, says that that [doctrine] was most precisely handed down by Ptolemy, and with the most exquisite and abstruse [reasons], but that by no one of the expositors before Cardan himself was it understood. However, we shall examine the first in this chapter, and the rest of them in the following chapters.

Therefore, Ptolemy says, with Cardan in agreement, that an eclipse portends for regions that are subject to the sign or the triplicity in which the eclipse occurred, according to the distribution of the signs to all the places on Earth. But principally to those, or to the metropolitan cities, that at the beginning of their construction had the eclipsed Light in that sign, or that sign in the ASC of the figure of their construction; or if the time of the construction and its figure were not known, those that are ruled by Princes or lords in the figure of whose nativities or of their succession to rulership or of their election to rulership, that ecliptical sign occupies the ASC or the MC.

But that doctrine of the rulership of the signs over regions and cities was already refuted by us in Chapter 7. And it only remains for Cardan to be emended when he says in his *Commentary*:

> "that where a city agrees with its constellation (that is, with a universal constitution, such as the chart of an eclipse), and the region does not agree by triplicity at least by sign; nevertheless, the effect will occur. In the case of men, however, even

though a proper nativity would agree, and the city in which the man is would not agree, there will be nothing [by way of an effect]. And on account of this, I believe (he says) that that eclipse[1] [that occurred] in Taurus in the degree of my ASC in the year 1539 produced nothing, because it was not agreeing with the City of Milan, where I was, or was living, or nearby."

These things, however, are alien to the truth. Both, because that agreement of the region or the city with an eclipse was already rejected above. And because, having conceded that a city is part of a region or a kingdom, so is a man a part of a city; therefore, if an effect occurs in a city without the agreement with the region, so it occurs in the case of a man without the agreement with the city.

Add that if besides the agreement of the eclipse with the nativity of a man, and agreement with the city would also be necessary, as Cardan will have it in his example; therefore, in a spreading plague, the city [would have to agree] with all the nativities of men who are attacked by the plague; which is very absurd to suppose, for it cannot agree with individual cases, just as a ship in the figure of its construction cannot agree with the individual [nativities] of those who are drowned in it, but that is the way it is.

Individuals living in a city exposed to the plague by a bad celestial universal constitution then in force, and not by reason of an agreement of that constitution with the figure of the construction of that city, are endangered by the plague through their being in that city. And those particularly whom that constitution will also affect; namely, if the eclipse occurs in their ASC, or in other significators of life, and they have a direction, or a lethal or sickly revolution in that same year.

---

[1] This was the total eclipse of the Sun that occurred in 7°11′ Taurus on the afternoon of 18 April 1539 as seen at Milan. The path of totality ran through the Mediterranean Sea south of Italy.

Less [affected] are those for whom only one of those happens; but least of all those for whom neither happens; or, on the contrary, those for whom some fortunate direction happens to the ASC, along with a healthy revolution, as [happened] to Cardan himself, to whom indeed the eclipse of the Sun occurred on the 8th degree of Taurus, when he had the 7th degree in his ASC. But in that same year his ASC was being directed to the trine of Venus, his ruler and ruler of the eclipse's place, and there was a very healthy Revolution, as is plain from Book 23, Chapter 7. And those things saved Cardan, who, while not aware of them, although they were very evident, fixed the cause for himself as being the discordance of his nativity with the figure of the construction of Milan that was unknown to himself.

But the principal reasons why Ptolemy's doctrine was deviating from the truth are: **First.** That every eclipse is only a lunation; and every lunation is subordinated to the annual Mundane Revolution of the Sun, from which it depends, as was shown in Chapter 4. Therefore, the annual Mundane Revolution of the Sun is the first and most efficacious universal constitution; but not an eclipse, unless it is part of that Revolution of the Sun.

Second. That from the figure of the universal constitution erected for any particular place, such as Paris, it is completely absurd to inquire and define [from it] what it might do in China or America. Since a celestial constitution acts by means of its universal influx only according as it is determined locally by an erected figure, as was shown in detail in Book 21, Section 2. And so, from a figure erected for the horizon of Paris, it should only be asked what that would do at Paris or thereabouts, so long as the rulership of the figure does not change, but remains the same. But not in China, where the effects of the same constitution will be defined similarly by a celestial chart erected for a place in China; for without that chart, neither the particular rulers of the constitution, nor by consequence its particular effects can be known in any possible place, as is plain from Chapter 10.

Third. That from common lunations, namely those in which no eclipse occurs, and from the figures erected for them, neither Ptolemy, nor any one of the old astrologers tried to get what effects those lunations would produce in foreign regions and those far distant from the place for which the figure was erected, but only those effects that would be produced in that very place, either in elements, or in plants, or in animals, or in men. But what is an eclipse of the Sun other than a new Moon? And what is an eclipse of the Moon other than a full Moon in the ecliptic, or without a latitude that exceeds the semi-diameters of the Sun and the Moon?

Or, therefore, must it be said that lunations with no latitude or with that latitude will signify for foreign regions, with greater [latitude], however, only for the place of the figure? It would be different, but it must only be said that lunations without latitude, or with an eclipse, are more effective, and they produce more notable effects; but without an eclipse they are less effective everywhere by reason of their own local determination by the horizontal chart of the *Caelum*, or a figure erected for the horizon of the place. And this is indeed common to all the Planets wandering away from the ecliptic, as the closer they are to the ecliptic, the more effective they are, and in the ecliptic itself they are the most effective. And from that [fact] has arisen the fictitious virtues of the Head and Tail of the Dragon of the Moon, by which indeed the more remote they are from the ecliptic, the weaker they are.

Nevertheless, in all universal constitutions—namely in annual Revolutions, eclipses, etc.—whose figures can be erected, we will be able to know for which nations that constitution will principally signify in this way. In the case of eclipses, see what nations or cities in particular have the Light being eclipsed, or the ruler of its ecliptical place, in the ASC, the MC, or the DSC; for the constitution of the Caelum principally signifies for those, by reason of the significators being angular. And to know this will not be useless to Kings, when great eclipses portend great effects; that is by erecting a figure for those locations.

In this case, if the constitution has signified wars, on account of the rulership of Mars in the primary point, see what nation may have, either the Light being eclipsed or Mars, determined for wars in the 7th, which is [the house] of wars, or in the 10th, which is [the house] of actions. For with those [positions] wars are actively or more certainly passively signified than in other [positions]. For those in which it was in the 12th, it portends illnesses or exiles; for those in which it was in the 8th, plagues and mortality; and so with the other [houses].. And this is from the *arcana* of the science. For the Planets act everywhere in accordance with their own determination, and not otherwise; but let this suffice for all of this. But see Book 15, Chapter 8.

Chapter 12. *The Times of the Events that will occur from the Universal Constitutions.*

Concerning these times, we must make four inquiries. **First.** How long will the effects of the universal constitution, such as the annual Revolution of the Sun, an eclipse, etc. last? **Second.** When will they begin? **Third.** When will they intensify or decline? **Fourth.** When will they end, or when will that constitution cease to act per se?

Ptolemy, along with Cardan, in *Tetrabiblos*, Book 1, Chapter 6, and the other old [astrologers] judge thus about these [questions] for eclipses, which he has principally speculated about.

First. The celestial figure is erected for the apparent time of the middle of the eclipse, that is the time of the true conjunction or opposition of the Lights.

Second. He calculates how many equinoctial hours the [period of] complete obscuration will last. For he says that that many years will the effects of the eclipse of the Sun last, and that many months will the effects of an eclipse of the Moon last.

Third. He considers the location of the place of an eclipse of the Sun with respect to the angles of the figure; and he says that if the place is in the ASC, the effects will begin in the first four months after the eclipse, and they will be more powerful in the first third of the total duration. Moreover, if the place [of the eclipse] is in the MC, the effects will begin in the second [period of] four months, and they will be more intense in the second third of the [total] duration. Finally, if the place [of the eclipse] is in the DSC angle, the effects will begin in the third [period of] four months, and they will be stronger in the last third of the total duration of the effects. Moreover, the particular intensifications and remissions will be indicated by the conjunctions and aspects of the Planets ruling the eclipse, when they have fallen onto the place of the eclipse, or the angles of the figure, especially when those Planets are in their own matutine or vespertine rising, or in their own stations. And that is Ptolemy's opinion.

But since the place of the eclipse rarely falls in those angles, so by the distance of that place from the ASC, they want to find precisely the time of the beginning of the effects of an eclipse of the Sun. *First*, the quantity of the day may be had from a common Table of the quantity of days. *Second*, it may be seen how many hours are counted from the angle of the east down to mid-eclipse in this way. If mid-eclipse is after the time of Sun rise, subtract the time of the beginning of the day from the time of mid-eclipse; but if mid-eclipse precedes the time of the rising of the eclipsed Sun, in a contrary way, subtract the hours and minutes of mid-eclipse from the [time of] the beginning of the day, or the night, and there will be left the time between mid-eclipse and Sun rise, which you put as the third number in the Golden Rule, or [rule of] proportion. For the second [number you put] the 365 days of the year, and for the first the quantity of the day, and there will emerge the number of days after the eclipse that its effects will begin. These will be stronger around the beginning of the middle, or the end of their duration, according as mid-eclipse is nearer to the east or the west of the MC. And similarly in the case of an eclipse of the Moon, it must be worked by the quantity of the night, having subtracted the time of the beginning of the night from the time of mid-eclipse as the third number above; but the first number will be the quantity of the night, and the second 365 as above.

In the first place, however, it must be shown that this doctrine of Ptolemy is alien to the truth for the following reasons. **First.** What he looks at for the duration of the effects. An astrologer ought only to agree with reason, or with experience, which never lacks a proper reason, although it is sometimes unknown to us or obscure. But Ptolemy and the other old [astrologers] display neither reason nor experience by which it might be proved that the hours of the duration of an eclipse of the Sun signify years, but for an eclipse of the Moon they signify months. Therefore, it seems to me that that doctrine ought to be rejected. Moreover, how much it may be alien to reason will be plain from this—for any Mundane Revolution of the Sun will complete its own effects within that very revolution, also according to Ptolemy's doctrine.

Therefore, the same thing should be understood about all Revolutions, both the periodic ones and the synodic ones of the other Planets. Then, if we were to suppose that an eclipse of the Sun in the DSC would last for 3 hours, and therefore its actual efficacy would last for 3 years beyond the delay of its effects when it is in the DSC. Therefore, since in several years more eclipses could be made, both of the Sun and of the Moon, no little confusion would occur in connection with the forces and effects of all the eclipses that would occur in 3 years, when many would be acting at the same time, which could not avoid occurring; nor would any intellect, at least any human one, be able to discern what effect would be due to the first, third, fourth, fifth one, etc.; and therefore, no [particular] force and effect could be clearly recognized for any event. In that confusion, all astrological knowledge of eclipses would vanish; and so it will be absurd to declare anything about their virtues and effects—that no astrologer would concede.

And it must be declared similarly about the total eclipses of the Moon, especially about those occurring around the DSC. Moreover, every eclipse would be subordinated in action to the Mundane Revolution of the Sun as a partial cause of the total, or a less universal one to the more universal one. But a revolution of the Sun completes its effects in a single year. Therefore, the effects of an eclipse are not extended past the Mundane Revolution of the Sun in which the eclipse itself occurs, unless the lunation ends within the following Revolution of the Sun.

Besides, if the hours of the duration of a solar eclipse are equivalent to years, and in the case of the Moon only to months, why does Ptolemy determine the beginnings of the effects at the same time, and why does he not accelerate more quickly the effects of the eclipse of the Moon than those of the eclipse of the Sun, when the latter and the former are eclipsed in the DSC? That is, if in the case of an eclipse of the Sun, he attributes the quantity of a day to a year, why in the case of an eclipse of the Moon does he not attribute the quantity of a night to a month, so that an equality might be preserved for both of them? Are not the effects of the Moon quicker than those of the Sun?

But as for that which pertains to the time of the beginning of the effects, it is certain that where the Sun and the Moon do not set within a 24 hour [period], Ptolemy's method collapses for defining the time in which the effects of the eclipse will begin. That method is therefore not universal and common to the whole circle of the lands [of the Earth], but it is only local, and consequently not scientific. In addition, in the case of the Mundane Revolution of the Sun and lunations that are not eclipses, the time of the beginning of the effects is not determined by Ptolemy by the distance of the Light from the ASC explained above. Why, therefore, should that be done in the case of eclipses, which are nothing else than lunations? Besides, it is absurd and contrary to the doctrine of Ptolemy himself to deny that any effects of an eclipse occur, when the eclipsed Light and the ruler of the eclipse come to themselves by body or by aspect, or when they come to the place of the eclipse or to the principal angles of the figure, which can happen immediately after the eclipse. Therefore, the beginnings of the effects are not only from that distance.

Finally, should the eclipse of the Moon be made in the DSC, its effects will begin only around the end of the year that has elapsed from it. But meanwhile another eclipse of the Moon can be made that is not in the rising; therefore, the later effect will precede the prior effect, against the order of the times by which that same eclipsed Moon is the cause of different effects. Or the intellect will be confounded by confusing the effects of those eclipses, when it happens (as can often be the case) that their effects begin and end at the same time. But much more when a total eclipse of the Sun is made in the DSC, whose effectiveness will only leave off in the fourth year after the eclipse; since in four years, more than 12 eclipses can occur, either of the Sun or of the Moon, and either above or below the Earth (even those that Ptolemy had wrongly declared to be ineffective), of which the greater part will act at the same time on these sublunar things. Which is certainly evidently convincing that there is either no knowledge about the effects of eclipses, or else it is other than Ptolemy's doctrine.

And so, we say first. The efficacy of any universal constitution flourishes and lasts until the closest following one of the same kind. And therefore, the efficacy of the Mundane Revolution of the Sun flourishes until the next following Revolution, or Ingress into 0°00' of Aries. And this is not disputed by that astrologer; and the efficacy of each synod of the Planets, whether they are both Lights, or one of them with other Planets, or of other Planets among themselves, lasts until the similar synod immediately following, and is not extended beyond [that time] at least per se; and this can be proved by many reasons.

The first one is. That if it should be conceded that the effective force of one new Moon lasts through one or more years, just as Ptolemy will have it in the case of a new Moon occurring in the ecliptic around the DSC, the greatest confusion will be introduced in connection with the forces and the effects of all the possible new Moons. And it will not be possible to define anything certain about them, unless having examined and distinguished the forces of the preceding and following new Moons, which would be impossible for the human intellect. But that confusion is not admitted by Ptolemy or the other astrologers, who do not even judge about one new Moon from the one preceding and the one following. Since, however, they judge about the Mundane Revolution of the Sun and its quarters from the next preceding new Moon or full Moon, since its force will not have ceased before the Sun's Ingress into the cardinal points. Therefore, the force and efficacy of any new Moon lasts only up to the [time of] the next new Moon, and it is not combined with that one's efficacy; otherwise, in the aforesaid Revolution of the Sun, the following new Moon would also have to be noticed.

The Second one is. Because in the synod of the Sun and the Moon, their forces, which are the principal celestial ones, are especially united, but particularly when [the synod] is in the ecliptic; therefore, at that moment they act very strongly upon these sublunar things, circulating the influx of their own conjunction by a common ray, which is the instigator of the effects that are going to happen from that synod. For what philosopher or astrologer, having supposed the force of the stars on these inferior things, will deny that from the Sun and the Moon conjoined they produce their influx so long as they are conjoined, since from the elements of astrology, those that are conjoined do one thing, [but they do] something else when they are in square, and something else when they are in opposition, or that that same influx [the conjunction], the most powerful of all, does nothing? For who would restrain the efflux of that influence onto these inferior things, since nothing in the *Caelum* is given to be more powerful than the Sun and the Moon conjoined, especially centrally, as Ptolemy himself states; but on the Earth it is not found, except as a passive force with respect to the celestial bodies?

Therefore, a new Moon, and especially an ecliptical new Moon, acts upon these sublunar things, from the very moment of that new Moon, and their effects on the sublunar World are not retained through many months or even through a year. And since about individual new Moons that are also non-ecliptical the same thing must be said; then without doubt either a confusion must be allowed with regard to the forces and effects of new Moons, and judgment will have to be made about anyone of the preceding and following ones, contrary to the practice of all astrologers, or it will have to be asserted that the efficacy of one synod lasts only until the next following synod, although nothing would forbid its effects to be continued by a following synod of similar virtue, as they can be restrained by a synod of contrary virtue; but each synod always acts during its own period with its own efficacy.

The third is. Because in other universal constitutions, namely the annual Revolutions of the World and their quarters, then in new Moons or full Moons that are not ecliptical, etc., Ptolemy neither retards nor prolongs their effect within the times of similar constitutions that follow; but in Chapters 10, 11, and 12 it is shown how judgment should be made about the effects of the individual ones during the period of each. Therefore, he has introduced the above said retardation and prolongation in the case of eclipses without any reason, since they would only be lunations without latitude, which because they ought to be more effective than the rest, and on the contrary ought to produce their own effects more quickly.

Add to these [reasons] that in the case of eclipses of the Sun, nothing that is different or new happens from the rest of the new Moons than what happens from the removal of the light and heat of the Sun with respect to the Earth for some hours [during the night]. Moreover, in the case of eclipses of the Moon, we are only deprived of the light from that same Sun reflected by the Moon; but besides that, the light of itself does nothing more than illuminate; both that subtraction of the light and the heat cannot of itself produce for us effects that are greater than their subtraction, when those Lights lying hidden under the Earth are eclipsed for us by the interposition of the Earth. When, nevertheless, to those daily eclipses and to those of many more hours—indeed of days in the polar regions—no particular effects are attributed.

And from this, the source of the error of the old [astrologers] is plain, namely that they thought with Aristotle that whatever the celestial bodies do to these sublunar things, they do through their light. For having taken this as a fundamental fact, it would then follow that eclipses of the Sun and the Moon are of very much different virtue from the rest of the new Moons or full Moons, in which the light of the Sun and the Moon does not fail, and therefore judgment must be made otherwise about them. But it is false that they are of different virtue on account of the deprivation of light, although those characteristics are greater on account of both of the Lights being in the ecliptic and on account of their central union.

And from that, I deduce that the whole influential force of an eclipse, insofar as it is an eclipse, that is the force of an eclipse is greater than that of another lunation, consists only of the coming together or the opposition of the Sun and the Moon in the ecliptic. And therefore, that eclipses taking place under the Earth are scarcely less effective with respect to us than those that take place above the Earth that we have already noted in Chapter 7. Therefore, it is not on account of the deprivation of light in eclipses that their effects are of a different kind and duration than the effects of the other lunations, and they are neither retarded or prolonged, either in many months or years; although some great effect started or produced by some eclipse can last for many months, indeed for years, no more by an act concurrent with the efficacy or virtue of that past eclipse, unless we would want to admit the confusion of the virtue of the lunations too that are not going to be made ecliptical at the same place on Earth.

And the things that have been said hitherto are to be understood not only about lunations, but also about the annual Revolutions of the World, Great Conjunctions, etc.; but it must be noted that an eclipse of the Sun is of greater virtue than an eclipse of the Moon. Not because in the latter we are only deprived of the accidental light of the Moon, and in the former of the Sun's own light; but because a conjunction of two Planets is more effective than an opposition of those same Planets. And besides that, the efficacy of an eclipse of the Sun lasts [only] one month; that is, until the next following new Moon. But the efficacy of an eclipse of the Moon lasts only half a month; that is, also until the next following new Moon; namely, because an opposition is only effective for the effects of a half period of each whole synodic Revolution.

We say secondly. The effects of universal constitutions begin at the moment when the constitutions are made. For then their influx, or seed, is ejaculated into the sublunar womb, which conceives effects conformable to those celestial causes, and produces them at suitable times. For having established the celestial cause most powerfully active, the passive power of the sublunar things, and the application due to both of them, the acting cause of the effects cannot naturally be hindered.

We say thirdly. Also, according to Ptolemy's opinion, that those effects arise and break forth when applications and conjunctions are made by the Planets ruling the constitution to its primary point, or to its opposition or square, either in the same triplicity or in the following angle and the ASC, or when the Lights come to those points with an aspect of the rulers of the constitution, or when they apply by body or by aspect to those rulers, or when they rise or set together with them or with the primary point of the constitution. And especially when the rulers of the annual Revolution of the Sun and its quarters, by body or by a conformable and strong aspect, come to the rulers of the subordinated lunations. Then in fact they bring forth, or reduce, or intensify the effects.

But in addition, they burst forth from the directions of the Lights or of the angles, especially of the ASC, to conformable promittors, then too of the rulers of the universal constitution. Moreover, the directions of the Mundane Revolution of the Sun should be set up completely, as [is done] in the case of the Revolutions of the Sun for nativities in accordance with Book 23, Chapter 15, and by that same Table. But the directions of the synodic revolutions of the Moon should be set up with the following Tables corresponding to the mean synodic month of the Moon—in short, in the same manner as the directions for the periodic Revolutions of the Moon, by the Tables put with the above said Book 23, Chapter 15.

First

Grad.	Dies	Horæ	Min.
1	0	1	58
2	0	3	56
3	0	5	54
4	0	7	52
5	0	10	50
6	0	11	48
7	0	13	46
8	0	15	44
9	0	17	42
10	0	19	40
20	1	15	20
30	2	11	0
40	3	6	40
50	4	2	20
60	4	22	0
70	5	17	40
80	6	13	20
90	7	9	0
100	8	4	40
200	16	9	20
300	24	14	0
360	29	12	0

Second or Converse

Dies	Grad.	Min.	Sec.
1	12	11	27
2	24	22	54
3	36	34	21
4	48	45	43
5	60	57	15
6	73	8	42
7	85	20	9
8	97	31	36
9	109	43	3
10	121	54	30
20	243	49	0

Third for Hours

Horæ	Grad.	Min.	Sec.
1	0	30	27
2	1	0	54
3	1	31	21
4	2	1	43
5	2	32	15
6	3	2	42
7	3	3	9
8	4	3	36
9	4	34	3
10	5	4	30
20	10	9	0

Table of Directions for Synodic Revolutions of the Moon.

[**Note:** in the Table above, the Latin column headings are: Dies (Days), Grad (Degrees), Horae (Hours), Min (Minutes), and Sec (Seconds).]

But if the figure of a new Moon is considered with the places in it determined as instructed in Chapter 5, the directions should be made as they would be for the periodic Revolutions of the Moon.

We say finally that to define the actual action of any universal constitution at the moment in which another similar thing begins, and not extended beyond its own limits; although an effect begun under one constitution is continued by a similar one immediately following, it can be extended and perfected on account of the conformity of those constitutions in their virtue and signification. And that is frequently evident in the particular constitutions of nativities; namely, because if a sickly Revolution of the Sun succeeds a sickly one, the sickness that started in the first one will kill in the later one. But that is from the later revoluttion, which if it would have been healthy, the sickness started in the first one would have ended in health.

And the reasoning is the same with other accidents, such as riches, matrimony, dignities, etc. And therefore the same thing is also [the case] in universal constitutions. For the stars act uniformly in the latter constitutions as they do in the former ones; for otherwise a universal effect could neither be deduced nor concluded from particular effects; and so there would be no astrological science. And therefore, for war, plague, or inclemency of the atmosphere, the Mundane Revolution of the Sun should be inspected, or an eclipse immediately preceding the beginning of that accident, but the following ones for the intensification, slackening, or ending, after having compared these with the preceding [indications].

It can be objected. That if Saturn or Mars is the principal ruler of the universal constitution, such as an eclipse, its effects will only begin when that ruler by its own motion comes by body or by aspect to the place of the eclipse or to the following angle. Moreover, since the motion of Saturn is the slowest, then that of Jupiter and Mars, especially around their stations, if it is by body or by aspect a long ways distant from the place of the eclipse or from the following angle, the effects will not even begin in that lunation, but perhaps after two or three lunations.

I reply. Whether the above said things are posited or not posited, it is not necessary that the effects of an eclipse should begin from an application of Saturn or Jupiter to the place of the eclipse or to the following angle by their own motion, since they should begin on the very day of the eclipse, as was said above, and powerfully and very strongly if the ruler of the eclipse aspects the place of the eclipse or the following angle, or if it is conjoined to either of those. But those effects will emerge from the sublunar womb, or they will be increased, either by the above said directions or by the above said application if it can be done in that same lunation; if not, it will suffice to have an application of the Sun or the Moon to the place of the eclipse, to the following angle, [or] to the principal ruler of the eclipse, whichever one it is, which applications the Moon by her very rapid motion most quickly completes. And the same thing must be said about the other universal constitutions.

He who objects will more sharply object that Cardan in his *Little Book on Interrogations* expounds an eclipse of the Moon that occurred in 11°11' Pisces in the year 1523 on the 25th of August at 15:15 PM at Milan with 15 Leo rising[1] and the Moon and Saturn conjoined in the 8th house; in which the Moon was distant from the ASC by 8:48; and the night then was 11:06. And from this, Cardan wants to deduce 9 months for the retardation of the effects of that eclipse, which, counted from the day of the eclipse, would fall at the beginning of May 1524, at which time a very fierce plague had arisen in Milan; and in that whole Duchy; in Milan [alone] it killed 30,000 people; moreover, in the Duchy as a whole it killed 100,000, and it lasted 3½ months—just as the eclipse lasted 3½ hours; although, however, no other place in Italy was then suffering from the plague. Therefore, Ptolemy's doctrine on the beginning and duration of the effects of eclipses is true by a noteworthy experience, but ours is false.

I reply first. Cardan is wrong in his calculation. For if the nocturnal time of 11:06 is equivalent to 365 days, then 8:48, the dis-

---

[1] These numbers are approximately correct. Calculation from modern data puts the eclipse at 11°18' Pisces, the time of mid eclipse at approximately 15:35 LMT (from preceding noon) or 15:36 LAT at Milan, with 20 Leo rising. If Cardan calculated the time when the Moon's ecliptical position at the time of the eclipse would have arisen, then the time interval was about 8:50, close to the 8:48 that he calculated; and the length of the night was just about 11:00 if we equate it to the Sun's nocturnal arc.

tance [in time] of the Moon from the ASC will be the equivalent of 289 days, which is 9 months and 19 days, which, counted from the day of the eclipse, fall on the day 11 June, and not on the beginning of May.

I reply secondly. It is far more probable that since Jupiter was the ruler of the eclipse in mutual reception by domicile with Saturn, which, conjunct the Moon, Mars was aspecting by trine from Scorpio, on the day on which a Grand Conjunction of Saturn, Jupiter, and Mars, and of the Moon itself in the 11th degree of Pisces was made, where the eclipse of the Moon itself had occurred, namely on 5 February 1524,[1] then the seeds of the plague would be ejaculated that would have begun to germinate on the 19th of February, when there was a synod of the Sun and Saturn on the very place of the Grand Conjunction; and on that same day, the Moon was opposed to Saturn, Jupiter, Mars, Venus, and Mercury, all of which were in Pisces. But the deep roots would have resulted from the Revolution of the Sun in that same year 1524, for which here are the places from Schöner,[2] but the time and the figure from our own abbreviated Rudolphine Tables, because in Schöner's time the Sun's motion would not have been rightly known.[3]

---

[1]This was the date of the famous stellium in Pisces in 1524. There were actually five planets in Pisces, their longitudes being Venus 6, Saturn 10, Moon 11, Mars 11, and Jupiter 11. And if the astrologers of the time had known it, Neptune was in 8 Pisces, which would have put *six* planets in close conjunction in Pisces. Since Pisces is a water sign, many astrologers of the time predicted a great flood. But Morin, writing a century later to contradict Cardan, ignores that and concentrates on the indications of plague.

[2]Johann Schöner (1477-1547), German mathematician, astronomer, and astrologer. Morin's reference is possibly to his *Tabulae astronomicae...* 'Astronomical Tables...' (Nürnberg: Johann Petreius, 1536).

[3]But here again the *Rudolphine Tables* led Morin astray. From them he calculated the time of the Aries Ingress as 8:15 PM LAT; but calculation from modern data puts it at 11:15 PM LAT. At that time the ASC was 30 Scorpio, most of the house positions are different, Venus was no longer the ruler of the ASC and the 8th, but rather ruler of the 6th and the 11th, and both the 6th and the 12th houses were empty.

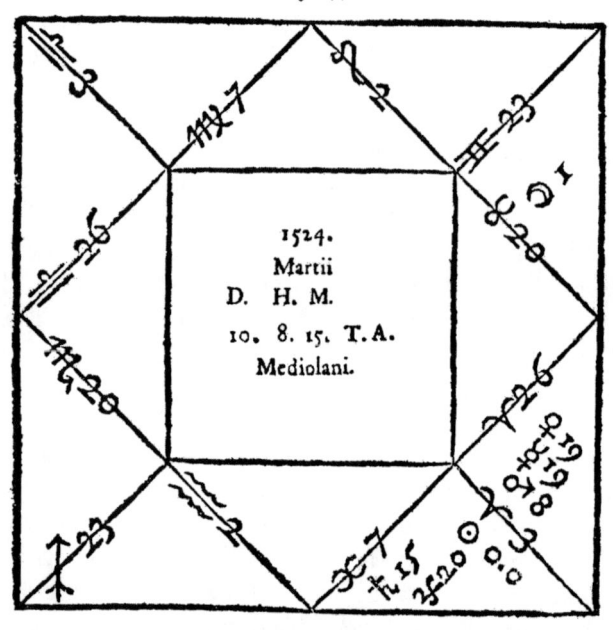

**Aries Ingress
Milan, Italy
10 August 1524 8:15 PM LAT**

In which figure the Sun, noticeably crowded, is in the 6th house applying to Mars; Venus, ruler of the ASC and at the same time of the 8th is also found in the 6th in exile and conjoined to Mercury, ruler of the Moon in the 8th. All of this, moreover, was proclaiming a sickly year in the region of the figure. And finally of course, the fruit of the plague erupted from the direction of the Sun in that Revolution to the 11th degree of Gemini, in partile square to the place in which the greatest conjunction itself was made, to which the Moon itself was applying by square in that same figure, which direction was completed at the beginning of May; moreover, the plague was ended in the middle of August, at which time, the Sun by direction had come to the 11th degree of Virgo, namely in partile opposition to the greatest conjunction.

Therefore, with all of these located thus, why should we seek for any causes of the plague other than the above said greatest conjunction of Saturn, Jupiter, and Mars and the other [configurations] that followed that have already been explained, since for such an effect they would have been most sufficient, and indeed most evident by the directions of the Sun for the beginning and duration of the plague? Therefore, since Cardan brings forth this sole experience of his and Ptolemy's doctrine, which was also crippled by [being in error] more than one month in the time of the beginning of the plague; and to which doctrine however the reasons put forth by us above are strongly contrary, it seems that it should rather be said that it was by accident that it happened that Ptolemy's doctrine however agreed with ours supported by the best reasons, and with perfect finish of experience as far as it was concordant for the beginning and end the plague.

Moreover, it does not seem that it ought to be sought why that plague should have raged in only the Duchy of Milan from the ASC sign, or from an eclipse, or from a Great Conjunction, or from the Sun's annual revolution. For that sign could have been common to many other places in France and Italy, and Planets could have been in the same houses; also, it does not seem that it ought to be sought from the sign in which there is a universal constitution, or in which there is an eclipse, or a Great Conjunction, or an annual Revolution, as Cardan thinks along with Ptolemy.

Those signs ought at least to be carefully inspected, but it seems that it ought to be sought from a particular temperature and constitution of the place in which the effect is produced, by reason of which constitution, that place particularly harmonizes with the sign itself or with its ruler, as was said by us in book 20, Chapter 4, [since it] was disposed to their effects more so than others, since the celestial bodies, just as other physical causes, always act in accordance with the disposition of the subjects.

Chapter 13. *The Quantity of Effects emanating from Universal Constitutions.*

In the case of eclipses, this must be chiefly determined by the magnitude of the eclipse, from which Ptolemy deduced the duration of the efficacy of the eclipse. For the greater the eclipse was, the more it portends major effects; not on account of the deprivation of light, as was said previously. But because the synod of the Sun and the Moon or their opposition are closer to the ecliptic, in which a greater force of the Planets exists.

But in general, the ruler of the primary point of any constitution, or the following angle, conjoined to them or coupled by a strong ray, in a strong celestial state, and angular in the figure, promises great effects and that they will appear quickly; but affected in a contrary manner, bad effects; and midway, medium effects.

If a single Planet is ruler of the constitution, or two Planets of the same signification and of a benefic or malefic nature, especially when they are strong, greater and more evident effects are signified than if there are many [rulers] of a diverse nature and signification. For with each one acting according to its own nature and determination, one hinders or reduces the effects of the other, and a force that is united is stronger than one that is dispersed.

The ruler of a constitution above the Earth, diurnal by day, nocturnal by night, and strong, and oriental to the Sun and occidental to the Moon, promises notable effects; but lesser ones when it is under the Earth.

Saturn, Jupiter, and Mars rulers of a constitution, with other things being equal, produce greater effects than Venus or Mercury because their virtue is greater. But the greatest effects of all are made if the Sun or the Moon is ruler of the constitution and notably well or badly disposed. For the forces of the Sun and the Moon are the greatest forces of the Planets.

The fixed stars of the first magnitude in the angles, the ASC, the

MC, and the DSC, presage great effects, and especially if they are vertical to the region and they occupy the angle next following the primary point of the constitution.

Universal constitutions that occur in cardinal signs, other things being equal, prevail over the rest by the magnitude of their effects, because those signs are the principal sources of changes in the first physical cause, and they are also the exaltations of the principal Planets; and those that are in the ASC or the MC or in those places have their own rulers. These give great effects in a house of the figure.

Chapter 14. *The Quality of the Effects produced by Universal Constitutions in general.*

In this chapter, nothing else will be looked into other than whether a universal constitution is favorable or unfavorable. Moreover, that can be defined from [the information in] many chapters.

For first, the malefic Planets ruling the primary point of the constitution and badly afflicted in their celestial state portend evils everywhere, but more serious ones in those places in which they also rule the principal angles of the figure or are in them. But the most serious evils of all when they are in those places, in which, in addition to their own site and rulership in the figure, they will be determined to evils, as if they would be in houses 4, 6, 7, 8, or 12. But on the contrary, benefic Planets ruling the primary point of the constitution and well disposed in their celestial state, presage good things everywhere; but greater things in those [places] in which they also rule the principal angles of the figure; but greatest of all in those [places] in addition to which, by their own site and rulership in the figure, they will be determined to good things, as if they were in houses 1, 2, 5, 7, 9, 10, or 11. But if the total rulership of the constitution belongs to two Planets, one of which is of a benefic nature, but the other of a malefic nature, from the nature of both, their celestial state, their determination and strength, there will be a mixed quality of the events.

Second. Universal constitutions in which violent fixed stars are dominant, such as the Eye of Taurus, the Heart of Scorpio, the Head of Medusa,[1] etc., are malignant. But those in which bright benefic fixed stars rule, such as Spica Virginis, Arcturus, Castor & Pollux,[2] etc., presage future good things.

Third. If the Lights or the rulers of the constitution apply first to Planets that are benefic and well disposed and determined to good, they signify good things. [But] if they apply to malefics badly disposed and determined to evil, they portend evils according to the nature of the Planet to which the application is made, and according to its determination.

Fourth. The synod of the Planets is threefold by reason of their nature. Namely, benefics with a benefic, malefics with a malefic, and benefics with a malefic. The first of these is good, the second is evil, and the third is middling. But the celestial and terrestrial state of those Planets must be considered.

Fifth. Both the goodness and the malice of a conjunction of two Planets is threefold by reason of the sign. **The first** of these is of goodness, when one of the Planets is fortunate in the sign of the conjunction, but the other is unfortunate, such as a conjunction of Jupiter and Mercury in Pisces. **The second** is when one is fortunate, but the other is peregrine, such as a conjunction of Saturn and Jupiter in Pisces. **The third** is when both of the Planets are fortunate in the sign, as when there is a conjunction of the Sun and Mars in Aries, or the Moon and Jupiter in Cancer.

The first of the evil ones is when both Planets are peregrine in the sign of the conjunction, such as a conjunction of Jupiter and the Moon in Libra. **The second** is when one of the Planets is unfortunate, but the other is peregrine, such as a conjunction of the Sun

---

[1] These are the stars Aldebaran or α Tauri at 4°54′ Gemini, Antares or α Scorpii at 4°53′ Sagittarius, Algol or α Persei at 21°18′ Taurus in the year 1650.

[2] These are the stars Spica or α Virginis at 18°58′ Libra, Arcturus or á Boötis at 19°21′ Libra, Castor or α Geminorum at 15°22 Cancer, and Pollux or α Geminorum at 18°23′ Cancer in 1650.

and the Moon in Aquarius. **The third** is when both of the Planets are unfortunate in the sign of the conjunction, such as the conjunction of the Sun and Mars in Libra, or Saturn and Mars in Cancer. However, in these [combinations] there is found the relationship of enmity, amity, sympathy, or antipathy of the Planets. For the conjunction of the Sun and Mars in Libra is very bad, because the Sun and Mars are enemies, and both of them are badly disposed in Libra. And the same thing must be said about the conjunction of Saturn and Venus in Aries.

And the same consideration can be applied to the oppositions of the Planets, in which the two signs must be looked at. Namely by seeing whether both [Planets] are fortunate or unfortunate in the signs that they occupy. Or whether one is fortunate and the other unfortunate; or finally, whether both of them are peregrine. Moreover, a notable doubt can arise about oppositions; for example, whether it would be worse for the opposition of the Sun and Mars to be with the Sun in Aries and Mars in Libra, than it would be with the Sun in Libra and Mars in Aries. Moreover, I think that the latter would be worse; for the bad influx of Mars is strengthened too much in Aries, and the benefic Sun is too much debilitated in Libra; the contrary of which is better. But in the opposition of the Sun and Saturn from Leo to Aquarius, it is better for the Sun to be in Leo and Saturn in Aquarius. For the nature of Saturn is mitigated in Aquarius, but in Leo it would be too much corrupted.

Besides, when every Planet is in its own domicile, it is benefic to the World; therefore, it is better for Planets to be in opposition from their own domiciles than the other way around; and therefore, in the case of the oppositions of Mars and Venus from their own signs, it is better for Venus to be in Taurus or in Libra than in Scorpio or in Aries, where experience proves that the nature of Venus is too much corrupted. And the logic is the same for the rest of the Planets and for the square and trine aspects, where the two signs in which they occur must be considered.

Sixth. In a conjunction of the Planets, it must be seen which of them may prevail. But they can prevail by nature, by celestial state, and by terrestrial state. By nature the Sun prevails over its own satellites and the Moon; but the latter prevails over the satellites of the Sun. By celestial state, if Saturn and Venus are conjoined in Taurus, Venus will prevail; and the one who is born then will be shamefully lustful. But in the case of terrestrial state, if the Sun and Saturn are conjoined in the 10th house, the Sun will prevail for honors on account of its analogy with them; but if they are conjoined in the 8th or the 12th, Saturn will prevail on account of its analogy with death and illness; and so the good or the evil quality of the effect may become known. And the logic is the same with the rest. And because the hour of the conjunction of the Moon with all the Planets can now be known; therefore, if at the times of those conjunctions the figures are considered, there can be prognostications deduced from them that should not be scorned, both universal and particular ones for any particular place; and this should be noted as a secret!

Seventh. If Saturn or Mars were rulers of the constitutions and in perigee, they will be less bad than in apogee. For the closer they will be to the Earth, the worse they act on it. However, think the contrary about the perigees of Jupiter and Venus; namely that they would be more beneficent and more effective in generating good.

Eighth. If the [principal] Planet of a universal constitution, such as the Sun in a Mundane Revolution, is the ruler of the ASC or the MC, in that year or at least in a quarter of that year, it will act very strongly in accordance with its own nature; [a consideration], however, to which the old [astrologers] paid no attention, but only to the rulers of the Sun and the principal angles, by which they certainly made no small mistake. For since all the Planets differ among themselves in their nature and virtue of acting, and each of them always acts in accordance with its own nature and force of acting; is it [then] erroneous in a Revolution of the Sun not to take note of what the Sun [does] by its nature and its own virtue, and so with the rest [of the Planets]?

Chapter 15. *Some things that should be particularly noted about the Natures and Actions of the Planets in both Universal and Particular Constitutions.*

The Planets are influentially hot, cold, moist, dry from the celestial material of which they are composed, which since it is unique in them, there is also given to each of them an equality of those influential qualities with the part of the celestial matter. But besides that, [they] were also composed unequally of the elements; and in the Sun, fire prevails; in Saturn, earth; etc., as was explained in Book 9, Section 2. Since there are also individual Planets prevailing in each influential nature, such as the Sun in heat and dryness; the Moon in cold and moistness, etc.; and both the elemental and celestial material is given to a Planet conformably and proportionally according to its own substantial form, which in them is the first principle of acting both elementally and influentially, each one of them is known by its elemental nature, more evidently contrary to its influential [nature], and prevailing over that influential [nature] similar to itself. Moreover, having said those things, the following can be inquired into.

First. Why in the case of the Planets, supposing a particular elemental nature from the predominance of the elemental material—as in the case of Saturn, cold and dryness from the predominance of earth—does that nature that prevails in Saturn not impede or hinder the effect of the contrary influence?

I reply. Contraries, properly said, are engaged in [things of] the same kind. But a hot elemental nature and a frigid influential or elemental nature, are not of the same kind; therefore, they are not formally contrary to themselves; and consequently, they are compatible in producing effects and acting. Nevertheless, because two [natures] are more powerful than one, therefore the active force of the Planet, consisting of an elemental nature and a similar influential nature, will prevail over another simple nature or a solitary influential one. And so, Saturn, seen as itself, at least cools and dries more than it heats and moistens. And therefore, in both universal and particular constitutions, the elemental nature of Saturn must be more attended to than the influential nature contrary to it, which by me is saying that its influential nature is less prominent, but the other elemental[1] nature is said to be more prominent, on account of the similar element being joined, by which is indicated the principal influential nature of each Planet.

Second. With Saturn posited in a sign of fire, air, water, or earth, what will it do?

I reply. In earth, determined to its elemental nature—cold and dry—it will chill and dry greatly, and especially in Capricorn, which is determined to the nature of Saturn. For then, the concourse of the cold and dry nature would be twofold, in addition to the elementals, Saturn and Capricorn—that is, the elemental Saturn and the determination of the sign. However, [when placed] **in air**, the determinative nature of the sign will not prevail over the elemental [nature] of Saturn, but it will only moderate it considerably. And **in a fire sign**, Saturn will dry [things] more intensely, but it will chill more mildly. But **in a water sign**, it will chill intensely, but it will dry more mildly; that is, in summer, vapors causing more intense cold by accident will humidify, and will meanwhile cause long-continued rains.

And yet it must be noted that if Mars, for example, should be posited in Cancer, from their combination more heat and dryness will emanate than cold and moistness; for the signs are only hot, cold, moist, or dry by determination; but the Planets are like that formally; and therefore Mars is hotter and dryer than Cancer is cold and moist. And from that it is also deduced that Mars imparts its own nature and influence more than Aries or Scorpio. And the logic is the same with the others.

Third. How do both the elemental and the influential natures act at the same time in the individual Planets?

---

[1] Reading *altera verò elementalis* instead of *altera verò influentialis*.

I reply. The influential [nature] only acts influentially, that is by reason of its site, rulership, and aspects in the houses of the figure; but the elemental [nature] acts not only elementally per se—that is, in accordance with the verticality or obliquity of its rays falling upon the horizon—but also, influentially by accident, since the elemental nature in Planets is subordinated to their own substantial form, and it complies with them in acting both elementally and influentially. And Mars under the Earth can heat influentially above the Earth by reason of its rulership in the ASC or in the place of the universal constitution.

Moreover, although both natures act differently as much as they can; yet, the effect of the elemental [nature] acting alone per se does not make a strong and constant impression on sublunar Nature; but the effect of the influential nature, either solitary or subordinating the elemental [nature] to itself is long lasting and fixed; both in the particulars of nativities, and in universal constitutions. And therefore its only astrological effect is usually seen to be in predicting the future.

Fourth. Which one of these natures is allotted its own effects more surely?

I reply. That the effects of the elemental nature both on the constitutions of the air and on the temperaments of natives depend more on particular sublunar causes, that is on the situation of the place, the quarter of the year, the proper constitution of the seed, etc., than on the elemental nature of the Planets; and therefore, prediction about these effects is less certain. But the effects of the influential nature, such as that someone is going to be fortunate in riches, honors, marriage partner, etc.; or that he may perish by a violent death, and similar things—because these do not depend upon the above said sublunar causes, since they occur at any time or place, and to men of any condition—can therefore be more quickly predicted and are accustomed to be.

Fifth. Why do the Planets imprint fixed qualities and temperaments on the nativities of those born on a particular day that last for their whole life? But why do they not do so for the air or for [conditions in] a whole region?

I reply. Because one born with his own radical celestial constitution does not change from one nature into another, but he is only the kind that he is. And for this, some particular arrangement of the *Caelum* is sufficient. But for the air or a region to be changed from one state to another, a greater force of the *Caelum* is required; and consequently, this can only be done by a universal constitution that pours forth the seeds of change on sublunar things.

Sixth. Why does Saturn cool and dry more with Capricorn than it heats and humidifies with Aquarius or in Aquarius, since Aquarius does not refer its hot and humid nature any less to Saturn from the celestial material of which Saturn itself is composed, than Capricorn refers a frigid and dry [nature]?

I reply. That is because Saturn is in addition cold and dry like Capricorn, but not hot and humid like Aquarius; and that elemental cold and dry nature agrees especially with its substantial form, which is the principal cause of Saturn's actions. Therefore, in Capricorn it acts with a doubled force, but not in Aquarius.

Section II.

Chapter 1. *In which some important things are mentioned first about the kinds of Effects emanating from Universal Constitutions, or are taught about the Kinds of Prediction.*

So much confusion is found among astrologers about prediction; and so much of a hotch-potch of aphorisms and opinions conflicting with each other, that one without natural light and an intelligence born for philosophy will have entered into a labyrinth that is truly inexplicable. Not withstanding any amount of study, he will remain for his whole life entangled in the obscurities of ignorance. And this should not seem remarkable to anyone, since this part of astrology is far different from that which is contemplated for the nativities and fates of men. For in this part, the influential qualities of the stars are almost solely or at least principally looked at, insofar as they are determined by the essential significations of the houses or the spaces of the figure with regard to that man being born; according to which determination the stars act according to rule, as is observed in nativities.

But in the other part of astrology, almost solely or at least principally the elemental qualities of the stars and the signs are looked at, insofar as they affect some whole region in its air, water, land, plants, animals, and men. And the force of the celestial bodies, at least for their elemental effects in this part of astrology is determined in another way for a region than for a native. For, only the first house is noticed for the temperament of a native, namely the signs and the Planets in it, its ruler, and the aspects to it. But for the temperature of the air or its condition, there are principally noted in which house of the figure the primary place of the constitution is situated, then the ruler of that place (both of which are common to the whole Earth), as well as the rulers of the preceding angles, but especially of the one following that primary place, all of which determine that constitution elementally to a [particular] region.

Whence, it is that from these rulers and their state astrologers unanimously pronounce about the future elemental effects in that region, about heat, cold, moistness, dryness, winds, sterility, fecundity, mortality, etc., although these things depend no little on the nature of the region and its situation, as well as upon the quarter of the year, so that the doctrine of the universal constitutions is far more difficult and uncertain than the doctrine of nativities.

Add that the latter is worked by everyone for the sake of profit or pleasure, but the former by very few, who judge only by blind acceptance and by chance from the decrees of the old [astrologers] especially in fact from those of the Arabs, that the individual masters of astrology have brought down to us by the *Cabala*, no one having been found hitherto, who will have tried to put that old doctrine to the [test] of reason and experience, as it is proper to recover and illustrate it. Since this task, undertaken by us, is no small one, namely to expound it. And indeed those things that were placed by us in the first Section seem especially to agree with correct reason. But so that those things that follow in this Section, should be better perceived, some must be stated in advance by us in this chapter.

First. Three methods have been seen by me for predicting the state of the air—from which many [procedures] follow for the land, water, plants, brute animals, and men.

The first is that of Jofrancus Offusius the German[1] by the altitudes of the Planets and the [length of time of] their stays above the horizon, and some other observations, which we discussed in Book 13, Chapters 2 & 3, and then in Book 16, Chapter 2; and we have already shown the use and the imperfection of the method noted also by that same Offusius.

The second is [the method] of Kepler, who has supposed the Earth to be a sort of *animal*, not only endowed with sensation, but also with a sort of intelligence, so that whatever things the syzygies of the Planets do in the *Caelum*, it perceives them in itself immediately, having been stimulated by them. It is excited by each stimulus, and it moves itself to the excretion of the vapors and exhalations that are contained in itself, which are the common material of all the meteors that are appearing in the air.[2]

And therefore, in his *Ephemerides from the Year 1621 to 1630*, in reporting the causes of changes in the air, he has no reference to universal constitutions, nor to celestial charts erected for them, nor to the diverse nature of the signs, the Planets, or the fixed stars; but whatever he advances for changes in the air, he attributes to a syzygy of the Planets, then to whatever beginning it is, and of whichever ones of the Planets, or to several of them occurring at the same time. And

---

[1] JoFrancus Offusius (c.1500-c.1565), M.D., *De divina astrorum facultate in larvatam astrologiam* 'On the Divine Power of the Stars against a Bewitched Astrology' (Paris: J. Royer, 1570).

[2] In Kepler's day, and in fact until the early part of the 19th century, it was generally believed that meteors were atmospheric phenomena.

indeed that method is worthwhile for this [reason], since every day there is some syzygy, either of the Moon with the other Planets, or of the Planets among themselves; and therefore no one is so ignorant, for whom this method at first glance is not very easy in practice.

But since the changes in the air are very varied and contrary among themselves, it is certain that from a future syzygy, Kepler did not predict by his method what sort of change would have followed. As is plain from this, that in the year 1623, from the conjunction of the Sun and Saturn in the 9th degree of Leo, he will have it that there was caused a dryness and great heat. In the year 1624, from the conjunction of the Sun and Saturn in the 22nd degree of Leo, thunder, lightning, and heavy rains. In the year 1625, from the conjunction of the Sun and Saturn in the 6th degree of Virgo, heat, thunder, lightning, and the very heaviest rains. In the year 1626, from the conjunction of the Sun and Saturn in the 19th degree of Virgo, serene weather, etc. Where to the same syzygies, in the same sign, and in the same quarter of the year, contrary states of the air are attributed.

Therefore, Kepler's method for predicting the state of the air cannot be said to be scientific or useful. Moreover, this is confirmed by two reasons. The **first** is that if any particular syzygy does nothing else than stimulate, and it suffices that the Earth is stimulated by any syzygy, so that of itself it is excited and discharges what must be discharged, it is plain that the diversity of future changes [in the air] will not be looked for from the syzygies, but rather from the various intrinsic dispositions of the Earth that are unknown, and so it will not have been possible for any prediction of what sort of changes there would be to be made by means of the syzygies.

Second. Since very certain experience is established by means of nativities, and then from Book 19, that the natures of the Planets are diverse among themselves, just as the nature of the aspects are also diverse; therefore, a different syzygy of different Planets will not stimulate the Earth in the same manner, and consequently it will not produce the same kind of effects. And in general a different syzygy of different Planets will not cause the same change [in the air], but each one of them will act on the same subject—that is, on the Earth—according to the nature and proper virtue of the Planets and the aspects; and so they individually produce diverse effects, also from the same disposition of the Earth, which whoever denies it will divulge his own ignorance of physics.

Add that if any constitution of the air that has arisen only depends objectively on a particular syzygy, why does that constitution happen in one [particular] place on earth, rather than in another above or below the horizon, since that syzygy is common to the whole Earth? If anyone says that a future effect [will occur] at a disposed place on Earth and where there is something that must be discharged; then, since that place is unknown, no prediction will therefore be possible for that particular place. Besides, what syzygy will make serenity and tranquility of the air, since then it could not be said that the Earth discharges anything that would produce serenity and tranquility of the air? Those things that we have said against that opinion of Kepler's may be seen in Book 21, Section 1, Chapters 4-7, then in Book 22, Section 3, Chapter 2.

Finally, the third method is that of Ptolemy and the other old astrologers by universal constitutions and their rulers, which we therefore adhere to, because the true astrology became known to the first men, and it remained to posterity through the *Cabala,* but indiscriminately depraved by the arts of the Devil and the ridiculous fictions of men, as we have made known in the doctrine of nativities. And therefore, by correcting what must be corrected, that method should be preferred to the opinions of Offusius and Kepler—men ignorant of the true astrology (as we have said elsewhere) and also disagreeing among themselves.

Second. The confusion and contrariety in the decrees of the old [astrologers] was introduced by this, that the twelfths[1] of the *Pri-*

---

[1] That is, the signs of the zodiac. Morin means the *tropical* signs.

mum Mobile were not known to them before Ptolemy's time; but they thought that the constellations of the zodiac were the true signs that are said to be the domiciles of the planets and to be subject to their rulership. Whence, it resulted that with the constellations lurking about under the twelfths, and with the strengths of both of them fighting among themselves, they would have produced contrary decrees,[1] when one astrologer attributed to a twelfth what was due to a constellation or stellar sign, and vice versa; and so contrary opinions are found about the same Planet in the same sign.

Third. The old astrologers judged very confusedly about the constitutions of the air. Since for the heat and cold of the air, for hail, rains, dryness, and, following from these on the Earth, sterility, plague, wars, etc., they judge about those individual things from the great conjunctions, the annual Revolutions, eclipses, lunations, and their quarters, [but] differently and in different ways, as if it ought to be judged one way about one constitution and another way about another, so that here and there to see it is in an English sum.[2]

Moreover, since one should predict in the same way from the individual universal constitutions (except in the case of their subordination); namely, because the stars act uniformly in all the universal conjunctions—of course, through the rulers of the constitution according to their nature and state—for the purpose of predicting whether there will be rain or fine weather, there is no need to define it by individual constitutions, but it is only needful to know what sort of effects the first of all the universal constitutions presages—that is, the Mundane Revolution of the Sun, and whether the later ones agree with it or are contrary, and which one would rule; and from that, judgment should be made, taking note of the fact that the year has three quarters subordinated to the prime

---

[1] Morin has condemned the attribution of the presumed characteristics of a constellation to the sign of the same name.

[2] An 'English sum' is evidently a slang term for 'a state of confusion'.

one or the Ingress of the Sun into 0°00′ Aries, and which quarter has more lunations subordinated to the quarters but especially to the prime one; and each lunation has 4 quarters, of which the last 3 are subordinated to the [preceding] synod of the Sun and the Moon.

Fourth. It is generally admitted by all the old [astrologers] that the Planets in the signs, i.e. in the twelfths, act universally, that is through the whole circuit of the Earth according to their own nature and that of the sign in which they are located, both elementally and influentially. Therefore, in a fire sign the formal heat and dryness of Mars is strongly increased; in a water sign, they are very reduced; in an air sign, its dryness is moderated; and in an earth sign, its heat is moderated, but its dryness is increased. And similarly, Saturn in an air sign is mostly temperate; in an earth sign, its cold and dryness are increased; in a fire sign, its dryness is increased, and its cold is reduced; and in a water sign, its cold is increased, and its dryness is reduced; and thus with the rest [of the Planets].

However, it must not be understood from this, that a Planet receives anything from a sign, or a sign receives anything from a Planet; but rather that from the concourse of a hot Planet with a fire sign, it produces a great heat on these inferior things, [but] from the concourse of a hot Planet with a cold sign, there is a mildness in heat; and thus with the rest [of the Planets and signs], as we have said in Book 20, Section 3, Chapter 5. And the same thing is done in temperaments.

And so in every universal constitution, it must be seen how the natures of the Planets, and the signs, and their rulers agree or disagree. For of whatever kind the concourse, or the celestial cause, will be, of that same kind will be its universal influx on all these sublunar things. However, the effects of which influx are diverse according to the diverse site and nature of the places, and the diverse part of the year. For the same heat liquefies wax and hardens clay[1];

---

[1] This is Morin's favorite saying to illustrate the fact that the same cause may have entirely different effects on different kinds of subjects. It appears in Origen (3rd cent.), *The First Principles*, I, 1, 13.

and the Sun causes heavy rains somewhere by elevating more vapors by its heat than it can resolve in its stay above the horizon,[1] when elsewhere it causes fine weather by dissipating everything that it elevates by its own heat.

For the Earth is the vessel of Nature, into which as a womb the individual elements, altered and set in motion by the celestial bodies, ejaculate their own seed. Moreover, the Sun is of the nature of a vivifying fire, which heating the womb of the Earth, and fostering the first generations on Earth—namely it produces the vapor and the exhalation and copious amounts in accordance with the intensity of the heat and the nature of the land. Moreover, from the vapor and the exhalation, or, as is pleasing to the chemists, from mercury and sulfur the remaining things are generated.

And consequently, what is asserted by many is false, [namely, that] conjunctions of any planets made in fire signs heat and dry; [and] in water signs, they cool and humidify. For thus the planets would not act in accordance with their own nature, but only in accordance with the sign in which they are posited, which is absolutely alien to nature, reason, and experience. Nevertheless, it sometimes happens that a hot celestial cause would cool, as when the Sun makes summer in the torrid zone; for because there it elevates the most copious vapors by its own ardent heat, which by their own brief stay above the horizon cannot be dissipated; and therefore, throughout the summer, rains are almost continuous in that zone, and the summer is cooler than the remaining parts of the year; but that cold is only *accidentally* from the Sun and not from the Sun *per se*. And similarly, the intense cold of Saturn or the Moon in the winter constricts the pores of the face of the Earth; and that cause is by accident, because the first region of the earth is made hotter and more humid.

And the logic is the same with the rest of the things that must be looked at for prediction—namely, having taken into account the

---

[1] Reading *super horizontem* 'above the horizon' instead of *semper horizontem* 'always the horizon'.

place and the quarter of the year for at least the elemental effects. For, in the case of the influential [effects], since they are determined to the significations of the houses, no notice must be taken of the place or the quarter of the year, nor by accident do effects appear that are contrary to the forces of the celestial bodies determined in that way, for Saturn in the 12th always and everywhere threatens illnesses.

Fifth. It is not sufficient to perceive that the primary point of a constitution, or a particular Planet, is in a fire sign or a water sign; but in addition it must be noted in which Planet's domicile it is posited. Then, because a Planet does one thing in Cancer, another in Scorpio, and still another in Pisces—namely, always acting in connection with the nature of its ruler—but then, because the effects of a universal constitution chiefly follow the nature of the ruler of the primary point, by the common consensus of astrologers.

Sixth. The proper natures of the Planets are helped or hindered by other extrinsic causes besides the signs and syzygies, namely by their position with respect to the Sun or the Moon, by a conformable or non-conformable situation resulting from their location above or below the horizon, by the length of their stay above it, as well as by their distance from the Earth, which was fully discussed in Book 13.

Seventh. From the same universal constitution, such as the Ingress of the Sun into Aries, or a new Moon, or a conjunction of Saturn and Jupiter, either in this or that sign, or under [the rulership] of this or that Planet, or in that way disposed by rulership; that is by the same universal constitution seen only celestially, the celestial influx of course produces the same thing for the whole circle of the Earth, but it provides different effects, both for a different site and nature of the parts of the terrestrial globe, and for the different position of the primary point of the constitution in the celestial figure—that is, above or below the horizon, in the angles, or outside of the angles, and with different rulers, both of the angles and of the primary point.

For by these, that universal constitution is determined to individual horizons, so that it can provide special effects conformable to the natures and state of the rulers, to the position of the primary point with respect to the horizon, to the nature of the place and the quarter of the year, all of which must be taken into account for the prediction. Whence it is plain how fallacious the judgment of a universal constitution would be when viewed only from its celestial state, or from solely the celestial state of the Planets, without any consideration of the horizon, as is often found here and there in the aphorisms of the old astrologers.

Eighth. A celestial constitution signifying humidity or rains is good in one place on Earth, namely in a sandy place, bad in another, namely in a marshy place; likewise, it is good in one quarter of the year, namely in the summer unless it overflows, but bad in the winter; likewise, it is good for some crops of the Earth, but bad for some that it does not suit. Moreover, all of these things must be distinguished by careful sagacity and with attention given to the [type of] agriculture.

Ninth. In any universal constitution, many Planets in fire signs presage spells of dryness; in water signs, waters; in air signs, winds; and in earth signs, hail, or snow storms and hail. However, attention must be paid to the Planets ruling those signs—namely, whether in their elemental nature they agree or disagree with the signs; for, when they are agreeing, their signification is intensified, and when they are disagreeing, it is reduced; then similarly, attention must be paid to the nature of the place and the quarter of the year, as has been very often stated.

Tenth. For predicting from a universal constitution, it must be known which Planet is the principal ruler of the year, which one is the ruler of the quarter of the year, which one is the ruler of the month or of the lunation; then, what is the nature, both elemental and influential, of these individual rulers, and what is the nature of the signs in which they are placed, and the nature of the ruling fixed stars, and how all of these are determined in the figures. And having made a mixture of all of these, one will have to judge according to the prevailing virtue about the future elemental and influential effects, taking into account the [nature] of the place and the quarter of the year, at least for the elemental effects, as was said above. And the knowledge [of the effects] depends upon all this!

Eleventh. Other things being equal, that Planet must be chosen for the primary ruler of a universal constitution that more agrees with the quarter of the year, such as Mars for the summer, or Saturn for the winter. And Saturn portending cold for the winter quarter will make that cold in the air, especially in the more northern places on Earth. And the logic is the same with the rest [of the planets].

Twelfth. In [judging] universal constitutions, not only must it be foreseen whether the future air will be serene, disturbed, mild, or hot, cold, humid, dry, or healthy or unhealthy, and for what living things; but especially, what sort of winds will there be, for the temperature of the air principally depends upon the winds. For those that blow from the colder parts of the Earth, such as the subpolar parts, chill; those from the hotter parts, such as from the equator, heat; those that are from the sea, carry clouds and waters; those from a distant tract of the Earth, such as Tartary[1] is from us, dry up and clear up [the atmosphere].

Moreover, a wind lasting for some days is a motion of the air following the rarefaction of the air itself in the hotter places, and which occasionally increases the motions by the rarefaction and dissipation of clouds, or vapors and exhalations, which the disturbed air itself drives; this is evident from the perpetual wind in the torrid zone, from the east to the west, which is nothing other than a motion of the air caused by the daily motion of the *Primum Caelum*, as we have said elsewhere.

Moreover, a wind that lasts an hour or is momentary, which is the sort that precedes a rain storm, is only from the dissolution of clouds and rains falling in close order, as if from a gust. Further-

---
[1] Roughly, Russia and the countries to the south of it that are east of Europe.

more, it is very difficult to predict which wind ought to last; that is, because when the air is rarefied, or vapors are elevated into the air (from which, to produce this and to be moved it is necessary for the parts to be weaker in their rarity). Mostly, it would depend upon sublunar causes prevalent in the place, from which is the beginning of its motion. Whence, it is no wonder if meteorological prediction often fails!

Thirteenth. The Planets that are rulers of the universal constitution, and of its primary point, then the rest of the Planets in that constitution, act influentially upon these sublunar things according to the characteristics of the houses with their own determination in the figure; however, with this difference from [their significations] in the figures of nativities; namely, because the first house in the figure of a native would only signify about the particular life and health of the native; but in the figure of a universal constitution it would signify about the life and health of all living things in the region of the figure.

The 7th house in the figure of a native is [the house] of marriages and the particular contentions of the native; but in the figure of a universal constitution it is [the house] of the marriages of that region in general, and then of the contentions and wars common to that whole region. And so with the other [houses]—namely, taking in general in universal constitutions what is taken only particularly in nativities, or with respect to the native alone. For the characteristics of the houses are the same; that is, the essential significations of the houses are the same in general figures and in particular figures; but in the latter, the constitution is only particular, and therefore signifying particularly; but in the former, the constitution is general, and therefore signifying generally.

And similarly, it will have to be seen which houses of the figure the Planet that is ruler of the sign rules, and which one it will aspect by a stronger ray, and from those it must be judged by a universal method. See what we will have said about these things at the end of Chapter 5, Section 2, Book 21.

Fourteenth. Hence it is deduced that those natives are more readily and strongly affected by a universal constitution, whose natal figures agree more in the significations of the houses with the figures of the universal constitutions; and they are affected by the things signified by the corresponding houses. As if the 10th house of a universal constitution agrees with the 10th house of a natal figure or the Revolution of a natal figure, the native will be affected in that year or month in those things signified by the 10th, according to the nature and the influx common to the same figure.

Fifteenth. Since for us the southern winds are hot, the northern ones cold, the eastern ones dry, and the western ones humid, from their appearance there mostly follows heat, cold, dryness, and rains in the air. Therefore, if it could be known in advance which wind would be going to blow, the future constitution of the air would also be known—at least most of the time; however, although we have said in Article 12 [above], that it would be very difficult to know on account of the sublunar causes on which it often depends; nevertheless, it is certain that if a universal constitution will have signified cold and dryness for us northerners, southern winds will not blow from that constitution; if it will have signified heat and humidity, the northern winds will not blow, etc.

And therefore, from universal constitutions it can thus be known in advance which winds will blow; but from that same universal constitution it can also be known in advance whether the future will be windy or not, and what kind of wind it presages; therefore, by comparing among themselves the elemental qualities and those of the winds that that universal constitution presages, the future constitution of the air, in heat, cold, rains, fine weather, and wind, will be more precisely determined.

Sixteenth. From universal causes, some future effects can be predicted with certainty; namely, those that cannot be prevented by any natural or artificial force, such as eclipses; but others can only be predicted conjecturally, such as winds, rains, etc. Because even those are necessarily produced by their own causes, we however do not know the combinations of those causes either of the active or the passive ones, and whether they are going to take place and how; nor do we know whether other causes may act to hinder them by their own concourse and combination with the previous ones.

And therefore, only conjectural predictions can be made about them—even more uncertain than predictions based on the figures of nativities. From which it is not surprising that Tycho Brahe will have worked more at natal astrology, but he did not deride its worthlessness, as Gassendi falsely imputed to him in his biography; and Tycho only bewails that the art itself had not yet been rightly established in his own time.

Chapter 2. *The Difference between the Periodic and the Synodic Revolutions of the Planets as regards their Efficiency.*

At the beginning of the World, the Sun and the state of the whole *Caelum* affected the whole Earth, but in various ways in accordance with the diverse respect of the state of the *Caelum* itself toward the individual places on Earth, or in accordance with the diverse determination of the *Caelum* in the charts of the *Caelum* erected for individual places on Earth. And in each place on Earth, the chart of the *Caelum* signified universally whatever can happen both elementally and influentially for that place from the motion of the *Caelum* and the Earth.

And therefore, in the annual Revolution of the World for any place on Earth, the Sun by itself, and by the figure of its Revolution, renews that universal signification by acting both elementally on the air, water, and land, and the various sublunar things, and influentially on all the things signified by the houses of the figure, with respect to the radical figure of the said place, and especially with respect to the house held by the Sun in that figure; and this is understood [to be in effect] during the year of that Revolution. And similarly, it must be judged about the periodic Revolution of the

Moon to its own radical place at the beginning of the World during the month of its Revolution, and yet also with respect to the current Revolution of the Sun.

Moreover, all these things were shown by us to be true in the periodical Revolutions of the Sun and the Moon for the nativity of a man, who is the *microcosm*, on which in the great World the Planets act uniformly. And it seems that it should not be thought otherwise in the case of the periodical Revolutions of the other Planets to their own radical places at the beginning of the World. But because the radical places of the planets are unknown, with the exception of the Sun, there only remains for us, therefore, their synodic revolutions to take note of.

And so, what concerns the synodic Revolutions of the Sun and the Moon, the primary Planets of the World, these too, and the state of the whole *Caelum* at the moment of the Revolution, affects the whole Earth universally, by reason of those Planets coming together, and of the sign in which the synod is, and the rest of the celestial state, but in different ways in accordance with the diverse determination of the *Caelum* at the individual places on Earth, taking account of the radical determination, especially of the Sun and the Moon, and then of the other Planets at the beginning of the World, or at the moment when all the planets were established and the Earth was exposed to their forces, which determination is unknown, on account of the unknown chart of the *Caelum*, then of the time for the individual places on Earth.

Then too, [there must be] taken into account the celestial figure at the beginning of the current annual Revolution, which is known, and that for the duration of the synodic month. Moreover, what I have already said about the synodic Revolutions of the Sun and the Moon among themselves, must also be understood about their synodic Revolutions with the rest of the Planets, and their Revolutions among themselves; always having observed the subordination of the universal constitutions, which was discussed [above] in Section I, Chapter 3.

But now, the nativities of men are subject to the effectiveness or the influx of universal constitutions; that is, of their periodic and synodic Revolutions, as we have spoken elsewhere—in which it must particularly be looked at [to see] how the primary point of the constitution affects the figure of the nativity and of its current Revolution during [the time of] that constitution. But, having made these advance statements, we now come to the special effects of universal constitutions.

Chapter 3. *The Kinds or Types of Effects emanating from Universal Constitutions. And first, the Effects of the Mundane Revolution of the Sun.*

Those who have truly philosophized about these things have proposed paying attention to only 4 causes or universal constitutions—namely, the great conjunctions, the eclipses of the Lights, the Mundane Revolution of the Sun, and the synods of the Sun and the Moon—wishing the magnitude of the causes to be retained therein in the order of their rarity. Since, however, the Mundane Revolution of the Sun is rarer than the eclipses, which happen several times in one year, either above or below the horizon; and, by reason of their virtue and dignity, preference should be given to the great conjunctions, although not by reason of their own duration, as was said in Section I, Chapter 3.

And consequently, we acknowledge only two primary universal constitutions—namely, the Mundane Revolution of the Sun, and the synodic Revolutions of the Sun and the Moon, of which the more effective ones are those in the ecliptic.[1] For that which pertains to the great conjunctions of Saturn and Jupiter, and the rest of the synodic Revolutions of the other planets, both among themselves and with the Lights; these should only be viewed as parts of the Mundane or Annual Revolution of the Sun, and then of the monthly Revolution of the Sun and the Moon, on account of the reasons set forth at the end of Section I, chapter 3.Concerning

---

[1] The *synodic revolutions in the ecliptic* are of course the eclipses of the Sun and the Moon.

which, however, we shall discuss separately in its own place; but it seems to us that we ought to begin with the Mundane Revolution of the Sun.

And so, **First.** The figure of the annual revolution of the World for the proposed location should be erected in accordance with Section I, Chapter 4.

Second. The rulers of the year should be chosen in accordance with Section I, Chapters 9 & 10. And indeed if Mars is in Aries with the Sun, or in Scorpio, especially if it is in an angle, it will be the most powerful ruler of the year; and the effects of the year will be solar in kind, on account of the Sun itself which is making the Revolution, but the effects are strongly determined to Mars; and consequently, they are for the greater part martial in their type. But if Mars is not in those signs, but for example in Sagittarius, since the Sun in Aries acts with Mars, and Mars in Sagittarius acts with its own ruler Jupiter; Jupiter will therefore be the ruler of the year in that Revolution of the Sun, but it must be especially looked at along with Mars for detecting the type of the principal effects of the Sun in that year.

And if Jupiter is in Aries or Scorpio, Mars will then be made the more powerful ruler, and it will prevail over Jupiter in the effects of the annual Revolution or over those determined to the Sun itself, because as Mars acts in accordance with the nature and state of Jupiter, or with Jupiter in such a state, so in turn Jupiter acts in accordance with the nature and state of Mars, which in addition rules the Sun but not Jupiter. Both of them will, however, be very strong on account of their reciprocally united rulership,[1] which is not otherwise distracted.

But if another Planet not ruling Mars is conjunct the Sun in Aries, that one is inferior to Mars as far as the rulership, because it acts in accordance with the nature of Mars or is dependent on Mars. But nevertheless, it will affect the future effects of that year

---

[1] Mars in Sagittarius and Jupiter in Aries are in mutual reception by domicile.

by its own qualities, as was already mentioned about a similar case in Section I, Chapter 9. And these things [relate] to the rulership of the primary point of the Revolution of the Sun.

But as for what pertains to the rulership of the angles, let the choice of the ruler be made as it was done for the [rulership of] the primary point, and as was shown in the above said Chapter 9. And similarly for the fixed stars ruling the constitution, the doctrine set forth in that same chapter should be observed; namely, in which all the things that are required for choosing the rulers of the constitution are sufficiently set forth. And it must be noted that in the case of a Mundane Revolution of the Sun (for example), it will make known no little, not only to know which Planet is the principal ruler of each quarter of the year, but also which one will principally rule all the quarters at the same time, for the effects of that one will appear in the whole year, and especially in that quarter of the year in which it will prevail; but the effects of the other [Planets] will be conspicuous in those quarters which they principally rule.

Having explained these things, we shall now teach how to make a judgment on the effects of a Mundane Revolution of the Sun (which we are taking as an example of all universal constitutions). And first let us say that it must be judged both elementally and influentially; that is, it produces a certain kind of temperature in the air, universally communicable to the water and the land, which are not mixed bodies; then it produces certain kinds of influential effects in men according to the things signified by the houses.

The temperature of the air is sought either at present, at the beginning of the Revolution, or in the future during the course of that revolution. The present condition can be known and determined by means of Offusius's [method], which is discussed in Book 13, Section I; for the stars act extrinsically by their own elemental virtue according to that method—at least by reason of their altitude and their stay above the horizon—and therefore, the proper elemental virtue of the individual Planets must be considered, even if they are not rulers of the year, as was shown in that method of Offusius that was corrected by us; but principally the virtue of those [Planets] that would have been angular in the figure and above the Earth. Also, not having omitted the brighter fixed stars in the angles, and especially those with the Sun and the Moon, or rising and setting with the rulers of the constitution; for by these, the present condition of the air can be caused, but not for many days.

But the future temperature of the air, during the revolution itself or its quarter, depends upon the influx of the stars. For the celestial bodies produce not only elemental qualities according to their own inclination of ray and their perpendicularity to the horizon, as [is explained] above in Offusius's method, but also by their influential virtue, as we have stated elsewhere; namely when in the figure of a universal constitution they are allotted the rulership or some [notable] force. For notable and long-lasting changes in the air and in sublunar things are not made by planets on individual days, but only by universal constitutions that are more powerful and that happen more rarely.

Therefore, either for the state of the air during a Revolution of the Sun, or for the general fates of men according to the things signified by the houses, judgment should be made from the rulers of that Mundane Revolution of the Sun. In which three things always occur that must be noticed—namely, the proper nature of the rulers, their celestial state, and their terrestrial state, which will be discussed individually in what follows.

Chapter 4. *The special Effects of the Planets that are Rulers of the Year, resulting from their Nature.*

For that which refers to the nature of a Planet, from which its own effects emanate, one must consult the Tables of the Universal Rulership of the Planets that is appended to Book 13, Section II, Chapter 3. From which it will be plain what any particular Planet rules over in the individual kinds of things from its own nature, or what it rules over by analogy to them. Or, one must follow Ptolemy, who in *Tetrabiblos*, Book 2, Chapter 8, before the rest of the astrologers, learnedly and in conformity sets forth the effects of the individual Planets, when acting alone and not mixed with others, they rule a universal constitution; and the Table mentioned above corresponds very closely to his doctrine. And therefore, it seems that those words of Ptolemy ought to be put here, to which also some truer things should be added by us from Haly, Cardan, and other astrologers.

Saturn, therefore (says Ptolemy), when he is the sole ruler, is generally the cause of corruption from cold, and properly in the bodies of men he makes long-lasting illnesses, wasting away, consumption that arises from catarrhs, disturbance of the humors, fluxes, quartan fevers, exiles, poverty, straitened circumstances, mourning, panics, deaths especially of old people; and the animals[1] that are left he afflicts with illnesses, so that indeed the contagion spreads to the men who use them.

In the air it excites a cold that is fearful, icy, misty, and pestilential. Disturbances of the air, dense clouds, fogs, heavy snows, not useful but harmful, and from which serpents are born that will be harmful to men. In rivers and in the sea, savage tempests and shipwrecks, difficult courses, scarcity and death of fish. And in the sea particularly the ebb of water leaving the sea bed and flowing back; but in rivers, overflows and the corruption of waters; on the land, high prices for fruits, scarcity and devastation, especially of the necessities of life, by withering [of plants] and locusts, or by floods and rain storms, or by hail, so that men ultimately perish by famine and similar evils.

However, consideration must be given to the sign in which it is placed, to the quarter of the year, to the climate, and to the temper-

---

[1] The Latin text has simply *eas* 'those', but both the Greek original (*alogôn zôiôn* 'dumb animals') and Cardan's Latin version (*Bruta* 'brutes') have a word meaning 'animals'. So perhaps the word *animales* was accidently shortened to *eas* by the typesetter of the *Astrologia Gallica*.

ament of men. For in a cold sign, a colder quarter of the year, and a cold climate, it will stir up a prodigious cold, and it will be very harmful to frigid temperaments; but in a fire or air sign, in a hot quarter of the year, and in a hotter climate, it will make the air temperate, and it will be useful to hotter natures.

When **Jupiter** is the sole ruler, it generally makes growth. And when the event pertains to men, it signifies glory, fertility, tranquility, and peace. It will enrich domestic things and foster good things for the body and mind; it promises benefices and good things from Kings, and it honors governors with glory; and in general, it is the cause of good things. And in fact, it signifies an abundance of those animals that serve the uses of men; and on the contrary, death for those that are harmful to men. Moreover, in the air it signifies a good temperature, healthy, windy, humid, nourishing the things being born on Earth; it helps the courses of ships; it makes moderate increases in [the flow] of rivers, and an abundance of fruits, and things similar to these.

To these add that when it is moderately hot and dry, it is the author of fine weather, and it excites pleasant and healthy winds, especially northern ones, and it moderates excessive heat or cold.

But **Mars** having obtained the sole rulership, is generally the cause of corruption on account of dryness. And when the events pertain to men, it will stir up wars, internal seditions, captivities, the fall of cities, tumult among the people, the anger of Princes, and sudden murders on account of those causes. Moreover, it will also cause tertian fevers, eruptions of blood, acute illnesses, violent illnesses, deaths of young people, violence, injuries, fires, homicides, looting, armed robberies. And in the air, it will cause hot spells, winds that are hot, pestilential, and withering, bolts of lightning, whirlwinds, droughts.

And on the sea, sudden shipwrecks on account of turbulent conditions, and lightning, and similar causes. And in rivers, it will absorb the waters, dry up springs, and corrupt the waters. It diminishes crops and things growing on the Earth, and either on account of the heat that it brought in previously, or else it destroys things brought in by fires.

Add to these, that since Mars is intensely hot and dry, if it is in a fire sign, in the summer and in a hotter climate, it will harm more seriously, and especially hotter natures, and it will make hot spells, lightning flashes, thunder, bolts of lightning, and hail. And in water signs, with watery or stormy stars, and especially with the Pleiades, it will stir up rains and strong storms.

Venus, when it rules alone, generally does things similar to Jupiter, with a certain pleasantness. But in general it bestows on men glory, honors, joy, abundance of years, happy marriages, and numerous offspring, pleasure in friendships and associations, increases in wealth, cleanliness in livelihood, affability, and reverence for religion; and besides, good bodily condition, and familiar association with Princes. And in the air, temperate winds, humid and fertile conditions, good and serene weather, fertile rains, fortunate and lucrative voyages, overflowing rivers, plenty of pack horses, and an abundance of fruits of the Earth.

Add to these things, that since Venus is moderately hot and very humid, it is not without cause said to be the "mother of rains," especially from [a position] in water signs, and then from [being] in Aquarius,[1] when no dry planet is aspecting it.

Mercury, when it rules alone, generally accommodates itself to that star to which it is joined, but it signifies rapid motions. In human affairs, it signifies rapidity, diligence, and skill in those things that are done. It is an instigator in armed robberies, thefts, and piracy. It makes difficulties in breathing when joined to malefics, and dry illnesses, and daily fevers, coughs, gasping for breath, wasting; and changes in religious usage, in religions themselves,

---

[1] Despite Morin's protestations against assigning the natures of the constellations to the signs with the same names, he here reverses himself and views the *air* sign Aquarius as a sign signifying *water*, since the constellation is that of Aquarius 'The Waterman'.

in royal revenues, institutions and laws, according to the nature of the star to which it is joined. In the air, since it is dry and quick and revolves closely about the Sun, it is stirring up winds that are irregular, swift, and suddenly changeable, thunder, lightning, fissures, earthquakes, and lightning bolts. And from these causes, it is occasionally deadly to animals and plants. When it is occidental, it diminishes [the flow of] rivers; when it is oriental, it increases them.

It occurs [to me] that it ought to be added here that Ptolemy and the rest of the astrologers make Mercury to be of a versatile nature and one easily changeable into another nature, which it receives either from the sign in which it is posited, or from some other Planet to which it is connected by body or by aspect. But if it were [like that], why did Ptolemy attribute particular effects to it that do not suit any other Planet? And so, the same thing must be judged about Mercury as about the other individual Planets—namely, that each one of them has its own fixed and immutable nature, according to which it acts individually. and that nature cannot be changed into another nature, either from [the nature of] the sign, or from a Planet connected to it; but Mercury does act with the sign in which it is posited, and along with the Planets with which it is connected as partner in its action, just as we have said about all the planets in Book 20, Section 3.

Nevertheless, it can be said that its nature is such that it is contrary to no other one of the Planets in such a way that it would suppress their effects; but it accommodates itself to all of them, and it aids all of them in their own actions, and it is aided by them in turn in its own actions, which are swiftness, mobility, ingenuity, art, science, skill, craftiness, etc.; so that, consequently it may be supposed to change its nature from its own nature into that of others.

But after these things, Ptolemy added[1]:

> "Such is the proper nature of each Planet as I have said, that the planets by themselves but

---
[1] *Tetrabiblos* II. 8, Section 88.

mixed with others according to the variety of the signs, and aspects, and positions with respect to the Sun, change their actions conformably, and various qualities result from the communication of natures. Moreover, since it would be impossible to set forth the qualities of the individual mixtures, and to recite all the configurations, of which there is so great a variety, this consideration may be left to the sagacity and prudence of individual mathematicians."

and this squares with the first Aphorism of the Centiloquy.[1]

Besides, it would disturb no one that he did not propose the effects of the Planets set down above for the annual Revolution of the World, but rather for eclipses, which he judged wrongly to be the prime and most effective universal cause of sublunar effects, [for which, see] *Tetrabiblos*, Book 2, Chapter 4. For in Chapter 10, where the quarters of the year are discussed, and in Chapter 12, where the months or the common conjunctions of the Sun and the Moon are discussed, he hands down a method of judging that is no different than that for eclipses, but he wants to erect celestial charts and select their rulers, and from them to render judgment, just as for eclipses.

And the truth of the matter is that the rulers of the year do not act otherwise than the rulers of eclipses or common lunations; but if Mars (for example) is ruler of the year, an eclipse, or a common lunation, it will make the same kind of thing in [all] these individual constitutions if its celestial and terrestrial state is the same, and the rest [of the indications] are in agreement; although it can produce far greater and more intense effects of its own nature if in that same

---

[1] For a translation of that Aphorism, *see* James Herschel Holden, *Five Medieval Astrologers* (Tempe, Az.: A.F.A., Inc., 2007): Ptolemy, *Centiloquy*, Aphorism 1. "From you and from knowledge, for it is not possible for the one knowing to proclaim the particular forms of affairs; wherefore, the perception does not receive the particular form of the perceptible thing, but something general. And the one searching must guess at the affairs. For only those who are inspired predict the particular things also."

year it is the ruler of the Mundane Revolution of the Sun, and if most of the lunations are also in the ecliptic,[1] especially immediately following themselves.

A major difficulty appears in this—[namely,] that Ptolemy in [his discussion of] universal constitutions excludes the Sun and the Moon from rulership. And then Julius Firmicus Maternus, running riot here and there in his astrology with the fictions and trifles of the Arabs,[2] excluded those same Lights from the rulership of a nativity, "as if (says Pontano) they would scorn the particular duty and descend to that slavery; and they therefore entrust that [task] to a subordinate Planet, in whose terms or in the terms of the Sun they are found by day, or [in those of] the Moon by night."

But this doctrine is absolutely false on account of the fictitiousness of the terms,[3] and the similar [statements] of stupid opinion by the old philosophers, who used to say that God does not concern himself with sublunar things, but He had entrusted their governance to intelligences and other causes inferior to Himself. But other astrologers do admit the Sun and the Moon to the rulership of universal constitutions; and Origanus reviews their effects in his *Introduction*, Part 3, Chapter 3.[4] But why they allow [this], and

---

[1] That is, if they are also eclipses.

[2] This statement seems to imply that Morin thought that Firmicus's book, the *Mathesis*, contained astrological opinions from the Arabs, which is of course false! Firmicus wrote in the 4th century, and the Arabs knew nothing about astrology until the 8th century. Perhaps, because Morin found statements in Firmicus that agreed with statements in the much later books of the Arabian astrologers, he assumed that Firmicus had copied them from the Arabs. Actually, the coincidence of opinions was due to the fact—unknown to Morin—that both Firmicus, and later the Arabs, had based their astrology on earlier Greek sources. So if Morin did not like some of their statements, he was actually criticizing Greek astrology, not Arabian astrology.

[3] Morin had concluded that the *terms* were worthless because he could not see any astronomical basis for them. See his discussion in Book 15, Chapter 13, where he even goes so far as to ascribe their invention to the Devil. Actually, unknown to him, they were devised by the Alexandrian inventors of Horoscopic Astrology in the 2nd century B.C., but since their early books are lost, we do not know what their rationale was.

[4] Perhaps a reference to David Origanus, *Astrologia naturalis...* 'Natural astrology...' (Marseille: J. B. Senius, 1645).

[thereby] depart from Ptolemy's opinion, neither they, nor Origanus offer any explanation. But from the principles and the doctrine previously set forth by us, the difficulty will be elucidated thus.

It is certain, and [the idea] is received by all astrologers, that the Sun and the Moon have their own natures, domiciles, exaltations, and triplicities, according to which they act, just as they are determined in every constitution, whether it is universal or particular, even as the rest of the Planets; therefore, by whatever reason they are admitted to the rulership of a constitution, the Sun and the Moon by that same reason should also be admitted to that rulership, and this is all the more just because the Sun and the Moon are the principal and primary Planets, as is also proven from Ptolemy's [statements] cited above, and is witnessed by astrology as a whole, just as it has been alluded to by us in many places; and no reason given above can be supposed to be more valid by which they are excluded, and a Prince is [thus made] inferior to his own satellites.

For if a comparison is offered to Kings, with which the Sun has a manifest analogy, and the one who entrusts the administration of his own kingdom to his own subordinates. I say that, with this comparison also having been admitted between physical and political things, a true King and one worthy of the name (namely, one who has the knowledge and practice of ruling), entrusts not only his own wars and battles to the commanders of his own army, his own justice to the Senate, and secret things and of greater moment to his own chancellor and to the Secret Council, but he even entrusts himself when things demand it in battles, to the senate and the Council personally he is in between; and by his own majesty, his experience in ruling, his magnanimity, his fairness and prudence not only in commanding, but also in accomplishing, he does more than any commander, or Senate, or the entire Council; and so truly solemnly and gloriously he rules his own kingdom; not, however, solely by the mask of his name, as we have heard has happened with Kings who were lazy, ignorant, effeminate, and incapable of acting, who, unable to perform by themselves the administration of the kingdom, abandon it to subjects; nor do they take any interest in those things that they do [that lead to] the destruction of the people and the ruination of the kingdom.

Similarly, therefore, when the Sun, the King of the Planets and the sublunar World—both by itself and through its followers—is the most powerful director, the most watchful and the fairest appointed by God; it will be prepollent in celestial charts; it itself by its own virtue governs principally the effects of a constitution. Moreover, when its followers are prepollent in rulership, the Sun regulates the effects more through them than through itself. But the followers of the Sun always respect its majesty and power in acting, both because they receive their motion from it, and because from their varied position with respect to the Sun or to the Moon, they vary their own virtue of acting.

Moreover, the difference of the effects [arising] from the rulership of the Lights and their followers consists especially of this, after the diversity due to nature and virtue; because when the Sun and the Moon have taken command, the effects are greater, more illustrious, and more famous than when one of the other Planets rules; and, among men, they mainly pertain to Popes, Emperors, Kings, Queens, Princes, Magnates, Kingdoms, Republics, and Universities.

Besides, something from Ptolemy must be noted here. **First**, by the name Saturn, not only the Planet should be understood, but also the saturnine nature in general, which is common to both Saturn, and to the fixed stars and signs of the zodiac that are of the nature of Saturn; and therefore, it must be noted whether the saturnine nature prevails by means of such bodies in a universal constitution; and the same thing must be thought about Jupiter, Mars, and the rest of the Planets.

Second. Mixtures of the rulers of universal constitutions must be understood to be not only mixtures of other Planets, but also of the fixed stars, and the signs in which the ruling Planets are posited, or with which they are conjoined.

Third. Ptolemy opined thus: "The Sun and the Moon in universal constitutions are the principal causes of events, and they control the rulerships of the stars and the powers of the rulers, either strengthening or weakening them." And Cardan in his *Commentary* explains this thus:

> "Namely, because the Lights in eclipses (about which Ptolemy is then talking) signify a disposition of that magnitude for the quantity of an eclipse; and the Lights can be compared to the fire in a lit furnace, which signifies nothing else except that many things can be done by the aid of it. And because if it is great, great things can be done; but if it is little, [only] little things; however, not whether bricks should be baked, or glass liquified, or silver refined, etc.; for these things belong to the 5 Planets—namely, to define the quality of the event."

However, that that is not a true explanation is proved thus. Because Cardan places no difference between the eclipses of the Sun and those of the Moon, as far as their events or disposition; and he seems to want the same disposition to be signified by either of the Lights experiencing an eclipse, which only consists of this, that many things can be done by the aid of a Light that is being eclipsed—not saying whether either of them rules this or that, since however the Sun and the Moon differ in nature between themselves, which Cardan cannot deny; and therefore they always differ in their effects, whether in an eclipse or not, and each of them always acts for itself by its own virtue, even as a fire by its own nature bakes bricks, or melts glass, or refines silver.

Besides, he does not put any particular difference for the Lights between the things effectuated by their eclipses by conjunction and the things effectuated by their eclipses by opposition, which however is opposed to the nature of their syzygies; and the Sun conjoined to the Moon does not do the same thing as when it is opposed to the Moon. Finally, because from that same fire, bricks are baked, and glass is liquified, which are two contrary effects, the reason for the contrariety cannot be sought from the action of the fire, which is the same, but from the subjects experiencing [its heat]. Therefore Cardan badly compares the 5 Planets to those subjects, which, in the case of the effects of eclipses are not experiencing causes but effecting causes, since they rule the eclipse.

And so, it seems to us that it should rather be said that from Book 13, Section II, Chapter 2, and the Table of Universal Rulership of the Planets mentioned above, that the Sun and the Moon have their own formal virtues and their own formal effects that are different from the effects of the other 5 Planets; then, they have their own kinds of things that they principally rule, either by nature or by analogy, in addition to their universal rulership over these sublunar things. So, the Sun and the Moon, in their periodic Revolutions back to their own radical places at the beginning of the World, renew their own force over all these sublunar things, and they principally renew their own kinds of things for themselves, but depending upon the other Planets when those Planets rule a universal constitution of the Lights themselves.

And therefore the Sun of course actively determines its own effects [as affected by] the other five Planets; and due to that it is not unreasonable that Ptolemy says that the Sun controls their rulerships, and he increases or diminishes their *forces* according to their position with respect to the Sun; but the *quality* of their own effects is not changed by those things, which is diverse in accordance with the diversity of the ruling Planet. And the same thing must be said about the Moon.

But in the conjunctions and oppositions of the Sun and the Moon, when even without an eclipse, the kinds of things, or the proper universal effects of the Sun and the Moon, are combined—like husband and wife—to which combination the other five Planets, having attained the rulership of the constitution, are also determined, as if they were compelled to act on those kinds of things and the whole sublunar empire of the Sun and the Moon, or as if the Sun and the Moon would be joined together to control and manage their own force and their own effects, because each Planet accomplishes [something] according to its own nature, force, and state, as is done between Kings and Dukes, or the commanders of their own armies, of which some act well, others badly, but each one acts according to his own force and inclination; or similarly, between a master and his servants.

Which explanation is consistent with the mind of Ptolemy and with experience, a thing which should be discussed more clearly. And from this it is plainly evident that the Sun and the Moon in universal constitutions are always the primary Planets, or the *Princes* as Cardan says, and they act primarily according to their own nature; but the rest [of the Planets] act only as satellites or secondary [Planets]; which is contradictory to the Copernican system.[1] And these things [are said] about the effects [resulting] from the nature of the rulers of the year.

Chapter 5. *The special Effects of the Rulers of the Year [that result] from their own celestial State. and first, by reason of the Sign in which they are posited.*

There are 4 things to be especially looked at in the celestial state. Namely, the sign in which [a Planet] is posited, its connection with the other Planets, its position with respect to the Sun and the Moon, and also its motion.

With regard to the first of these, the old [astrologers] have handed down to us a very vast forest of aphorisms on the effects of the Planets in the individual signs, the greater part of which are not to be trusted, and they do not agree with experiences; besides which, some of them are contradictory to others. And this has

---
[1] Remember that Morin was opposed to the Copernican system.

arisen from this—that the starry signs[1] were confounded with the [true] signs that were unknown at that time; or effects were not ascribed to their own genuine causes, as is still the case here and there in nativities, from which the true principles of astrology have not yet been deduced.

However, it has been received by all astrologers, and it is certain that the qualities of the Planets, signs, and fixed stars should be combined. And hence it must be judged that the latitude of the place and the quarter of the year must be taken into account. And this must be taken for a firm foundation, without which it does not appear that anything else could be substituted, and it could not be judged to be in any way scientific. Add that no small part of the aphorisms received from the old [astrologers] chiefly squares with that foundation. That is, the virtue of the signs surpassing the virtue of the fixed stars, or the fixed stars following the nature of the signs in acting, as is the case with all the Planets.

But truly in this place there occurs something that is most worthy of note. Namely, that the division of the signs into fire, air, water, and earth seems to have been unknown to Ptolemy.[2] For even though in *Tetrabiblos*, Book 1, Chapter 11, discussing the natural properties of the 12 signs, he divides them into tropical, equinoctial, fixed, and bicorporeal (which division is better explained by mobile, fixed, and *common* signs); and Chapter 12 divides them into masculine and feminine signs; and Book 2, Chapter 11, discusses the particular force and nature of the signs for varying the constitutions of the air. And yet, neither in these places, nor in Book 3, Chapter 11, where he discusses the form and temperament of the body, nor anywhere else, does he make any mention of the signs, as if they are inherently of this or that elemental nature; and

---

[1] That is, the *constellations*.

[2] This is true. Nor was this division mentioned by Dorotheus (1st century), Porphyry (end of the 3rd century), or Paul of Alexandria (4th century). However, it was mentioned by Teucer of Babylon (1st century) and Firmicus Maternus (4th century)—although only Aries and Pisces survive in the MSS of the *Mathesis*—and by Rhetorius (beginning of the 6th century).

only in that Chapter 11 of Book 2, does he determine the natures of the signs by the fixed stars that in his age or thereabouts were perceived in the signs, whose essence had scarcely become known in that age, but their proper natures had even much more escaped notice.

Whence, it is not surprising that the astrologers of that time, having perceived the very slow motion of the fixed stars into the following [signs], should have thought it to be the signs that did not have any action from themselves, and that their action was from the fixed stars that they had in them; and to call anything [done by] them according to what the Sun does in them, as Firminus[1] notes from Haly in his *Repertory*, Part 1, Chapter 1, which is evidently to assert that those signs themselves are of no virtue. But posterity discovered this to be false; and we have shown its falsity here and there in the present work.

It is also no wonder that Ptolemy had followed his predecessor astrologers, not otherwise for the nature of the signs, which he had defined by the fixed stars that he had included within them, and that each sign was not of the same nature [throughout its extent], but he said that it was different in the beginning, the middle, and the end[2]; and again he made the northern part of the sign to be different in virtue from the southern part, which cannot be said of the true signs, each one of which is the same per se and of a single nature throughout the whole expanse of the sign. But from this, another evil follows—certainly, that by confounding the true signs with the constellations slowly crawling along under them, they were not able to know the proper virtues of either the constellations or the true signs. And consequently, it is no wonder that from that source of ignorance, an amazing hotch-potch of aphorisms flowed, but of uncertain truth.

---

[1] Firmin de Beauval (fl. 1338), *Repertorium de mutatione aeris* 'A Treatise on Changes in the Air' (Paris: Iacobus Kerver, 1539. folio). Not Firmicus (4th century), as Hieroz mistakenly translates the text.

[2] Perhaps because he had in mind that each sign contained three decans.

It was added to these, that after Ptolemy, the elemental nature of the true signs having been detected, and with them divided into triplicities of fire, air, water, and earth, as Albohazen Haly[1] did in Part 1, Chapter 1, Al-Kindî[2] and the other Arabs divided the fixed stars of the Zodiac into 28 equal spaces, each one of 12°52′, which they call *Mansions of the Moon*,[3] during its synodic Revolution with the Sun, having made their beginning from the first star of Aries,[4] which in this year 1648 is found in 28°18′ of the sign Aries; and they assign the proper nature to each mansion in imitation of Ptolemy; and they have handed down a *Table of the Mansions*.

They will have it that when Planets, and especially the Moon, are posited in one of those Mansions, they act upon these inferior things in accordance with the elemental nature of that space of the Mansion—that is, of the fixed stars occupying that Mansion. But since Ptolemy had made the signs to be in a constant site, when he said that some are tropical, and others equinoctial, from that it results that these Mansions of the Moon are ambulatory through the signs of the zodiac according to the motion of the fixed stars.

But about that Table of the Mansions, which is held to be an *arcane* thing, there is not lacking a cause to be distrustful.

First, because from many Tables of that sort that I have seen, no mansion is hot or cold; but they are only put down as humid, dry, or temperate; which, however, does not agree with Ptolemy, who

---

[1] Albohazen Haly is another name for Haly Abenragel or ʿAlî ibn abî al-Rijâl (11th century). The reference is to his book, *The Complete Book on the Judgments of the Stars*, where in the third paragraph of Book 1, Chapter 1, he says, *And these signs are fiery, earthy, airy, and watery*.... And in the next paragraph he identifies them, *Aries, Leo, and Sagittarius are fiery*, etc.

[2] Yaʿqûb al-Kindî (9th century), Iraqi astrological writer. Probably Morin's reference is to his book *De nubibus et pluuiis*... 'On Clouds and Rains...' in an omnibus volume of astrological tracts (Venice: Peter Liechtenstein, 1507.)

[3] See the Table in question at the end of Chapter 6 below.

[4] The star Sharatan or β Arietis, in 1648 was in 29 ♈ 04. Morin states its longitude as 28 ♈ 18, which is close to its longitude 28 ♈ 23 in Tycho's Catalogue as presented in Kepler's *Rudolphine Tables*. Morin perhaps forgot to add the precession from 1600 to 1648.

acknowledges many parts of the signs to be hot, though none to be cold; and it cannot agree with the truth, since many of them are firmly hot, humid, cold, dry, or of the nature of the individual Planets, some of which are hot and dry like the Sun and Mars; some are hot and humid, like Venus; some are cold and dry, like Saturn and Mercury; and others are cold and humid, like the Moon; with Ptolemy himself acknowledging that.

Second, because with the nature of the true signs unknown, Ptolemy could not have known the natures of the constellations or the fixed stars; and therefore the natures of the Mansions (which cannot be said to be the Mansions of the *Moon*, rather than the Mansions of some other Planet) taken from that, could not be true. And if God, the Best and the Greatest, shall have given us life, for expounding brief observations on the text of the *Tetrabiblos*,[1] it will be evidently plain what should be felt about such a book of names, whose individual words Cardan has indeed faithfully honored, and whose principal fundamentals have already been justly condemned by us many times.

But meanwhile, in such difficulties, what should we feel obliged to do? Should we also pass down to posterity the particular aphorisms about the universal effects of the Planets in the individual signs of the zodiac, along with the Table of the Mansions of the Moon that have been handed down to us by the old [astrologers]? Certainly, while it is alien to my intelligence to expound things that are evidently uncertain, and I would prefer to make public a defect in this part of astrology, so that what was not accomplished by our predecessors, our successors might try to supply by their own efforts and observations—namely, by observing the true and proper natures of the fixed stars—[but] it seems safer to hand down only general aphorisms regarding this matter, based on the above said foundation. The truth of which no astrologer initiated in the legitimate principles of the science can call into doubt or even

---

[1] This seems to imply that Morin had in mind to write a brief commentary on parts of the *Tetrabiblos*.

overturn, if indeed those aphorisms also make known something to disclose the natures of the fixed stars.

For, since the nature of a sign is the same in its beginning, middle, and end, when it happens that a Planet, especially the ruler of a constitution, being posited for a long time in a sign, produces something new on these inferior things, apart from a connection by body or by aspect with another Planet agreeing with the effect, or with another place in that constitution. It can safely be said that that effect is from the fixed stars to which the first Planet is conjoined, or with which it rises, culminates, or sets, especially if it was one of the first or second magnitude. And therefore, we do not advise a student astrologer against experimenting with the aphorisms handed down by the old [astrologer], so that the truth that they may contain may be discovered and observed, provided that they may not be deterred by a labyrinth of confusion and the frequent encounter with contrary aphorisms.

And so:

First. If the Planet that is ruler of the year is in its own sign, it will act powerfully according to its own nature; but if the Planet agrees by its own extrinsic nature with the sign, it will act more powerfully elementally according to the nature of the sign; otherwise, it will act more powerfully influentially according to the nature of the sign. And therefore, Mars in Aries will heat more and will dry elementally; but in Scorpio, it will chill more and humidify influentially; with the nature of Mars itself flourishing and common to both. But the Sun, a Planet of a single nature, when it is in Leo, only heats and dries per se, both elementally and influentially. And so with the rest [of the Planets].

Second. If the planet that is the ruler of the year is not in its own sign, it will act with the nature of the sign in which it is posited, and the ruler of that sign, which, if it is in that same sign, such as with Saturn ruler of the year posited with Jupiter in Pisces, Jupiter will powerfully concur per se and by its own sign with the future events of that year. But if it is in an alien sign,[1] but one of the same triplicity, as with Jupiter posited in Cancer or Scorpio, its concourse will also still be powerful on account of the same nature of the sign and the trine aspect of the Planets. But if it is in a sign that is altogether of a diverse nature, but in its own domicile—as Jupiter posited in Sagittarius—when Saturn ruler of the year is in Pisces, it will still act strongly jointly, indeed it will prevail over Saturn; but if it is peregrine in a sign of a diverse nature—as with Jupiter posited in Taurus or Gemini—then the virtue of Jupiter on the effects of the year will be weak, and therefore the effects of Saturn would be less.

Third. When the planet that is the ruler of the year is in an alien sign, not only must that sign be taken into account, but also its ruler; for Gemini, Libra, and Aquarius do not do the same things, even though they are of the same triplicity, because they belong to 3 different Planets. It must therefore be seen which Planet is the ruler of that sign, and what its nature is, and what its state is, so that it may be plain whether it supports the proper effects of the ruler of the year, or whether it contradicts them.

Fourth. When the ruler of the year is in an alien sign, and its ruler is similarly in an alien sign, and without any mutual reception, there must also be taken into account the ruler of that second sign, but not its ruler; for the virtue of a ruler vanishes beyond the second rulership, and it does not go around in a circle.

Fifth. Saturn in all the water signs does not give water, at least not always, even though by its own nature it is disposed to rains on account of its frigidity; but the state of the Moon, Mars, and Jupiter, the rulers of Cancer, Scorpio, and Pisces, which by their own nature and state either help or hinder, must be taken into account, and especially if they aspect Saturn. And the rule is the same with the rest of the Planets, at least in accordance with the rational laws of judgments.

---

[1] That is, a sign which it does not rule.

Sixth. It sometimes happens that by accident Planets act in [a manner] contrary to their own natures. For example, that the Sun in Leo may cause rains in place of mild weather—namely, when it incites more vapors than it can dissipate—either on account of its noticeable heat with the briefer stay that it makes above the horizon, or on account of a region that has too many vapors, all of which the Sun cannot dispel, even with a longer stay above the horizon, or on account of an aspect from a Planet that is rainy by nature or by its celestial state.

Seventh. Any Planet, [posited] in signs agreeing extrinsically with its own nature, acts in accordance with that nature. Such as the Sun, Jupiter, and Mars in fire signs naturally bringing heat; Saturn in water and earth signs bringing cold; the Moon in water signs bringing moisture.

Eighth. It must be seen from the ruler of the year and its celestial state what quality will rise up and what it may be able to do to sublunar things, in the air, in the water, on Earth, and in kinds of mixed and living things, having taken into account the place and the quarter of the year.

Ninth. Those effects that do not agree with the above said causes, and that will not be from syzygies or transits producing them, must be thought to be made by the fixed stars with which the rulers of the year are located, or with which they rise, culminate, or set, or with which there are new Moons, eclipses, great conjunctions, and other universal constitutions.

Chapter 6. *The special Effects of the Planets that are Rulers of the Year by reason of their Connection with other Planets or Fixed Stars.*

That the Planets according to their diverse connection among themselves by body or by aspect, produce diverse effects upon these sublunar things, both universal in universal constitutions, and particular ones in particular natal charts, was shown in Book 19 and elsewhere. And no astrologer can be in doubt about this, nor indeed can any philosopher (except perhaps one who is truly ignorant of celestial things) doubt it. For the terrestrial Globe of itself would always be the same and would not experience any changes, except from extrinsic causes, namely those that would be caused by the celestial bodies.

And if the Planets were to revolve only in a single annual motion, always at the same distance from each other, as the fixed stars do; then in no way could a reason be given why the individual parts of individual years would be different, but there would be a plain cause why they should be equal. But since, therefore, in the truth of the matter they are unequal, and no summer is entirely similar to the one closely preceding or following it, and neither are the years similar, it must necessarily be declared that their dissimilarity is caused by the different motions and mutual combinations of the planets. Therefore, having assumed this, we should now say from [the writings] of the old astrologers what each one of them connected with the others does, [and] in what thing they agree among themselves, so that this doctrine may seem to have been handed down minimally from our predecessors to our posterity.

But five things must be noted here in advance.

First. There are only seven different legitimate configurations among the Planets, namely the conjunction, the semi-sextile, the sextile, the square, the trine, the opposition, and the quincunx, whose foundation in Nature has been shown by us in Book 16, Section I, Chapter 4. Moreover, the rest of the aspects introduced and approved by Kepler and others ignorant of astrology, are rejected by us as illegitimate.

Second. Although all these configurations are effective [in their action] on these sublunar things, the old astrologers, however, only expounded three of them in the matter of universal constitutions—namely, the conjunction, the square, and the opposition. And that is because those are more powerful than the rest of them, for the reason that was stated by us previously—namely, because when one of the configured Planets is in an angle of the chart, the other is also found in an angle, which indeed increases the strength of both Planets; and therefore the configuration of both of them acts more strongly.

Third. The conjunction is the strongest and most effective one of the configurations—not by reason of its light, as Magini[1] thought in the Introduction to his *Ephemerides*—since the other configurations are not lacking in the light of the configured Planets; but because a united force is stronger than a dispersed one; but in the case of the conjunction, it is the greatest union of the Planets that can be, for they are in the same line and in the same place in the *Caelum* with respect to the Earth. In the case of the opposition, they are in fact in the same line, but not in the same place in the *Caelum*. In the case of the square and the rest [of the aspects], they are neither in the same line, nor in the same place in the *Caelum*. And consequently, after the conjunction, the opposition is the stronger, then the square on account of the cause mentioned previously.

Fourth. The old [astrologers], at least in universal constitutions, attribute the same effects to those three configurations, the conjunction, the square, and the opposition, which however is contrary to the elements of astrology. And although the conjunction, square, or opposition of Saturn and Jupiter can affect the same sublunar material; nevertheless, it is alien to reason that they would affect it in the same manner or to the same extent, and that Saturn would do the same thing or act in the same manner when conjoined to Jupiter as when it is square or opposite Jupiter, especially in the case of human affairs, in which the square and the opposition of the malefics are accustomed to stir up unfortunate [conditions].

---

[1] Giovanni Antonio Magini (1555-1617), professor of astrology, astronomy, and mathematics at the University of Bologna. The reference is to his *Ephemerides coelestium motuum...ab anno 1608 ad annum 1630... cum supplemento isagogicarum ephemeridum...* 'Ephemerides of the Celestial Motions . . . from the Year 1608 to the Year 1630... with a Supplemental Introduction to the Ephemerides . . .' (Frankfurt: Wolfgang Richter, 1610.).

Fifth. In the aphorisms that follow, note must always be taken of the quarter of the year. Spring, moreover, is hot and humid; Summer is hot and dry; Autumn is cold and dry; and Winter is cold and humid. And therefore, some quarters of the year are more favorable to the causes of heat; others are more favorable to the causes of cold; some are more favorable to the causes of rain; and others are more favorable to the causes of dryness. But having noted these things in advance, the opinions of the ancient [astrologers], collected by us from their aphorisms, are as follows.

Saturn and Jupiter in conjunction, square, and oppositions on account of the slowness of their motion, for many days before and after their [exact] connection stir up changes in the air according to their own nature and that of the sign that they occupy. If indeed in fire signs, they produce heat, but especially dryness. In water signs, great rains and [outbreaks of] plague. In air signs, many winds and storms. In earth signs, spells of cold weather, frost, dense clouds and turbid air. In the spring, moreover, particularly humid and turbulent air; in the summer, hail and thunder; in the autumn, winds and heavy rains; in the winter, turbid weather, snows, and frost.

But it must always be noted which Planet rules in the place of the conjunction, not only by the dignity of rulership, exaltation, or triplicity; but also by its nature, both elemental and influential. For Saturn in earth signs, and especially in Capricorn, will prevail over Jupiter; then too in air signs and especially in Aquarius. But in fire signs, and especially in Sagittarius, Jupiter will prevail over Saturn, then too in water signs, and especially in Pisces. Moreover, a Planet that prevails in the place of a conjunction, will also prevail over changes, whether they pertain to the air, the water, and the earth, or to men. Moreover, in the case of the square and the opposition, it must be seen which [Planet] is stronger in the sign that it occupies, then which one of them is above the earth and angular. And for Jupiter to prevail is good, but for Saturn it is evil; and the same thing must the judged about the other Planets.

Saturn and Mars in conjunction, square, and opposition act similarly, taking into account [the nature] of the sign. And in fire signs they generate great and destructive drynesses; in water signs, rain showers, and heavy rains with hail; in air signs, strong winds, storms, lightning, thunder, lightning flashes, and corruption of the air; in earth signs, intense cold, icy cold, snows, and in Capricorn thunderbolts. In particular, moreover, in the spring they cause rains and thunder; in the summer thunder and hail storms; in the autumn rains and turbid air; but in winter a reduction of cold.

Saturn and the Sun in conjunction, square, and opposition, cools the air, especially in cold signs, and it provides rains and hail storms; then in air signs, strong and corrupting winds, and especially in Aquarius and Libra. In particular, moreover, in the spring, cold and rain; in the summer, hail storms and thunder with a reduction of heat; in the autumn, rain and cold; but in the winter, wet weather, turbid, and snows.

Saturn and Venus in conjunction, square, and opposition, generates showers and cold spells, especially in water signs, where it also causes hail storms, and in Virgo inundations. In particular, moreover, in spring, rains and cold; in summer, sudden rains; in autumn, cold rain; and in winter, rains and snows. And therefore, almost always the connection of Saturn and Venus is rainy.

Saturn and Mercury in conjunction, square, and opposition, in wet signs makes turbid air and rains; in fire signs, it produces dryness; in air signs, strong winds; and in earth signs, cold, and icy cold; so that in truth these configurations very often generate cold spells that are harmful to the fruits of Earth. But in particular, in spring, winds and rain; in summer, winds and hail storms; in fall, strong winds; in winter, winds and snows. And therefore, always, or at least most often, they generate winds.

Saturn and the Moon. It generates cold, clouds, rains, and now and then hail storms, especially in water signs. In particular, moreover, in spring, it makes the air turbid and humid; in summer, humid and cold, then too it makes hail storms; in autumn, foggy weather; but in the winter, very cold, foggy, and snowy.

Jupiter and Mars in conjunction, square, and opposition, in fire signs produce heat and excessive dryness; in water signs, rains with lightning flashes, thunder, and thunderbolts; in air signs, fine weather; in earth signs, dryness. In particular, moreover, in spring and autumn, it makes turbid air, and windy weather; in the summer, heat, thunder, and tempests; but in winter, it reduces the cold. But it must be seen which Planet prevails. For with Jupiter prevailing, it is healthy and fertile; but with Mars prevailing, unhealthy and corruptive.

Jupiter and the Sun in conjunction, square, and opposition. It causes delightful and fine weather, temperate heat, and healthy winds, especially in air signs; and in wet signs, fertilizing rains; in fire signs, it increases the heat, especially in Leo; and in earth signs, it dries up and clears up the weather. In particular, moreover, in spring and autumn, it generates winds; in summer, thunder and thunderbolts; but in winter, reduction of heat.

Jupiter and Venus in conjunction, square, and opposition, makes delightful and fine weather and calm air. Moreover, in water signs it makes clouds and healthy rains; and these configurations are for the most part fertile, especially when occurring at a suitable time; and they cause an abundance of fruits. And if Jupiter prevails, fine weather is more likely produced; but if Venus prevails, rains are more likely.

Jupiter and Mercury in conjunction, square, and opposition, usually provokes dry spells, especially in fire or air signs, and this [occurs] in any quarter of the year.

Jupiter and the Moon in conjunction, square, and opposition, usually causes fine weather and mildness of the air in any time of the year, and favorable winds; and some times it scatters white clouds all over the sky.

Mars and the Sun in conjunction, square, and opposition, acts in accordance with the nature of the signs, but usually with vehemence. In water signs, it certainly stirs up rain showers, thunder, lightning, hail storms—especially in summer—and with injury; in fire signs it causes an excess of heat and dryness harmful to living creatures; in air signs, burning winds; and in earth signs, it reduces rains. In particular, moreover, in spring and autumn, it causes winds and dryness; in summer, great heat, thunder, lightning, and hail storms; and in winter, it causes a reduction of cold.

Mars and Venus in conjunction, square, and opposition, in water signs produces much water; but in other signs it makes fine weather and temperate conditions and few rains. In particular, moreover, in spring and autumn, it bestows rains, also on the very day if the conjunction is made in Scorpio[1]; in summer, fine weather and few rain showers; in winter, a reduction of cold.

Mars and Mercury in conjunction, square, and opposition, in fire signs, especially in Leo, it causes a harmful excess of heat and dryness; in water signs, rain showers; in air signs, strong winds changing direction with rapidity, because both Planets are impetuous. In autumn, it makes hail storms and winds driving clouds. In winter and spring, it causes snows; in summer, thunder, and hail storms.

Mars and the Moon in conjunction, square, and opposition, in water signs, it excites rain; in fire signs, almost always dryness, but sometimes yellow and reddish clouds scattered over the sky, sometimes rainy conditions; in air signs, lightning flashes, thunder, and hail storms, especially in the summer, and sometimes a rainbow and rain.

The Sun and Venus in conjunction in water signs bestows rains; and in spring, autumn, and winter, in fire and air signs, fine weather.

---

[1] The conjunction in Scorpio can only happen in the late summer, autumn, or early winter.

The Sun and Mercury in conjunction in air signs causes winds; in water signs, rains; and in fire signs, dryness.

The Sun and the Moon in conjunction, square, and opposition, acts with the nature of the signs and their rulers. And therefore, it sometimes produces dry spells, sometimes winds, and sometimes calm weather. Besides, the conjunction in the summer is judged to be hot; in the winter, very cold; but the opposition acts in a contrary manner, unless Saturn confuses things.

Venus and Mercury in conjunction certainly acts according to the nature of the signs, but it inclines more to rain showers; and it produces inundations when it occurs at the time of a conjunction, square, or opposition of the Sun and the Moon.

Venus and the Moon in conjunction, square, and opposition inclines to gentle rains, rain showers, and snows; it produces cloudy and foggy weather, and it reduces the heat.

Mercury and the Moon in conjunction, square, and opposition acts according to the nature of the signs, but it inclines more to winds; and it varies the weather quickly on account of the velocity of their motion.

Besides, the above said configurations of the planets have a greater force for the above said effects when the Moon also affects other configured Planets by her own conjunction, square, or opposition. Moreover, when not just 2 but 3 or 4 Planets at the same time are conjoined, squared, or opposed, greater effects are signified, and more commingled, which can nevertheless be conjectured from the simple configuration given above, unless one wishes to consult the English Summary,[1] where one comes upon a huge hotch-potch of aphorisms. And when many Planets are posited together in the same triplicity, they act powerfully according to the nature of that triplicity. That is, in fire they produce an excess of heat and dryness, and from that, illnesses and sterility; in

---

[1] Probably a reference to some Latin astrological treatise by an English astrologer.

water, a harmful abundance of rains; and Mars and Saturn especially cause that to be evil.

But since the Moon's power on these sublunar things is the greatest on account of her distance from the Earth being the least of the Planets, her applications to the other Planets must be carefully noted in her synods, especially those with the Sun immediately preceding the Sun's Ingress into the cardinal points. For applying to Saturn, she will advance his own effects upon the elements and upon mankind; and so with Jupiter, Mars, etc. Besides, when she is increasing her light and applying to Planets that are direct, she bestows fine weather, but if she is applying to retrograde Planets, she bestows rains.

In addition, the configurations of the Planets must also be understood to be not only mutual configurations among themselves, but also with the fixed stars, and especially with those that by their own magnitude or nature, or by their particular association (such as the Pleiades or Scorpio) are perceived to be more effective for altering these sublunar things. For which, you will either consult the following Table of the 28 Mansions of the Moon, constructed according to the mind of Ptolemy[1] and the other old astrologers, and accommodated to this century; or your own particular experiences made by careful judgment, which will perchance be safer.

Moreover, the first Mansion of the Moon, corresponding to the experience of the old astrologers with the fixed stars, will begin in the year 1660 according to Tycho at 28 ♈ 28, where the first star

---

[1] Ptolemy knew nothing of the Mansions of the Moon. They were traditional among the Arabs and first became known in the West during the Middle Ages. Several books by Arabian astrologers mention them, and there were also some tracts wrongly attributing them to Dorotheus and the Indians (due to confusion with the Hindu *nakshatras*). The book by the famous twelfth-century translator John of Seville, *Epitome totius astrologiae* (Nürnberg: Montanus & Neuber, 1548), Book 4, Chapter 18, has a table of them with the name of the determinant star, the longitude (measured at intervals of 12°51' from the first star), the effect on the weather (dry, humid, etc.), and whether the mansion is fortunate or unfortunate. A convenient modern source is Vivian E. Robson, *The Fixed Stars and Constellations in Astrology* (London, 1923. often reprinted).

of the constellation Aries is put, which is south in the preceding or Right Horn.[1] For Stoeffler [1452-1531], Gaurico [1476-1558], Pitatus [fl. 1535-1568][2], and other astrologers agree that the first Mansion begins with the stars that are in the Right Horn of Aries; and those natures of the Mansions that they have related, we are putting here, with the warning that the nature of each Mansion coincides with the one of the stars that it includes, as they will have it, which you will nevertheless sometimes experience to be false! And besides, that is a greater reason, why the Moon's motion through these Mansions should be looked at, rather than the motions of the other Planets, the Sun, Saturn, Jupiter, Mars, Venus, and Mercury; since the fixed stars agree with their actions, just as they do with the actions of the Moon. But it must be feared that until now the true nature of each Mansion is not known, on account of the natures of the fixed stars that are not yet well known.

Finally, for the certainty and magnitude of the effects from the configurations of the Planets shown above, both among themselves and with the fixed stars, the power of the configured Planets in the signs of the configurations does much. For if they are conjoined in a sign where each Planet has the power of its domicile or exaltation, each Planet will act strongly, such as the Sun and Mars conjoined in Aries, Saturn and Mars in Capricorn, or Jupiter and the Moon in Cancer. If only one is powerful, that one will prevail in the effects, especially if the other one is unfortunate in the place of the conjunction, as when Saturn and Jupiter are conjoined in Capricorn, or Saturn and Mars in Aries.

---

[1] Again, as mentioned in the Note to Chapter 5 above, Tycho's Catalogue, as repeated in Kepler's *Rudolphine Tables*, gives the longitude of the star as 28 ♈ 23; and the precession to 1660 would put it in 29 ♈ 03. Modern figures would put it at 29 ♈ 14 in 1660. It is south of the other bright star Hamal or α Arietis, but both stars have north latitude.

[2] Pietro Pitati of Verona. Morin apparently refers to his *Almanach Novum...Tractatus perbreves de electionibus revolutionibus annorum et mutatione aeris...* 'New Almanac...A Short Treatise on Elections, the Revolutions of Years, and the Changing of the Air...' (Tübingen: Ulrich Mor., 1544). See Lynn Thorndike, *History of Magic and Experimental Science* (New York: Columbia University Press, 1923-1958. 8 vols.), Vol. 5, pp. 264-265. Parts of Pitati's book are dedicated to Pope Paul III (1468-1549), a patron of astrology.

Table of the Mansions of the Moon.[1]

1	a little dry	28 ♈ 28	15	wet	28 ♎ 27
2	temperate	11 ♉ 11	16	cold & wet	11 ♏ 11
3	wet	24 ♉ 03	17	wet	24 ♏ 03
4	cold & wet	6 ♊ 55	18	dry	6 ♐ 55
5	dry	19 ♊ 47	19	wet	19 ♐ 47
6	temperate	2 ♋ 39	20	temperate	2 ♑ 39
7	wet	15 ♋ 31	21	wet	15 ♑ 31
8	a little wet	28 ♋ 23	22	temperate	28 ♑ 23
9	dry	11 ♌ 15	23	wet	11 ♒ 15
10	wet	24 ♌ 07	24	a little cold	24 ♒ 07
11	a little cold	7 ♍ 00	25	dry	7 ♓ 00
12	wet	19 ♍ 50	26	a little dry	19 ♓ 50
13	temperate	2 ♎ 43	27	wet	2 ♈ 43
14	a little wet	15 ♎ 35	28	temperate	15 ♈ 35

---

[1] As noted above, this table begins at 28 ♈ 28 instead of 29 ♈ 03. But aside from that, nearly all the longitudes are slightly off. They should all be multiples of 12°51 26″ + 28°28′. But they have an average error of 4 or 5 minutes, with a maximum error of 8 minutes and a minimum error of 1 minute. However, if the actual extent of the asterisms that make up the Mansions of the Moon is wanted, then for each Mansion the longitude of the marker star should be used. This table is for the 17th century. See Appendix 5 for a Table for the Year 2000.

Moreover, in the case of the square and the opposition, if both planets are powerful in their own signs, both will act strongly; and therefore, great effects must be expected from both Planets. As if Jupiter is in Cancer, and Saturn is in Libra or Capricorn; but if only one is powerful in its own sign, that one will prevail; and all the much more if the other Planet is unfortunate in its sign, as if Jupiter would be in Cancer, and Saturn in Aries; or the Sun in Aries, and Mars in Cancer. But about these things, let what has been said suffice.

Chapter 7. *The special Effects of the Planets that are Rulers of the Year, from their Position with Relation to the Sun and the Moon.*

From their position with relation to the Sun and the Moon, the planets are called *oriental* and *occidental*; and in both positions they may appear *direct, stationary,* and *retrograde*. Moreover, Albumasar, in his *Great Introduction*,[1] Book 4, Difference 7; then al-Kindî in his *Epistle*,[2] Chapter 1, along with many other old astrologers, will have it that neither the Planets, nor the fixed stars, nor the signs are hot, cold, wet, or dry due to their own nature, nor do they generate [these conditions] per se, nor do they corrupt [the air]; but all these [conditions] are made by a planet's own motion in its own epicycle, and not by its direction, station, and retrograde [state], nor by its closeness to or elongation from the zenith. And therefore, here and there among the astrologers, the greater part of the sublunar effects is referred to the Planets, according as they are ascending to the upper or lower part of their epicycle. And yet this doctrine is plainly and evidently false on many counts!

First. Because the Sun itself is the true and hottest fire, and its

---

[1] Albumasar, *Introductorius maior* 'The Great Introduction' translated by Hermann of Carinthia (Augsburg: Erhard Ratdolt, 1489; often reprinted).

[2] Presumably, al-Kindî, *De pluuiis* 'On Rains' (Venice: Peter Liechtenstein, 1507). The full title of the edition is *Liber Alkindi de nubibus et pluuiis et tonitruis et fulgetris et uentis et accidentium suorum; Epistola Alkindi de aeribus et pluuiis...* 'al-Kindî's Book on Clouds and Rains and Thunder and Lightning and Winds and their Occurences; The Epistle of al-Kindî on Airs and Rains...'

rays are pure flames, as can be seen by means of a concave mirror. **Second.** Because now from a more accurate consideration of the system of the World, there are no epicycles for the motion of Saturn, Jupiter, Mars, Venus, and Mercury, but only eccentric or simple elliptical orbits, in which they move. **Third.** Because motion is not active of itself, but it is only distributive of the active virtue of the Planets, as we have already said elsewhere. And if the effects were not from the virtue of the Planets, but from their motion in epicycles or orbits; and these effects would be at least of the same kind from Saturn, Jupiter, and Mars, then from Venus and Mercury, because they have the same type of motions, even though they are faster than the others.

Therefore, such an absurd opinion ought to be cast out from the science of astrology, [as being] plainly contrary to experiences with the planets and the signs. and then with their own natures as set forth by us; and there should only be retained that which cannot be denied—namely, that the closer the Planets are to the Earth, the more effectively they act upon the Earth, and especially on those places that they are directly above; and the more remote they are, the more ineffectively they act. As was already proved by us elsewhere, namely by their own virtue.

Besides, as for that which pertains to the oriental and occidental state of the planets, it should be seen what we have stated in Book 13, Section I, Chapter 3, and then in Section II, Chapter 1[1]; since it is conformable to the reason and the mode of acting of the Planets, as they act differently when preceding the rising of the Sun from what they do when following it; and as when they are first freed from the solar rays, they operate more evidently, more powerfully and more purely according to their own nature, than they do when they are falling into those rays and being absorbed by them.

And at least, the immense elemental heat of the Sun restrains or moderates the elemental cold of Saturn, Mercury, and the Moon;

---

[1] See my translation in Jean-Baptiste Morin, *Astrologia Gallica, Books Thirteen, Fourteen, Fifteen, and Nineteen* (Tempe, Az.: A.F.A., Inc., 2006).

but it increases the heat of Mars and Jupiter. And the astrologers will have it that if all the ponderous Planets, namely Saturn, Jupiter, and Mars, happen to be oriental, they produce much dryness; but if they all happen to be occidental, they produce much humidity and rains, especially in winter. The Moon acts similarly with Saturn, Jupiter, Mars, Venus, and Mercury, by increasing or decreasing [the intensity] of the effects from their own proper natures. But what has been handed down to us about this state of the Planets by the old [astrologers] and especially by Albumasar in his book on *The Great Conjunctions*,[1] we shall put here.

The Planets in Aries.

Saturn in Aries under the Sun beams[2] makes dark air, and dense clouds, and runny noses.[3] But when oriental, it causes a good constitution of the air; when occidental, cold winds; when static, thunder and lightning.

Jupiter in Aries under the Sun beams generates rains; when oriental, fine weather; when occidental, dews and clouds; when static, an abundance of fruit.

Mars in Aries under the Sun beams makes fine weather; when oriental, it disturbs the air; when occidental, it causes rains; when static, lightning and thunder.

Venus in Aries under the Sun beams produces humidity; when oriental, thunder and rains; when occidental, winds; when static, humidity.

---

[1] *De magnis coniunctionibus,* translated from the Arabic by John of Seville and edited by Johann Engel (Augsburg: Erhard Ratdolt, 1489). An extensive and very detailed work on mundane astrology in eight books, dealing primarily with Jupiter-Saturn conjunctions, but secondarily with other conjunctions and with Aries Ingresses (Revolutions of the Years of the World). Another account of the effects produced by the outer Planets in different phases is given in Albumasar's, *The Book of Flowers*, Chapter 11. See my translation in *Five Medieval Astrologers* (Tempe: A.F.A., Inc., 2008.

[2] The Latin has *sub radiis Solis* 'under the rays of the Sun', which could be translated as *combust*, but I prefer the older expression 'under the Sun beams'.

[3] The Latin has *catarrhos ab humore frigido* 'catarrh from a cold humor'.

Mercury in Aries under the Sun beams is stormy; when oriental, fine weather; when occidental, well tempered weather, and almost always windy. [when static, is not given]

The Planets in Taurus.

Saturn in Taurus under the Sun beams brings about mild air, but it produces illness of the neck; when oriental, it brings healthy conditions; when occidental, dryness; when static, thunder, disturbances in the air, dense clouds.

Jupiter in Taurus under the Sun beams, temperate conditions; when oriental, an abundance of fruits and especially of figs; when occidental, rain showers; when static, it makes fertile and healthy conditions.

Mars in Taurus under the Sun beams makes the air tranquil; when oriental, it sets winds in motion; when occidental, serene conditions; when static, it dries things up.

Venus in Taurus under the Sun beams, lots of thunder; when oriental, healthy and fertile conditions; when occidental, dry and fine conditions; when static, moderate in all things.

Mercury in Taurus under the Sun beams, stormy; when oriental, humid and unsettled; when occidental, temperate. [when static, is not given]

The Planets in Gemini.

Saturn in Gemini under the Sun beams, dry; when oriental, a good period; when occidental, dry; when static, sickly.

Jupiter in Gemini under the Sun beams, then too when oriental, occidental, or static, conditions are temperate, healthy, and fertile.

Mars in Gemini under the Sun beams, illnesses; when oriental, it brings about quarrels and lawsuits; when occidental and static, it multiplies the heat and dryness.

Venus in Gemini under the Sun beams dries things up; when oriental, temperate; when occidental, it blows; when static, it is moderate.

Mercury in Gemini under the Sun beams excites, then also when oriental; when occidental, it presages a good state of things; when static, it is unstable.

The Planets in Cancer.

Saturn in Cancer under the Sun beams makes dark days, strong winds, and storms at sea; when oriental conditions are temperate; when occidental, it renders the seas suitable for voyages; when static, it produces chronic illnesses.

Jupiter in Cancer under the Sun beams makes a tranquil sea; when oriental, occidental, or static, conditions are temperate, healthy, and fertile.

Mars in Cancer under the Sun beams burns things up; when oriental, it stirs up lawsuits; when occidental, illnesses; when static, it heats up and dries out things very much.

Venus in Cancer under the Sun beams makes the air tranquil; when oriental, occidental, or static, it makes temperate and fertile conditions.

Mercury in Cancer under the Sun beams causes winds and storms at sea; when oriental, temperate and healthy conditions; when occidental, tranquil conditions. [when static, is not given]

The Planets in Leo.

Saturn in Leo under the Sun beams causes dry winds and catarrhs; when oriental, temperate conditions; when occidental, it dries things up, and also when static.

Jupiter in Leo under the Sun beams causes healthy winds; when oriental, it elevates people to honors or riches; when occidental, it moderates everything; when static, it reduces illnesses and restores health.

Mars in Leo under the sun beams portends illnesses for Magnates; when oriental, the destruction of things; when occidental, dryness; when static, illnesses

Venus in Leo under the Sun beams causes heat; when oriental, temperate and fertile conditions; when occidental, illnesses among cattle; when static, it harms women.

Mercury in Leo under the Sun beams is windy; when oriental, it brings forward wise men and makes the air temperate; when occidental, it is suffocating; when static, it stirs up illnesses.

The Planets in Virgo.

Saturn in Virgo under the Sun beams is sickly and also when static; when oriental, it dries things up; when occidental, it disturbs the air.

Jupiter in Virgo under the Sun beams and also oriental, occidental, or static, causes temperate conditions, plenty of everything, health, and joy.

Mars in Virgo under the Sun beams is sickly; when oriental, it produces lawsuits and wars; when occidental, it suffocates men; when static, it dries things up.

Venus in Virgo under the Sun beams dries things up; when oriental, it humidifies; when occidental, it makes temperate conditions; when static, it hinders women.

Mercury in Virgo under the Sun beams is stormy; when oriental, it is humid; when occidental, it is dry; when static, it is harmful to men of a mercurial type.

The Planets in Libra.

Saturn in Libra under the Sun beams causes illnesses, especially in the eyes; when oriental it causes cold, dry winds; when occidental, it disturbs the air; when static, it generates quartan fevers.

Jupiter in Libra under the Sun beams, as well as oriental, occidental, or static, is temperate, healthy, and fertile.

Mars in Libra under the Sun beams dries things up; when oriental, it disturbs the air and causes thunder; when occidental, rains; when static, dryness.

Venus in Libra under the Sun beams is humid; when oriental, [conditions are] unstable; when occidental, they are temperate; when static, it is harmful to women.

Mercury in Libra under the Sun beams is windy and stormy; when oriental, humid and fertile; when occidental, temperate; when static, harmful.

The Planets in Scorpio.

Saturn in Scorpio under the Sun beams chills; when oriental, it arouses northern winds; when occidental, it freezes; when static, it makes turbid air.

Jupiter in Scorpio under the Sun beams is rainy; when oriental, it is temperate and increases [the number of] fish; when occidental, the weather is fine; when static, it makes the air tranquil.

Mars in Scorpio under the Sun beams is humid; when oriental, it is windy; when occidental, it is tranquil; when static, much thunder and lightning.

Venus in Scorpio under the Sun beams, as well as when it is oriental, occidental, or static, stirs up rains, but more so when it is oriental. And when it is under the Sun beams or static in whatever sign it must be thought to be mostly rainy.

Mercury in Scorpio under the Sun beams is tempestuous; when oriental it is rainy; when occidental, dry; when static, variable conditions.

The Planets in Sagittarius.

Saturn in Sagittarius under the Sun beams is rainy and cloudy; when oriental, it is cold; when occidental, dry; when static, sickly.

Jupiter in Sagittarius under the Sun beams makes a good state of things; when oriental, the weather is fine; when occidental, it causes many rains; when static, it signifies favorable conditions for men.

Mars in Sagittarius under the Sun beams dries things up; when oriental, it starts wars; when occidental, many illnesses; when static, it is harmful here and there.

Venus in Sagittarius under the Sun beams is rainy; when oriental conditions are temperate; when occidental, windy and cold; when static, moderate conditions.

Mercury in Sagittarius under the Sun beams is very watery; when oriental, temperate; when occidental, dry; when static, harmful to the learned.

The Planets in Capricorn.

Saturn in Capricorn under the Sun beams stirs up southern winds; when oriental, northern winds; when occidental, cold and frost; when static, turbid air.

Jupiter in Capricorn under the Sun beams is humid; when oriental, an agreeable state; when occidental, rains; when static, tranquil conditions.

Mars in Capricorn under the Sun beams generates clouds; when oriental, it dries things up; when occidental, it heats things up; when static, it is temperate.

Venus in Capricorn under the Sun beams, cold spells; when oriental, rainy; when occidental, cold spells; when static, it is temperate.

Mercury in Capricorn under the Sun beams is rainy; when oriental, it darkens the air; when occidental, it bestows rain; when static, variable conditions.

The Planets in Aquarius.

Saturn in Aquarius under the Sun beams is cold; when oriental, rainy; when occidental, dangerous on the sea and in waters; when static, cloudy, snowy, and icy.

Jupiter in Aquarius under the Sun beams, an agreeable state of things; when oriental, healthy conditions; when occidental, much rain; when static, useful rains.

Mars in Aquarius under the Sun beams makes dryness; when oriental or occidental, winds and storms; when static, dangers on the sea.

Venus in Aquarius under the Sun beams is cloudy; when oriental, rainy; when occidental, hot and windy; when static, humid.

Mercury in Aquarius under the Sun beams is snowy; when oriental, rainy; when occidental, frosty and turbulent; when static, it disturbs the air.

The Planets in Pisces.

Saturn in Pisces under the Sun beams is cloudy and snowy; when oriental, a good condition; when occidental, rainy; when static, variable conditions.

Jupiter in Pisces under the Sun beams, as well as oriental, occidental, or static, bestows a good state of things, health, and an abundance of fish.

Mars in Pisces under the Sun beams is harmful to fish; when oriental, it lightens and thunders; when occidental, it dries things up; when static, it makes illnesses.

Venus in Pisces under the Sun beams is cold and frosty; when oriental, agreeably temperate; when occidental, watery, snowy, and windy; when static, variable conditions.

Mercury in Pisces under the Sun beams is stormy and rainy; when oriental or occidental, tranquil and agreeably temperate; when static, it causes variability in the air.

In addition, to the aphorisms above, many will be found, whose logic cannot be recovered, either by way of a mixture of the qualities of the Sun and the Planet, or by way of the Table in Book 13, Section I, Chapter 3. And so, experience should be consulted, with respect to the quarter of the year, and carefully distinguishing the effects of the Planets that are harmonizing with the latter per se, and with the former by accident; for the Sun per se heats and dries up the Earth, but by accident it irrigates by means of rains and it cools, when it cannot dissolve all the vapors that it draws up on account of its short stay above the horizon, or being impeded by other causes. And so with the rest [of the Planets].

Chapter 8. *The Special effects of the Planets that are Rulers of the Year from the Mode of their Motion.*

The individual Planets arranged around the Sun are apprehended to move in different ways—namely, direct and retrograde; between which, they appear to be static in two ways; and in both of these ways they are seen to be moved some times swiftly, sometimes slowly, and at other times moderately. Moreover, by these modes of their own motion, they act influentially and elementally. And indeed they act influentially by analogy, as it was explained by us in Book 13, Section III, Chapter 3. For when they are direct and swift, they signify the progress of the human things to which they were determined; and when they are swift, they signify swift progress; and when they are slow, they signify slow progress; and when they have middling speed, they signify moderate progress. But when they are retrograde, they signify an interruption of the progress of things, or a turning aside from them, or their destruction. And finally, when they are static, especially in fixed signs, they signify firmness, constancy, and the endurance of those things. But they act elementally principally in accordance with their own distance from the Earth and through their own nature.

Moreover, it is certain. **First**, that when a Planet is static, it is very active in accordance with its own nature and the place in the *Caelum* where it stands—that is, the sign in which it is located and the fixed stars among which it stands; for these by their own conjunction particularly determine the virtue of a Planet to an association of action—that is powerfully—on account of the length of time of the static condition. And from that, the true nature of the fixed stars can be discovered if it happens to be unknown; and take note of this!

Second. That when a Planet in its first station[1] begins to retrograde, then it inverts and disturbs its own past actions or effects [arising] from the association of the sign and the fixed stars down to the end of its retrogression; and when it again begins to be direct, it renews and perfects them, always taking into account the quarter of the year and the nearness of the Sun to the conjunction or opposition.

Third. That in the middle of their retrogression, Saturn, Jupiter, and Mars are opposed to the Sun as seen from the Earth, and they approach each other mutually, as if they will be fighting in turn from opposition, but, from the middle of the direct motion, the Sun touches them by conjunction and passes over. However, Venus and Mercury, in the middle of their direct motion and retrograde, are conjoined to the Sun with respect to us, but in direct motion they pass over the Sun, and they are passed over by the Sun when they are retrograde.[2]

Fourth. That the hot Planets, Jupiter, Mars, and Venus, when

---

[1] That is, when it is Static Rx.
[2] That is to say, when Mercury or Venus is conjunct the Sun and direct, it is on the far side of the Sun as seen from the Earth, but when it is conjunct the Sun and retrograde it is on the near side of the Sun and closest to the Earth.

they are retrograde—because then they are closer to the Earth—do therefore indeed raise up vapors by their own elemental heat; but they cannot dissolve them by their own heat alone. Therefore, they are justly said to be rainy, and particularly Venus, the least hot of all and the most humid. Moreover, the cold Planets, Saturn and Mercury, when they are retrograde—because then they are nearer to the Earth—do more powerfully condense the vapors raised up somewhere else, whence there are rains; and therefore they are also deservedly said to be rainy.

But when the Sun is found with the Planets Venus and Mercury retrograde, or when it is opposed to the others, Saturn, Jupiter, and Mars, then they are dry and serene, rather than rainy. For the Sun dissolves by its own heat that which cannot be dissolved by the other [Planets], either during the day by Venus and Mercury, or at night by Saturn, Jupiter, and Mars, unless the Sun's stay above the horizon is shorter than the mean and has blocked it; as occurs in the summer in the torrid zone, and with us in the winter.

Having stated these things in advance, some aphorisms on the Planets' direct and retrograde motion follow:

First. All the Planets are rainy per se when retrograde, especially in feminine signs, and most of all in water signs and in a humid Mansion, or with rainy fixed stars, and most of all with Venus and Mercury. And that squares with what was already said above.

Second. The more Planets that are thus disposed, the more certainly rain can be predicted; and if three are found thus in Cancer, Scorpio, and Pisces, applying to each other, a flood is portended.

Third. Many Planets retrograde in the northern part of the zodiac presage rains and winds in the northern part of the World; and when retrograde in the southern part of the zodiac, rains and winds in the southern part of the World. The reason is because Saturn, Jupiter, and Mars retrograde in the northern part of the zodiac have the Sun in the southern part of the zodiac, which consequently will have a short stay above the horizons of the northern people. And when the Planets are retrograde in the southern part of the zodiac, they have the Sun in the northern part of the zodiac, which makes short days in the south.

Fourth. Planets that are direct make rather dry and serene conditions. Because by nature the hot [Planets] raise up few vapors; but the cold [Planets] are weaker in making vapors more dense on account of their distance from the Earth. Nevertheless, they act as much as they can in accordance with their own nature, the sign, the [fixed] stars, and the quarter of the year.

Fifth. Planets that are retrograde in the southern part of the *Caelum* at the time of summer in the north, make thunder, lightning, and much hail for those [in the north]; but in the time of autumn, they make rains.

Sixth. In all of these [considerations], the position of the Planets themselves with respect to the Sun must be taken into account. For whether they are direct or retrograde, they are allotted some variety in their effects, according as they are oriental or occidental with respect to the Sun, according to the Table in Book 13, Section I, Chapter 3.

There are many other aphorisms in al-Kindî, Chapter 2, but none of which have valid and self-consistent reasons, but indeed they are contrary to astronomy. For those aphorisms must especially be understood of the Planets Saturn, Jupiter, and Mars when they are retrograde. But al-Kindî puts them many times retrograde in the same quadrant of the zodiac with the Sun, such as when he says:

> "When Planets are retrograding from the head of Cancer to Libra, and the Sun is with them in the same quarter." Then also, "when they are retrograde from Libra to Capricorn, and the Sun is with them"

But since Saturn cannot begin to be retrograde until it is distant from the Sun by more than a quadrant of the circle, and it should be between a quadrant and a third; but Jupiter should be distant by a third; and Mars by more than a third. And consequently none of them could be retrograde in the same quadrant of the zodiac with the Sun.

Chapter 9. *The special Effects of the Planets that are Rulers of the Year due to their Terrestrial State, or their position with respect to the Horizon.*

In the case of the Terrestrial State of the Planets that are Rulers of the Year, these things must be taken note of. **First.** In what house of the figure the Ruler of the Year is found, and under what mode it is contained—whether it is in an angle, a succedent, or a cadent house. **Second.** Which houses does it rule. Which houses does it aspect more strongly, certainly by opposition or by square aspect.

Haly, in Book 8, Chapter 7, discusses the *First* item at length, and after him Origanus, in Part 3, Chapter 3, where it is described what the individual Planets do as rulers of the year; but [they do not discuss] the *Second* and *Third* items. But how judgment should be made about the First, Second, and Third items—at least, for their influential effects—has been sufficiently stated by us in Book 21, Section II, then in Chapter 2 of that section; so that consequently it would be altogether superfluous to repeat here again in detail those things that were determined in general there; but it must only be added or rather recalled that the Planets are more effective in angles for [doing] those things that they signify, provided that their celestial state is strong for good or evil, or for whatever quality of the air—that is, other things being equal—but in cadent houses, they are weaker; and in the succedent houses, they are moderate, according to the commonly accepted opinion of astrologers, which is especially perceived to be true for the elemental effects.

For as regards the influential effects, Saturn in no house of the figure signifies a bad, disgraceful, or difficult death more than when it is posited in the 8th house, even though that house is not angular. And Jupiter is more fortunate in the 9th for travels, piety, and ecclesiastical dignities, than in any other house of the figure, other things being equal, even though the 9th is cadent. And in the 2nd it is especially fortunate for riches. And the logic is the same with the rest [of the houses].

Besides, for the elemental effects of a universal constitution, and especially for the temperature that will prevail in the horizon of the figure,[1] during [the effective time] of that constitution, it seems to agree with the reason, so that, just as in nativities judgment about the temperament of the native is made from the 1st house and its celestial state—that is, from the sign occupying it, its ruler, and the planets and fixed stars in it by body or aspecting it; just so in a universal constitution should judgment be made about the temperature of a region by taking note of what sort of sign is ascending; for just as it is an air, water, or earth sign, airy, watery, or earthy qualities will be principally produced, and air, water, or the Earth will be principally affected in themselves, and in their fruits and their inhabitants. And this method must not be rejected, since in particular many of the old astrologers along with Haly would have judged about the temperature of a whole region solely from the ascending sign in the figure of a universal constitution.

Furthermore, here one must beware of the error of Cardan, who, in his *Commentary* on Book 2, in Text 56, will have it indeed rightly with Ptolemy that two figures must be inspected for the Solar Ingress into the 4 individual cardinal points of Aries, Cancer, Libra, and Capricorn; namely, 4 for the Solar Ingresses, and 4 for the new Moon or full Moon immediately preceding them. But by his own opinion and without any authority from Ptolemy, he thinks indeed that figures must be erected for those new Moons and full Moons, since their time can be more accurately known. But for the Solar Ingresses, a figure cannot be erected [accurately],

---

[1] That is, in the location on Earth for which the figure is set.

because their time cannot indeed be accurately known.

However, since the exact knowledge of the time of a lunation principally depends upon an exact knowledge of the Sun's motion at that time, the time of the Solar Ingress ought therefore to be more exactly known than the time of a lunation.[1] As for the figure of the Solar Ingress into Aries, Cancer, Libra, and Capricorn, it should be the principal one for making judgment on the year and its quarters. See the end of Section I, Chapter 4, above.

In addition, in Text 58, Cardan attributes two effects to the conjunction or opposition preceding the Solar Ingress into a cardinal point; namely, a particular one, that only extends down to the [time of] the solar Ingress, and a general one that begins from [the moment of] that Solar Ingress. e.g. into the beginning of Aries, down to the next Ingress into Cancer; and so with the rest [of the Ingresses], but wrongly; for the virtue of a synodic Revolution of the Sun and the Moon lasts down to the similar Revolution next following, as we have taught elsewhere; and it does not cease for the Ingress of the Sun into a cardinal point; otherwise, there would be no reason for the Solar Ingress. For it only has a reason because the Solar Ingress happens with lasting effects and the virtue of that synod, of which the remains of the virtue or the effects pertain to the Ingress itself, in so far as they agree with its virtue; but they leave off with the next following synod; and they are not extended down to the Ingress of the Sun into another cardinal point.

In addition, Cardan is mistaken in his above said Comment on Book 2, in Text 56; when he will have it that if between the Ingress

---

[1] Not so! If there was an error of 7' in the Sun's position at the vernal equinox (which was true of the *Rudolphine Tables*, although unknown to Morin), then the error in determining the *time* of the equinox was nearly 3 hours, while even though the maximum error in the Moon's position at a lunation was about 14' (again from the *Rudolphine Tables*), the calculated time of the lunation would only be in error by 14'12°08' times 24 hours, or 28 minutes, and the average error would be one half of that or 14 minutes, which is a much smaller error than the nearly 3 whole hours error for the time of the Ingress! But since Morin thought that the *RudolphineTables* gave the exact longitude of the Sun, he supposed that the possible error in the time of the lunation was the more uncertain.quantity.

of the Sun into some cardinal point, e.g. the beginning of Aries, and an immediately preceding eclipse there happens to be a conjunction or opposition of the Sun and the Moon, since the figure of the eclipse had also occurred many months earlier, it will have to be looked at first, as being of the principal virtue in the quarter of the year, "because," he says, "if it can be [effective] over the whole year, much more can it be over the quarter of the year, to which it is closer." But the next place in strength, he attributes to the figure of the Solar Ingress, and finally the figure of the new Moon or the full Moon more closely preceding the Solar Ingress. For since an eclipse is only a lunation, its actual effectiveness will not be extended beyond its own period, as was said by us in Section I, Chapter 7.[1] And therefore the figure of the Ingress will have to be the one primarily considered.

Chapter 10. *The Effects of the Quarters of the Mundane Revolution of the Sun.*

Although the Mundane Revolution of the Sun[2] is the general and primary cause of the effects of the whole year; and the celestial charts of the quarters only act as they are transits of the Sun through the squares and opposition of the beginning of Aries, and that is with respect to the chart of that Revolution itself; yet, because the constitution of the *Caelum* and the state of the Sun—both celestial and terrestrial—at that transit more evidently manifests the quality and the force of that transit for the part of the year in which it falls for promoting or hindering the things signified by the Mundane Revolution of the Sun, or for undertaking something new; and besides, the cardinal points of the zodiac are in turn the beginnings of contrary changes or causes with respect to sublunar things. Therefore, having erected the figures necessary for each quarter of the year—namely, for the Ingress of the Sun into the beginning of Cancer, Libra, and Capricorn; then for the

---

[1] This may have seemed logical to Morin, but it contradicts common astrological opinion going all the way back to the Babylonians.
[2] That is, the Aries Ingress.

new Moon or full Moon immediately preceding [each of them] in accordance with Section I, Chapters 4 & 6, their rulers may be found in accordance with Chapter 9.

And if the same Planet should be the ruler of both figures, that one will be the most powerful in the whole quarter. But if different Planets should rule in both figures, their forces resulting from their own natures and their celestial and terrestrial states may be combined; and it should be seen how they are mutually disposed in the figure of the solar Ingress; then, whether by their own natures they are mutual friends or enemies, so that from these [considerations] it may be plain whether they help or hinder each other. And from that, judgment may be made about the figure of the Mundane Revolution of the Sun, while avoiding Cardan's errors that were exposed in Chapter 9, then too in the one following.

For in fact, with Ptolemy he will have it that if an opposition of the Sun and the Moon should have immediately preceded the Ingress of the Sun into a cardinal point, all the months of that quarter should begin from [the time of] the opposition of the Sun and the Moon; but it is clear that this is absurd from this—that since years are [reckoned] by the Sun, so months are [reckoned] from the synodic revolution of the Moon with the Sun; and that *synod* is its primary and independent beginning, not the *opposition* of the Sun and the Moon, which [only] acts with respect to the celestial chart of the preceding synod, and through the mode of a transit; if not through the place of that conjunction of the Lights, at least through the places of the other Planets and angles in that chart.

Add that according to Ptolemy's and Cardan's opinion, the order and time of the months is many times mixed up in the year, and [sometimes] only 15 days could be give to the months, which is another absurdity, and [also] the force of one synod would not last down to the next one following, which has nevertheless already been proven many times.

And so, in every quarter of a Mundane Revolution, first of all the new Moon immediately preceding it should be looked at; and secondly, either the opposition or the square that will occur between the new Moon and the Ingress of the Sun into the cardinal point; and if a square occurs between the opposition and the Solar Ingress, the square must be preferred for the judgment of that quarter of the year. For both the square and the opposition are certainly subordinated per se to the independent conjunction; but the opposition is not subordinated per se to the first square, nor the second square to the opposition; and they therefore act separately according to their own force, since they are dependent on the conjunction. Therefore, the Sun's Ingress into a cardinal point will no less depend upon an immediate square than upon an immediate opposition, in the reckoning of the principal disposers of sublunar things to the effects or changes caused by that Ingress, although the opposition is more powerful.

Besides, although the synod of the Lights may here be said to be independent, this however is only understood to mean that it is independent of any [other] syzygy of the Lights in the synodic month, but not that it is absolutely independent, since it primarily depends upon the preceding Ingress of the Sun into the beginning of Aries; for any synod of the Lights is a part of the whole year, dispensing and accomplishing its own effects according to its mode.

And therefore it will not follow that there is a progress into infinity, because the Solar Ingress would also depend upon [still] another previous synod. For the synod immediately preceding the Ingress of the Sun into Aries, since it is the final synod of the preceding year, is of very little virtue for that year, which it terminates and whose effects leave off, so that it should rather be thought to pertain to the following year, which begins with its own effects; and consequently, the progress into infinity would cease. Just as if the Ingress of the Sun into Aries should happen on the last day of the immediately preceding synodic Revolution of the Sun and the Moon; since then the force of that Revolution is exhausted and would cease, rather there will have to be taken into account the one that begins with the Ingress of the Sun into Aries, or the one that follows it by one or two days, especially since [both] Ptolemy and experience testify that the effects of a new Moon begin around three days before it; and the force of each house of the celestial figure is greatest at the cusp and continually decreases down to the cusp of the following house, where it leaves off altogether.

Furthermore, it seems that the Rule of Eudoxus[1] should not be omitted here, which Pliny mentions at the end of Book 2, Chapter 48,[2] of his *Natural History*, and which Origanus seems to approve in Part 3, Chapter 4; namely, that every four years the same conditions return, not only of the winds, but also of the storms for the most part; namely because every four years the figures of the Solar Ingresses into the cardinal points are very similar to each other for each cardinal point; and consequently, with the Sun and the fixed stars similarly posited with respect to the Earth the same effects ought to recur from them.

But besides the fact that the celestial and terrestrial state of the rest of the Planets is very varied, there also occurs a difference of 0:48 hours between two adjacent four-year periods,[3] which amounts to 12 equatorial degrees for the difference in right ascension of the two MC's or the oblique ascensions of the ASC's; from which, the position of the *Caelum* is also sufficiently markedly varied, and perhaps the rulership of the Planets over the angles of the figure; whence, it is no wonder if in the next four-year period there is perceived to be little likeness in the storms and the other effects in the individual quarters of the year.[4] But it can be perceived

---

[1] Eudoxus of Cnidus, a Greek mathematician and astronomer who lived in the 4th century B.C.

[2] Morin says "Chapter 47," but in the Loeb Classical Library edition it is Chapter 48 and Section 130. "Eudoxus however thinks that (if we choose to study the minimal circuits) there is a regular reoccurrence of all phenomena – not only of winds but largely of other sorts of bad weather as well – in four-yearly periods, and that the period always begins in a leap-year at the rising of Sirius." (H. Rackham's translation).

[3] Actually, it is a little less than that, or about 0:45.

[4] In his translation of this long sentence, Hieroz misses the point altogether.

more in 120-year periods,[1] because then at least the same MC returns, and consequently the same state of the fixed stars and the Sun, which have the greatest power over these inferior things; but the state of the rest of the planets will [still] differ greatly from that of the first year, as is evident in the ephemerides.

Chapter 11. *The Effects of the Synodic Revolution of the Moon with the Sun and its Quarters.*

If the true place of the Moon that it occupied at its own creation could be known to us, its Revolution to that same place would be the periodic and true lunar month for us; and the celestial chart of the Revolution would be the principal and genuine cause of monthly effects in general, as was similarly evident in the periodical Revolutions of the Moon for nativities. But about that place we are not certain, even though we have supposed by a most probable reason in Book 2, Chapter 10, that the Sun and the Moon by true motion were centrally conjoined at the beginning of Aries on the very day of their creation—having rejected the opinion of Kepler, who in his *Rudolphine Tables* thinks that they were conjoined in the 28th degree of Gemini.

And consequently, it is right for me to recommend that the periodical Mundane Revolutions of the Moon to the beginning of Aries should be looked at attentively, so that it might be observed whether they have any general effects, even greater ones than those of its synodic Revolution; however, because we are left with those synodic Revolutions of the Moon with the Sun that are very well known to all astrologers—indeed, even to rustics—from which true predictions about the general effects of the month are commonly made; therefore, we shall discuss only those in this chapter, beginning the individual months from the new Moon, or the conjunction of the Sun and the Moon, as from a primary and

---

[1] If we accept Morin's figure of 0:48 for the difference in 4 years, then in 120 years the difference would be 30 X 0:48 = 24:00 = 0:00; but since the true difference for 4 years is about 0:45, it would require 128 years to return to nearly the same time for the Ingress.

independent syzygy, just as was explained above.

And so, according to Section I, Chapter 6, let the figure of the conjunction of the Sun and the Moon be erected, whose rulers may be found from [the rules in] Chapter 9. And then let the judgment of that figure be made in accordance with the proper nature of the rulers and their celestial and terrestrial states, as is done in the Annual Revolution and its quarters. Since there is one and the same method for all those, the subordination must be taken into account, and consequently there is often no need to repeat the same things.

And similarly, it will be necessary to proceed to the judgment of the quarters, in which the angles and the Planets; especially the rulers, will not have to be looked at by themselves, but with respect to the figure of the new Moon on which each of those quarters depends, and because per se it is the beginning of the lunar month. For the quarter that will have a greater agreement with the new Moon by reason of its angles, rulers, and transits will produce greater effects and will more strongly advance the things signified by the new Moon during that same quarter. But we shall now explain here the place in Ptolemy's *Quadripartite* about the lunations and their quarters that Cardan calls the most difficult in the whole volume.

Therefore, in Ptolemy's Book 2, [Chapter 12], Text 63 in Cardan's *Commentary*,[1] since he explained his own opinion about the quadrants of the Annual Revolution of the Sun, or the four quarters of the year, and he added his doctrine of the monthly new Moons and full Moons, and then, asserting that there is a third cause of the particular storms in the air, he says,

> "in this there fall the particular configurations of the Sun and the Moon, not only of the new Moon and the full Moon, but also of the intermediate times, that is the squares; where it must be noticed that about three days before [them] the

---
[1] Textus 63 begins on p. 231, col. 1.

significations of almost all the storms commonly exist, or even after three days of the equated path of the Moon with respect to the Sun."

Which words have been explained in various ways by Lucio Bellantio and Junctinus, who want these words to be understood by a figure of 16 sides[1] for a consideration of the aspects, then by Cardan, Naibod,[2] and Magini, who think that they can be understood from a figure of 8 sides.[3] Cardan himself wants there to be observed not only the conjunction, opposition, and squares of the Moon with the Sun, but also their intermediate positions, because when the Moon will be placed in those intermediate positions, it may be customary to judge which changes it is going to make when it will have come to the next following conjunction, opposition, or square, or which changes should be expected from the next preceding conjunction, opposition, or square.

But how much this deviates from Ptolemy's opinion and the truth of the matter will be easily proved by [the words] of Ptolemy himself, who, for the third day before or after the equated path of the Moon to the Sun, does not understand it to mean anything other than the place in which the Moon last appears before the conjunction, or is first seen after the conjunction—that is, when it sets or rises heliacally—which day is more frequently the third day before or after the conjunction,[4] rather than the fourth, second, or first day; and among the ancients and also the rustics, it was always the most principal consideration for judging the particular state of the whole month.

---

[1] By which he means a consideration of aspects of multiples of 22.5 degrees.

[2] Valentine Naibod (1527-1593), *Enarratio elementorum astrologiae* 'A Description of the Elements of Astrology' (Cologne: Arnold Birckman's Heirs, 1560. 4to.)

[3] This would mean aspects of multiples of 45 degrees.

[4] This should probably be understood to mean the *second* day before or after the conjunction, because the elongation of the Moon from the Sun is a little more than 12 per day; and twice this would be about 24°, when the slim crescent of the Moon would be visible just before sunrise or just after sunset. (The ancients usually counted both ends of an interval, so what we would call the *second* day, they would call the *third* day.)

And that this is Ptolemy's opinion is established by this—because the lunar path is only equated to that of the Sun at [the time of] the new Moon, namely when the Moon arrives at the [the place of] the Sun. Besides, although in this place he also wants the triangular and sexangular figures[1] of the Moon with the Sun to be noted, but he doesn't mention the octangular or sextodecangular figures.[2] For in fact because in Book 1, Chapter 13, having counted up all the figures or aspects that ought to be considered in astrology—the opposition, trine, square, and sextile—he says then, "many aspects or intervals or differences of figures are not received among astrologers"[3] on account of the reasons that he enumerates there. Therefore, Cardan along with the others deviated from Ptolemy's opinion; and those things that he tried to prove by an 8-sided figure in the case of the decline of illnesses can be better proved without such a figure, as we shall say in [our book] The *Practice of Astrology*,[4] God willing.

But, from a genuine explication of the things mentioned above, it follows that in the heliacal setting and rising of the Moon with respect to us, diligent notice must be paid to the celestial and terrestrial state of the Moon, and especially with what fixed stars and constellations it appears, and which Mansion it occupies, and what constitution of the air is then evident.[5] For it is commonly thought that

---

[1] The trines and sextile aspects.

[2] The aspects that are multiples of 22.5 degrees and 45 degrees.

[3] This statement does not occur in the Greek text of the *Tetrabiblos*, nor in the Latin translation printed in Cardan's *Commentary*. But Cardan adds this statement at the end of Textus 45 (p. 144, col. 1), "Why did Ptolemy not consider the sides of an octagon, which consist of 45 degrees, and those of the duodecagon, which consist of 30 degrees? I reply that it was because the sides of the octagon do not include whole signs, but the [sides of] the duodecagon because they are too weak. Therefore the [previously mentioned] aspects are sufficient by themselves." Morin agreed with the first part of this statement, but he disagreed with the latter part, because he accepted the semi-sextile and the quincunx aspects that correspond to the sides of the duodecagon.

[4] A book that Morin intended to write, but which he did not live long enough to complete.

[5] Here Morin says that the existing condition of the air must also be taken into account, rather than relying solely on the astrological indications.

whatever is [the condition of] the Moon on the third day before and after the new Moon, that is all; that is, as far as the disposition of the air during the whole month. And that is not said without cause, both because then the Moon is approximately in semi-sextile to the Sun, which aspect is effective and the first one that it makes after its conjunction with the Sun; and also because if the heliacal risings and settings of the other Planets and also the fixed stars are of notable virtue on account of the same reason, [then] how much more should the heliacal rising and settings of the Moon be important, [since it is] a primary Planet and the one closest to us?

In addition, the following aphorisms about the lunations and their quarters may be noted.

1. If the Planets that are rulers of the conjunction or the opposition preceding the Ingress of the Sun into a cardinal point are hot by nature and in hot signs, and connected by body or by aspect with Planets or fixed stars of a hot nature, either partilely or by application; and if they are also in a hot quarter of the figure, and if the quarter of the year is of a hot nature, a tremendous heat will be produced in that quarter of the year, and especially at its beginning. And the reasoning is the same about the others.

2. The monthly lunations and their quarters increase or decrease the temperature of the quarter of the year in which they occur, with their own nature and quality. And therefore judgment about the whole quarter must not be made solely from the [chart for the] quarter of the year, unless the monthly lunations have been inspected; and also not even from a lunation can an exact judgment be made, unless the general nature of the quarter of the year has been looked at from its figure, and from the preceding new Moon.

3. Great changes are not made without the concourse of Saturn, Jupiter, or Mars with the rulership of the figure, with either a connection by body or by aspect with the Sun or the Moon. And calamities are not accustomed to happen unless the malefics are predominant.

4. A lunation occurring in the 1st or the 10th house, and especially in a mobile sign, will have sudden and swift effects; and these will be great if Saturn, Jupiter, or Mars rules the angle of the lunation; but greater still, if the lunation is with an eclipse; and the effects will begin to appear on the very day of the lunation.

5. Planets that are direct and swift cause fine weather; when stationary, they cause winds; when retrograde, waters.

6. Fine weather is caused especially by the Sun, Saturn, Jupiter, and Mars. But storms are caused by the Moon, Venus, and Mercury. And therefore, fine weather is compatible with great heat and cold; but rain showers are never compatible with great cold.

7. In the summer, the causes of cold must be many or strong; then in the winter, those of heat must also be many and strong; in order that that [such] notable effects could be allotted against the nature of the quarter of the year.

8. The Planet to which the Moon or the ruler of the lunation first applies must be carefully observed. For the air is very often changed by [that body's] nature and both its celestial and terrestrial state, having taken into account the quarter of the year; and if it applies to Mars, hail and thunder will have to be expected, unless the nature of the quarter of the year prevents it; if it applies to Saturn, rains and cold spells; if to Jupiter, fine weather, etc. But very often a change happens [at the time of] a separation rather than [at the time of] an application; and the reason is because a change or an effect is conceived or generated by an application, but it is born by a separation, or it is produced aside from its own causes; however, if the strong causes were from its celestial state, and they were angular, an application will produce an effect that a partile syzygy will reinforce.

9. Great attention must be paid to the eastern angle and its rulers. For a Planet in the place of the conjunction, opposition, or square, and in the ASC, will have many dignities in the figure; it will then have to be preferred to any others. But in these same places, the nature of the sign and the Mansion must be looked at, and in the case of their ruler, its nature, sign, Mansion, and house in the figure; and judgment must be made from these.

10. If the ruler of the lunation is of a humid nature, in a humid sign, applying to a humid Planet, also in a humid sign, and if the Moon first applies to a humid planet, etc., great humidities and rains will have to be expected in [that] quarter of the year, especially in a humid one such as winter. And the reasoning is the same with hot, cold, and dry. But if there should happen to be a contrariety of qualities—as that the ruler is hot by nature, but in a cold sign—and the votes of both are equal, moderation in heat and cold will have to be predicted; but if they are unequal, the stronger part will win out; but it will [also] have to be seen in which quarter of the year, the nature favors.

11. Causes of heat in the summer increase the heat in accordance with their strength; [but] in the winter, they diminish the cold. Causes of cold act against the heat in the summer; and they increase the cold in the winter. And similarly, the causes of humidity moderate the dryness of summer; and they increase the humidity of winter; from which it is evident what in general the causes of dryness would do.

12. The fixed stars that are conjoined to the Lights or to the rulers of the lunations must be diligently noted; for they are very powerful for changes in the air; then, those that rise, culminate, and set with them. See also the fixed stars that are rising and setting at the moment of the figure.

13. If in any figure of a lunation there happens to be a conjunction or opposition of the other Planets, and especially one of the superior Planets [either] among themselves or with the inferior Planets, that [aspect] will be of greater virtue than one [happening] at another time, and especially if it is partile. But they will be of the greatest virtue if they also aspect the Sun and the Moon.

14. The change signified in a lunation will happen when the

Moon, after its conjunction or opposition with the Sun, is connected by a strong ray with the ruler of the constitution; or when it will come by its own motion to the sign or the degree of the ASC, especially if that sign is angular in [the figure of] the Revolution of the Sun, or its quarter. But the syzygies of the Moon with the Sun will not cause those changes by themselves.

15. If Saturn, Jupiter, and Mars are conjoined among themselves, or with Venus and Mercury, or if they are opposed in the lunation; and at the same time the Moon applies to them, the air will certainly be changed in accordance with the nature of the strongest planet.

16. When the Planets that are rulers of the constitution are subordinated or inferior, and by their own motion they come to the signs of the angles, or to those angles of the figure of the superior Planets, they act according to their own nature and that of the sign.

17. Some astrologers, according to Mizaldus's *Book on the Judgments of the Air,* Chapter 2, direct the ASC of the Lunation to the ruling Planet or its square or opposition, giving 13°11' to each day. And then they want the change to be [one that is] made according to the nature of the Planet, the nature of the sign that it is in, and the Mansion, unless that Planet is weak. However, this aphorism must only be understood to refer to a new Moon and the places determined in it, as we have said elsewhere for the periodical Revolutions of the Moon in nativities.

18. Planets that are conjoined are more disposed to fine weather, but those opposed are more disposed to rains. And when many Planets, such as 4 or 5, come together in any sign, the judgment about the air must be made rather from the nature of the planets and the ruler of the sign, than from the nature of the sign; [but] with this [nature] not neglected, nor [that of] the ruler of the sign.

19. In the case of a new Moon, a full Moon, or a square [of the Sun and the Moon], the Moon's latitude must not be omitted, nor that of the planet that rules the chart, nor the triplicity in which they are placed, since from that a conjecture may be made about the part of the World in which the change in the air may be expected.

20. Great changes in the air are called the *Opening of the Gates* or *Cataracts of the Sky*.[1] For there is a double opening—that is, a minor one *Of the Gates*, and a major one the *Cataracts* or the *Double Doors*. The minor one is when the Planets that have opposite domiciles, such as Saturn & the Sun, Saturn & the Moon, Jupiter & Mercury, and then Mars & Venus, are mutually conjoined, in square, or opposition to each other.

But the major one is when the Moon, [separating] from a conjunction, square, or opposition of one of those, immediately moves to an aspect of the other; that is, from Saturn to the Sun, from Jupiter to Mercury, and from Mars to Venus; or the reverse; for then [there will be] furious winds, storms, heavy rains, plentiful rains, hail, thunder and lightning, according to the quarter of the year; and the *Opening of the Gates* of the planets must be expected; especially if the Planets from which the Moon has separated, or to which she applies in a universal constitution are fortified, and they are with tempestuous fixed stars, and they are aspecting themselves.

Moreover, a change in the air is sometimes made with the nature of a superior Planet, sometimes with the nature of the stronger one, but more often with the nature of the one to which the Moon applies. As, if when departing from the Sun it will apply to Saturn, there will be a saturnine change in the air, taking into account the sign that Saturn occupies, the fixed stars to which it is joined, and the quarter of the year. And if Mercury by body or by aspect should be joined to a Planet that is *Opening the Doors*, it will excite winds and noisy tempests. Moreover, a retrograde Planet [excites] abundant rain; two retrograde planets excite even more abundant rain.

---

[1]These expressions for heavy downpours of rain correspond to the popular English expressions, *pouring down rain*, *raining cats and dogs*, and *A Noah's Flood*.

And it must be noted that if the Sun is around its own perigee, along with the inferior Planets, they will be inclined to the rains of the *Opening of the Doors*, especially in a water sign. But if the Sun was around its own apogee along with superior Planets, they will be inclined to fine weather and dry spells, unless the nature of the sign and its ruler prevents it.

And besides, it must be noted that the *Opening of the Gates* is stronger, when the Moon has separated from an inferior planet and is applying to a superior one, than if it should be separating from a superior planet and applying to an inferior one. Finally, it must not be omitted here that both a minor and a major *Opening of the Gates* singularly confirm the bond of sympathy, by which the planets are connected with their own celestial domiciles, and that they act not only by reason of their proper nature, but also by reason of their rulership.

Chapter 12. *The Synodic Revolutions of Saturn, Jupiter, Mars, Venus, and Mercury, both among themselves, and with the Lights, and their Quarters; and then about their Effects.*

Now that the Revolutions of the Sun and the Moon, the primary Planets in the World, have been sufficiently discussed, the order of the doctrine demands that we should at least speak of those things about the Revolutions of Saturn, Jupiter, Mars, Venus, and Mercury, that do not exceed the strength and capacity of human intelligence.

First, therefore, their periodic Revolutions to their own radical places at the beginning of their own creation are even much less known to us than the periodic Revolutions of the Sun and the Moon. And that which pertains to their synodic Revolutions, both with the Lights and among themselves, although it can be known in what sign and degree of the zodiac they occur, yet at what hour they may exactly be made is still unknown on account of the deficiency of the astronomical tables; and the hour can scarcely ever be known about the revolutions of Saturn, Jupiter, and Mars among themselves, on account of the slowness of their motion, especially when they are located near their stations.

Therefore, on account of these reasons, a celestial figure of those revolutions cannot be erected from the tables[1]; whence, it is not known which one of them is the ruler of a particular house, [as judged from] the angles, and [consequently] what special effects they may be going to produce because of the house [positions] at individual places on Earth; but it can only be known what they would signify for the whole Earth by reason of their celestial state, when they are at least considered separately. And that was perhaps done by Divine Providence, so that at the time of great, threatening, unfortunate conjunctions, the individual nations might have to be fearing God and assigning the cause to Him.

Moreover, having supposed that the tables of the motions of the Sun, the fixed stars, Saturn, Jupiter, Mars, Venus, and Mercury were accurately restored, and also that figures of the synodic Revolutions of the Moon with all the Planets might be accurately erected, and especially those with Saturn, Jupiter, and Mars; and that there will be possible figures of the Revolutions for the Sun, Venus, and Mercury among themselves, and more so with Saturn, Jupiter, and Mars; and consequently only the figures of the revolutions of Saturn, Jupiter, and Mars among themselves will remain, which, if anyone tries to erect them, he will have to attempt that by observations and not by tables, because the tables cannot be brought to such precision and that for every day.

But [instead] it will be necessary to proceed thus. Let the diurnal motion of both Planets be observed in some circle, especially in the meridian circle, on the day before their conjunction [as shown in] Problems 2 and 4 of Part III of our *Astronomy Restored*,[2]

---

[1]This was true in Morin's time, but it is no longer true in our days, since astronomers are now able to calculate the planets' positions with great accuracy.

[2]Morin's book, *Astronomia jam a fundamentis integre et exacte restituta...* 'Astronomy now from its Fundamentals completely and exactly restored...' (Paris: the Author, 1640. 4to 361 pp.).

but having avoided a time in which they are moving more slowly. And when the difference of longitude of the Planets will be established by observation and the diurnal [motion] of the slower Planet at the same time added to make the sum, which does not exceed the diurnal [motion] in longitude of the swifter Planet; then by the golden rule, the difference of both the diurnal [motions] may be put for the first number, 24 hours for the second number, and the above said difference in longitude for the third number; for the fourth will be the proportional hour and minute[1]; at which time after the observation the conjunction of those Planets will be made. And since this observation does not seem to be impossible, especially when the conjunction will be one of Planets, it is certain that if it rightly succeeds, it will sometimes be of the greatest utility on account of the noteworthy force of those conjunctions.

But now, whether the figure of the conjunction was erected or not erected, the following things should be noted about its celestial state.

1. What are the natures of both of the conjoined Planets.

2. In what trigon is it made, and into which one will it next proceed.

3. In what sign is it made, and who is its ruler; then, what is its celestial state; then, whether and to what extent does it aspect the place of the conjunction.

4. Whether the conjoined Planets and their ruler are oriental or occidental to the Sun or the Moon.

5. Whether they are well or badly disposed in the sign, and which one of them is stronger, and also which one of them is more familiar to the ruler of the place of the conjunction.

6. What is their latitude and declination.

---

[1] That is, find the time to conjunction from the equation, (Difference in longitude / Difference in motions) X 24 hours = time to conjunction.

7. Which Planets are aspecting the place of the conjunction and its ruler; and to which Planet do both of the conjoined Planets first apply and also the ruler of the conjunction.

8. To which fixed stars are they also conjoined, and in which Mansion.

Moreover, by having combined all of these, the universal virtue may be elicited, by which that sort of conjunction will act upon the whole Earth.

But if the figure of the synodic Revolution can be erected, from that can also be known its terrestrial state and what kind of effects it may be going to produce according to the things signified by the houses for any horizon.[1] For since it is certain that those things will be made in any house of the figure that is made with respect to any horizon, it is also certain that it will do those things that are signified by that house and by those [Planets] that are in it, or which the rulers of that conjunction rule on account of their determination.

And so, if the conjunction is made in the 1st house, it will act upon the beginnings and arising of things, and the nativities of men; and it will perhaps cause the birth of some notable man of the nature of the Planets that are conjoined. If it is made in the 10th, it will act upon kingdoms, republics, dignities, and undertakings. If it is in the 9th, it will act upon religions and sects; if in the 7th, upon marriages, lawsuits, and wars; if in the 8th, upon deaths, natural disasters, and violent [occurrences], according to the force of the conjunction.

But the conjunctions of Saturn, Jupiter, and Mars produce greater effects than the others; and they are commonly believed to excite the overthrow or change of kingdoms, new religions, sects, wars, savage plagues, floods, and other stupendous effects—namely, in regions where they are in houses conformable to such things, or in regions where they are overhead, and there is a

---
[1] That is, for any particular location on Earth.

disposition of the lower things conformable to the notable strength of that conjunction. And therefore, astrologers are accustomed to pay close attention to these conjunctions, having scorned the rest of the conjunctions. And Albumasar in his book on the *Great Conjunctions* states why they should be more effective in certain signs; and in this matter he follows the principles of Hermes [as reported] in Haly,[1] *Judgments of the Stars*, Part 8; but their doctrine is confused, so we think that it ought to be omitted here; and we have only added some aphorisms below that are common to all synodic Revolutions and in keeping with the tables included in Chapters 6 & 7 above, that will provide more light and certainty for making predictions.

1. The synodic Revolution of any two Planets in the same triplicity in which there was an immediately preceding conjunction of those same Planets, continues its effects, or produces similar ones again; in a complementary triplicity, it produces effects partly of the same kinds, and partly different; but in a triplicity of a contrary type, it produces contrary and extraordinary effects—not however always the greatest effects—for the magnitude of the effects will correspond in all synods to the strength of the Planets ruling the conjunction.

2. If a conjunction and its ruler are in the same triplicity, the effects of that conjunction will be greater by reason of the triplicity, both in the air and on the regions of the Earth ruled by that triplicity.

3. Great conjunctions in cardinal signs always produce great effects; and they will be greater the closer they are to the beginnings of those signs; both on account of the maximum strength of the cardinal points, and because those signs are the exaltations of the principal Planets.

---

[1] Haly Abenragel, *Praeclarissimus Liber completus de iudiciis astrorum* 'The Very Famous Complete Book on the Judgments of the Stars' (Venice: Erhard Ratdolt, 1485. often reprinted elsewhere). Book 8 discusses the Revolutions of the Years of the World (Aries Ingresses). Morin probably used one of the later editions.

4. The conjunction of Saturn and Jupiter presages great things more than the others, because both Planets are of the greatest virtue and authority in the Caelum, as has hitherto been observed by astrologers. No wonder! Since both of them are accompanied by their own satellites like the Sun, which was [a thing] unknown to the old [astrologers]. But their conjunctions in the cardinal signs are more effective than in the rest of the signs.

5. Many Planets in cardinal signs always signify something great, both in universal constitutions and in particular ones; for either they are conjoined or square or opposed, which in those signs very often causes some huge evils.

6. The conjunction of Saturn and Jupiter is always very evil, unless the benefic Planets powerfully rule that conjunction. Moreover, it is worse in cardinal signs, and worst of all in Cancer, which is the exile of Saturn and the fall of Mars. And this conjunction is always followed by corruption of the air, plagues, floods, the destruction of fish, wars, and the death of Princes.

7. All the conjunctions of Planets in malefic signs are ruinous; but they are even worse if the malefic [Planets] badly afflict them, or if they are badly configured with the place of the conjunction.[1]

8. In all conjunctions of the Planets, great notice must be taken of the Sun and the Moon, whether they are conjoined with or configured with the conjoined [Planets]. For the resulting effects are more universal, more conspicuous, and they pertain to Kings and Princes.

9. A conjunction in fire signs excites heat and dryness; in air signs, winds and storms; in earth signs, icy cold and snows; in water signs, rains. However, note must be taken of the quarter of the year and the nature of the Planets that are conjoined; which, if they agree with the [nature of] the signs, there will be a harmful excess;

---

[1]This entire paragraph is omitted by Hieroz, and the following paragraphs are misnumbered – Par. 8 being numbered Par. 7, etc.

if they disagree, there will be a moderation of the natures.

10. The stronger one of the conjoined Planets in the place of the conjunction, and the one that is higher in its eccentric path, and the one that is raised up higher above the horizon, will be superior in the effects; and if it is benefic by nature, it will do something beneficent; but if it is a malefic, it will do something harmful.

11. If the ruler of the conjunction is benefic by nature and is well disposed, it will do something beneficent; if it is a malefic and badly disposed, it will cause evils.

12. If the conjunction is in a fixed sign, its effects will be slow and long-lasting, especially if Saturn is one of the conjoined Planets, and if in addition it is stationary or slow in its motion. If the conjunction is made in a mobile sign, the effects will be swift and of a brief duration, especially if Mars or Mercury is one of the conjoined Planets and swift in its motion. If the conjunction is made in common signs, the effects will be middling.

But that which pertains to the squares and opposition of these conjunctions is two-fold—namely, by determination and by syzygy; which, since they deploy the effects of the conjunction by advancing, increasing, diminishing, suppressing, or doing something new, as was stated in connection with the synodic revolutions of the Sun and the Moon; also, the judgment of these comes about similarly—namely, account being taken of the virtue and determination of the conjunction, and of the celestial constitution that is in effect.

Finally, the times of the effects of each synodic Revolution are detected by bringing the conjoined Planets to the angles of the figure or to the places of the rulers, or by bringing the rulers to the angles and place of the conjunction, or by directions defined by the diurnal mean [motion] of the swifter one of the conjoined Planets of the periodic or synodic revolution, as was done for the Moon in Section I, Chapter 12; but it must be noted that both here and for the Moon, the directions must not be started from the figures of the quarters or the opposition, but only from the figure of the conjunction, down to the next following conjunction, taking note of how the celestial charts of the quadratures and the opposition agree with the determination, or disagree with the directions to those times.

Chapter 13. *The Composition of the Subordinates of the Universal Constitutions of the* Caelum, *and their mixed Effects.*

In Section I, Chapter 3, the subordination of the Universal constitutions of the *Caelum* was fully discussed; and it was shown that the synodic Revolutions of Saturn, Jupiter, Mars, Venus, Mercury, and the Moon, both with the Sun and among themselves, are subordinated to the Mundane Revolution of the Sun. But then we have hitherto only discussed simple constitutions—that is, the Mundane Revolution of the Sun, and the synodic Revolutions of the Moon, Saturn, Jupiter, Mars, Venus, and Mercury, both among themselves, and seen separately with the Sun, and their effects. Now, therefore, it remains that we should talk about their mixtures and say a few things, but particularly necessary ones, about their mixed effects.

And so, for judging the effects of the Mundane Revolution of the Sun, the proper significations of the celestial charts must be combined—both that of the Revolution itself, and those of the new Moon, the full Moon, and the squares of the Sun and the Moon immediately preceding that revolution. Taking note that the signification of the squares and the full Moon depend upon the signification of the new Moon, as was already said previously; and consequently, particular notice must be paid to the new Moon itself, even though between it and the Sun's Ingress into the beginning of Aries, the full Moon or a quarter comes in between; so nevertheless that that new Moon should only be viewed as the cause that is disposing or preparing the sublunar Nature for the proper effects of the Solar Ingress into Aries, but not as the efficient cause [of those effects]. And the celestial charts of the squares and the opposition of the Moon to the places determined at the time of the new

Moon, for which there is no small force, should not be spurned.

Moreover, in the case of the lunations in the first quarter of the year—that is, those occurring between the Sun's Ingresses into Aries and Cancer—the proper significations of the quarters and the full Moon will have to be combined—first, indeed, if they are close to the signification of their own new Moon itself—but then all of the significations or what results from them, will have to be combined with the signification of the chart of the solar Ingress into the beginning of Aries; and no more should note be taken of the chart of the new Moon preceding that Ingress, whose efficacy has passed and lapsed.[1] And it will have to be done similarly for the individual quarters of the year.

But for that which concerns the other synodic Revolutions of Saturn, Jupiter, Mars, Venus, and Mercury, with the Lights, and among themselves, it must first be seen which [Planet] the Sun last encountered before its Aries Ingress, and the Moon before the new Moon preceding that Ingress. And note will have to be taken of that sort of synods as the causes disposing sublunar Nature to the effects of the Sun for that year, and the effects of the Moon for that month; and the transits of the Sun and the Moon through the squares and opposition to the places of those synods will [also] have to be looked at until the time when the Sun and the Moon come together with them again—also not having omitted the squares and opposition through the syzygies.

But as for the other synods of Saturn, Jupiter, Mars, Venus, and Mercury among themselves, there are noted in the charts of the Sun and the Moon, their current synodic Revolutions, but especially those of Saturn, Jupiter, and Mars, and the transits of both the Lights and Saturn, Jupiter, Mars, Venus, and Mercury through the places in which they last came together; since none of the above said things are superfluous in Nature or can be indifferent,

---

[1] He means that the lunations and their quarters occurring *after* the Solar Ingress need no longer be compared to the lunation *preceding* the Solar Ingress, because its signification has lapsed.

but the individual things come together with their own force to alter and change these sublunar things. Whence the breadth of this marvelous science and the difficulty thrown to human intelligence can easily be inferred. But so that this may be at least in part removed, the following rules may be noted.

First. If the same [Planet] is the ruler of two subordinated figures, and is in the same sign in both cases, that one will be very effective in the latter figure for the common signification of both figures, also with the ruler of that sign strongly concurring. If the rulers are different but in the same sign, see in the latter figure whether the ruler of the sign is connected by a strong ray with the rulers of the figures or with one of them, or whether it is in the principal angles of a figure; for then, the latter figure will also be very effective with regard to the common significations of both figures. Finally, if there are different rulers of the figures, and they are in different signs that are not in the same triplicity, nor do they receive themselves in the latter figure, nor are they connected by a strong ray, the latter figure will be of small virtue or of none at all with regard to the signification of the former figure, at least to move it forward.

Second. If two subordinated figures have the same ASC sign, and its ruler is also the ruler of the primary points in the constitutions, or in at least one of them, and especially if it is the first one, or if it aspects those points by a strong ray, and if that one is strong in its celestial state and is angular, the latter figure will strongly move forward the things signified by the previous figure.

Third. A universal constitution that is prior in order and superior will burst forth into its own significations through later and subordinated constitutions that occur during its own period [of effectiveness] if those constitutions signify things similar to the prior constitution; but they are retarded or impeded if they signify the contrary; for the prior and superior constitutions always retain their own future effects in potential, which are reduced to actuality by later or inferior constitutions, not indeed by all of them; but only by the proper virtue of those that are similar and concordant., as is similarly plain from the genethliacal figure of a native and its Revolutions.

Fourth. Many constitutions occurring at the same time, such as a new Moon along with a synod of Saturn & Jupiter, or a similar synod, or a new Moon along with a Mundane Revolution of the Sun, produce the greatest effects, especially if the ASC of the constitutions that occur at the same time is the same, or the ruler of their primary point is the same.

Chapter 14. *The Dependence of the particular Constitutions of Nativities on the Universal Constitutions already discussed; and how they act upon individual Natives during their Lifetime.*

The doctrine contained in this chapter is of great moment in astrology—that is, because *particulars* are subject to *universals*, as Ptolemy rightly instructs in the Preface to [*Tetrabiblos*] Book 2.[1] And this is plain in the case of any native who depends upon his own genethliacal constitution for his temperament, habits, intelligence, and the future accidents of his life, that universal astrology gives evidence to that experience; in fact that his particular constitution of the *Caelum* will depend upon the preceding universal constitutions—namely upon the Solar Ingresses into Aries, Cancer, Libra, and Capricorn, and upon the lunations, of which the former can only be a part, not one acting independently entirely, which form a potentiality that it reduces into actuality according to its own mode.

But neither Ptolemy, nor Cardan in his *Commentary*, have set forth and elucidated this doctrine as is right. For Cardan erred in his *Comment* on Textus 2 when he says[2]: "No one thing can be sig-

---

[1] Ptolemy says (*Tetrabiblos* ii. 1): "And since weaker natures always yield to the stronger, and the particular always falls under the general..." and also (*Tetrabiblos* i. 3) "...for the lesser cause always yields to the greater and stronger..." [Robbins's translations]
[2] Cardan, ibid. pp., 169 col.2 – 170, col .1.

nified generally for the whole Earth; and therefore general constitutions are not given by way of an acting cause, but only by way of the place." That is, no celestial cause can be given that signifies some one thing for the whole Earth, but it will only signify different things by way of the different places. If indeed it is certain from the elements that a conjunction of Saturn and Jupiter viewed by themselves with their own celestial state, does some other thing in respect to the whole Earth, than a conjunction of Saturn and Mars, and both the latter and the former signify some one thing generally for the whole Earth. That is, the latter is the effect or impression from Saturn and Mars conjoined, but the former is the effect from Saturn and Jupiter conjoined.

For from the elements it is also certain that the conjunction of Saturn and Mars is, at the same moment of time, in the individual houses of the figure, not with respect to one place, but with respect to the whole Earth. And for those for whom it is in the 10th, it certainly signifies about the accidents of the 10th; for those for whom it is in the 8th, it signifies about the accidents of the 8th; for those for whom it is in the 7th, it signifies about the accidents of the 7th; but in each house, it produces effects and makes an impression according to its own force; and that is other than what the conjunction of Saturn and Jupiter would do; therefore, it signifies some one thing for the whole World, but only generally; and the same thing must be said about the Solar Ingress into the beginning of Aries, about an eclipse, or any particular new Moon, etc.; from which it is plain that that universality of celestial cause was not known to Ptolemy nor to Cardan.

Furthermore, such a cause or universal constitution is determined for the whole Earth by the individual places on Earth through its own terrestrial state with respect to each location, which state is pronounced by the celestial figure erected for each place; and from it arises the universal cause with respect to the kingdom, province, city, and country district, which Ptolemy and Cardan admitted; and about which we also must discuss.

Therefore, Ptolemy in Textus 3 and Cardan in his *Commentary*, divide this universal cause into those that are determined to the whole kingdom, the whole province, a single city, and a single country district; and as the country district, the city, the province, and the kingdom are subordinated, just as a part is to the whole, so it is insinuated from that that those universal causes are subordinated. However, neither Cardan nor Ptolemy have said how an inferior [cause] can depend upon a superior one in acting, or how it can determine it, nor how a celestial figure for a whole kingdom should be erected, so that it can be known from it what may be signified for the whole kingdom.

And since Cardan in his Commentary, in Textus 7, has asserted with his customary audacity that after the year 1583 and down to the year 1782 before the middle, a monarchy will begin and everything will be ruled by a single will; and this [prediction] perhaps stimulated the Kings of Spain to their desire for a monarchy, to which they were directly proceeding for a sufficiently long time, and finally under Philip III (1578-1621) they became stationary; and under Philip IV (1605-1655) they turned retrograde, having lost the kingdoms of Catalonia and Lusitania, along with the East Indies and much other wealth; it is certain that for such a monarchy, no figure of any universal constitution could be erected, such as for a new Moon, a Solar Ingress into Aries, or any eclipse.

For if it should be said that it can be erected in a city that is the metropolis or headquarters of a whole monarchy, in which the monarch himself stays, surely since it is by the will of the monarch whatever city of the World he wishes to make his metropolis and in it to fix his residence, it is plain that individual nations would be subject to a universal constitution, not by reason of their terrestrial status or site proper to a [particular] horizon, but [simply] by the will of the monarch, which is entirely alien to the mode of acting of the stars. And this reason is valid not only for monarchy in general, but for any kingdom or empire. For what astrologer would have said that the Philippine Islands would be affected by an eclipse, with its figure erected in Spain, where the Prince who rules those island stays, unless perhaps by accident as will be explained below?

And so, all these universal causes, whether they are of a natural kind found between the Solar Ingress into Aries, and the following new Moon seen only in the *Caelum*, or a local kind that is found between the figure erected for the whole kingdom and a figure erected for any of its cities, it seems to us that it must be defined according to the following rules.

First. No place on the face of the Earth naturally rules another and per se. For in the Terrestrial Globe looked at as itself, the individual parts of its surface are in themselves equal; and having taken one part as A, no valid natural reason can be offered why that one should be subject to part B rather than to part C, or D, E, F, etc., placed around it, or to the closer part L rather than to the more distant part M.

Second. The metropolitan city[1] of a kingdom can be constructed at any place on Earth, as is self-evidently known. Therefore, no place on Earth per se and naturally will depend upon another as the designated metropolitan city.

Third. Any place on earth is naturally affected by the constitution of the *Caelum* through a celestial chart determined for that place on Earth, and not for another place in which the chart of that constitution admits a noticeable diversity of the angles with regard to the degrees, but especially the signs [on the angles]. Otherwise, universal astrology would collapse, if a judgment about the accidents in each place could not be made from a figure erected for that place.

Fourth. No man is naturally subject to another man except his parents, from whom he receives his existence as a man and his life; and this natural liberty still endures amongst the people of the forest. But politically, each man can be subject to another; and thus a

---

[1] By *metropolitan city* Morin evidently means *capitol city*.

servant is subject to his own master, a client to his Prince or King, and a captive Emperor to his conqueror, as was the case with Bajazet[1] and Tamerlane,[2] and it is known for many others.

Fifth. But from these it follows that this country district depends upon some city, and that city depends upon some kingdom; this must not be understood of the *natural dependence* of those same places, but [only] of the *political dependence* of the men inhabiting those places, who are *politically* subordinated to some King or Prince—which is a *dependence by accident*, as mentioned above, and frequently changeable by the accidents of Fortune.

Sixth. The accidents or fates of each place are of two kinds. For some of them are *natural*, such as dispositions of the air, and the plagues, sterilities, and floods that follow from that, then those that pertain to the things signified by the houses per se. But others are *political*, such as laws, edicts, taxes, etc. The fates of the first kind in each place depend primarily and per se on the constitutions or the universal celestial causes by charts erected for that place. But fates of the latter kind depend particularly on the personal nativity and Revolution of the King or Prince or their plenipotentiary minister; but universally by the same universal constitution, according as it is received by the King and his Minister and Council in the place, in which these are found at the moment of that constitution. For that constitution affects individuals according as it is determined with respect to those individuals.

And therefore, individuals act and experience [its effects] according as they receive it, according as by their own nativities and directions they agree or disagree with it. And so if the figure of a universal constitution is erected in the metropolitan city of any province, and it is compared with the figure of that same constitution erected for the place, where the King and his Prime Minister was [at that time], by having consulted the figures of their nativi-

---

[1]Bajazet I Yilderim (1347-1403), Ottoman Sultan, was defeated and taken prisoner by Tamerlane in 1402.
[2]Tamerlane or Timur Lenk (1336?-1405), the great Mongol chieftan.

ties and [current] Revolutions along with their directions, it will be possible to conjecture what will be signified by such a constitution for that same province. Moreover, by the title 'King' is to be understood not only the King himself or the Queen, but the royal primates, amongst whom there is an absolute power of acting, in which case it must refer to those primates rather than to the King or Queen, namely because they will govern everything according to their own free choice and impulse.

Seventh. The native receives the influx of the Solar Ingress into Aries, in the place where he is then found; and that Ingress allots its own effects in that place by reason of its celestial and terrestrial state during that revolution of the Sun. Moreover, the native who receives that kind of influx with both its states in that same place; if he [later] proceeds to another place, he of course carries with him the influx received by him according to both its states; but by traveling he frees himself from that influx of the terrestrial state received in his former place, and he becomes liable to the effects that the same Ingress produces by its own terrestrial state in the places that he traverses, or in which he resides, just as when going through a city in which a plague is raging, or making a stay there, he may be greatly exposed to the plague. And from that it can happen that in the prior place death or illnesses may be signified for the native and in the latter place health and life

Therefore, for the best remedy for the plague, it was said not unhelpfully by the ancients that one should go a long distance away from the place where the plague is raging—namely, beyond the limits of the celestial figure that stirred up the plague in that place, namely where the angles [of the figure] are changed, or the rulers of the constitution signifying the plague, and one must be slow to return for fear of remnants [of it remaining]. And let these things that have been said about the dependence of one place on another by reason of a celestial constitution, and then about the dependence of the native on individual [places], be sufficient.

Consequently, moreover, we should say how the native may be

subject to the universal constitutions of the place in which he is located—whether he would receive [the influence of] that constitution in the place where he is located, or whether he would receive that constitution in the place of his nativity, or where he stays for a time, or in another place from which he has departed. For which, the following rules should be noted.

First. All of the universal causes are [made] powerful by the dignities of the planets, the strength of the rulers, and the state of the universal constitution, namely its celestial and terrestrial state; but some of them are weak. Moreover, they must be compared among themselves and with the particular ones.

Second. The celestial causes that are the most universal and most powerful produce the greater and more powerful and longer lasting effects. And so, the Solar Ingress into the beginning of Aries, then the conjunction of Saturn and Jupiter, are the more universal and produce greater and longer lasting effects than a new Moon and an eclipse, at least other things being equal compared to the strength and debility of conjunctions in turn.

Third. Other things being equal, a universal constitution prevails over a particular one; and a more universal constitution prevails over a less universal one. But a weak universal constitution will not prevail over a strong particular constitution; and a weak universal will not prevail over a strong particular. Therefore, if the Solar Ingress into Aries weakly signified dryness, and a following new Moon strongly signified rains, it will rain in that month. And similarly, if both the Solar Ingress into Aries and the new Moon would have signified a good and healthy condition of the air. Moreover, if a native had in that year and month the signification of a severe illness from his directions, Revolutions of the Sun and the Moon, as well as from transits, which he did not foresee and which he did not resist, he will certainly be ill. And so with the rest [of the indications].

Fourth. Other things being equal, the effects of a constitution on many people, such as that a plague signified by a universal constitution, will kill many people, is more certain than the effect of a particular constitution on one person, such as that a native from his own direction and revolution is going to die. Since it is easier to prevent a single particular effect than [one affecting] many people.

Fifth. Particular constitutions agreeing with a universal constitution will undergo the effect of that universal constitution, whether it is good, or evil—and that entirely or in part, according as they agree strongly or weaker between themselves. And therefore, if in a universal constitution of the *Caelum* while repeating the synods or syzygies of the Sun, the Moon, or a Planet, they may have been similarly disposed as in the figure of the radix or a Revolution of the native, he will certainly be affected by the universal constitution in accordance with its significations.

Sixth. If the significator of illnesses or death in the nativity, or in a Revolution of a native, will be the same as the significator of calamitous illness in a universal constitution, and if there is a concordant direction, he will die in that same year or month. And similarly, if a Planet that is the significator of dignities in a nativity is the same as the ruler of the MC of a universal constitution, and if it should be strong and fortunate in either one [of those charts], that native will get honors or a dignity.

Seventh. In those nativities in which there are the same angles or places of the Lights along with the angles and the places of the Lights in a universal constitution, those nativities are well or evilly affected, according as the universal constitution is good or evil. If the places in the nativity are opposed or in square to the places in the universal constitution, they will be evilly affected, [but] if they are in trine or sextile, they will be well affected.

But if the principal rulers of the nativity, and especially those of the ASC, the Sun, and the Moon, should have a connection by rulership or aspect with the place of the new Moon or full Moon immediately preceding the nativity, or the ruler of its place; and should Saturn and Mars be in the principal angles of the natal figure, or if the Lights should be afflicted, such nativities will be base, unlucky, and monstruous.

But if the degree of the conjunction of the Sun and the Moon immediately preceding the nativity is fortunate in its celestial and terrestrial state in the natal figure, then some notable good will be signified according to the nature of the house of the figure in which that degree was. As, if it was in the 10th, it will signify notable dignities; if in the 7th, great fortune in marriage, etc. If it was unfortunate in its celestial and terrestrial state, it will signify some huge evil—as, if it was in the 8th square Saturn or Mars, a premature or violent death. If it was well disposed in its celestial state, but in a bad house, the native will fall into misfortune [signified] by that house, but he will overcome or evade it, and he will not succumb to it. And that is evident in my case, since I have that degree in the 12th house which is [the house] of illnesses, enemies, and prison. Finally, if it was evilly afflicted in its celestial state in a good house, it will prevent the good things of that house, or it will throw them into confusion.

Eighth. Unfortunate constitutions from which none or few escape are those whose rulers are very powerful for evil and [posited] exactly in the principal angles.

Ninth. If the ruler of the nativity or of the ASC of the native is a benefic and strong and rules the primary point of the constitution or its ruler, he will escape [the effect of] the evil constitution, but especially if that constitution is not very evil, and the native's revolution is also contrary to it. But there is nothing that renders him more safe from a bad universal constitution than when the ruler of the nativity or its ASC is also the ruler of that bad consitution, and especially if it is a benefic; for if it is a malefic, he will be saved at the beginning, but he will perish at the end, especially if the direction and the Revolutions are in agreement.

Tenth. The nativity and the Revolutions of the King are universal causes with respect to his subjects. And therefore, a subject of the court who has a discord with the King's nativity or Revolution, should fear for himself from the [actions of the] King; but he who has a concordance will be made fortunate with him, especially with his own nativity or revolution inclining to good or evil. And what is said about a King or a Prime Minister of a kingdom should also be understood to be said about any Prince.

Chapter 15. *The General and Particular Significations of Comets.*

Among the new phenomena of the *Caelum*, there is none that disturbs the minds of men so much as a Comet, which by almost everyone is thought to be some threatening scourge of God, and a portent of some imminent huge evil on the Earth, whence this [verse] of Claudian[1]:

"And never is a Comet seen in the sky with impunity."

Moreover, Ptolemy says a few little things about Comets in *Tetrabiblos*, ii. 9, on which Cardan commented diffusely; then in Aphorism 100 of the *Centiloquy*,[2] of which Ptolemy is however not the author, as I have proved in my *Astrological Notes* on the *Commentary*[3] on that same *Centiloquy* published by Lord de Villennes.[4] But from those things that have been handed down by Ptolemy and others, selecting those that are more conformable to

---

[1] Claudian (c.370-c.404), Roman poet.

[2] See now James Herschel Holden, *Five Medieval Astrologers* (Tempe, Az.: A.F.A., Inc., 2008), where the latter part of Ptolemy's Aphorism 100 reads as follows, "And the comets, whose stand is in the eleventh sign from the Sun, if they appear in an angle of some kingdom, that king or some great man of the kingdom will die; but if they appear in a succedent house of it, the things of the treasuries of it will have good, and it will change the government of it; but if they appear in the cadents, they produce sick people and sudden deaths; and if they move from the west to the east, some other enemy will attack those regions; but if it does not move, the enemy will be indigenous."

[3] *Remarques astrologiques de Iean Baptiste Morin...svr Le Commentaire du CENTILOQVE de PTOLOMEE...* (Paris: Pierre Menard, 1657)

[4] Nicolas de Bourdin, Marquess of Villennes (17th century), *LE CENTILOGVE DE PTOLOMEE* (Paris: Cardin Besongne, 1651)

the principles and the truth of astrology, and repudiating the rest, the following presages about Comets may be noted:

First. What is the nature of a comet; for since comets are the offspring of the Planets in the Ether,[1] and they are therefore said to be pseudo-planets; therefore, in its effects a Comet will principally emulate the nature of that Planet whose color it resembles. And therefore, the one that appears dark is of the nature of Saturn; the one that is very white is of the nature of Jupiter; the one that is very red is of the nature of Mars; the one that is yellow is of the nature of Venus; the one that is variegated is of the nature of Mercury; the one that is pale white is of a Lunar nature; the one that is brilliant is of a Solar nature; and each one according to its own nature produces various changes on sublunar things, and thus the kinds of its future effects may be foreseen.

Second. The greater, longer-lasting, and brighter a Comet will be, the greater, longer-lasting, and more conspicuous effects it will produce. And the same thing must be said about its tail, the longer it is. And contrary things are signified by the contraries.

Third. The swifter a Comet is in its own motion, the quicker and more rapidly will it give forth its effects.

Fourth. Comets retrograding into a preceding sign by their own motion portend huge changes of kingdoms and religions, and a great deprivation of all natural order in those. But when direct, changes that are more conformable to Nature and to reason.

Fifth. During a Comet's own apparition, any Planet or notable fixed star that it is continually pointing to with the end of its tail, portends that that Planet or fixed star will be the principal cause of the future effects.

Sixth. A Comet during its own motion passing from one sign into another is always under the rulership of the Planet in whose

---

[193] In Morin's day, comets were thought by some to be generated by the Planets.

domicile it is, and it acts with its nature and state, especially if it is connected to it by body or by a strong ray.

Seventh. A Comet acts with the strong aspects that it receives from the Planets, especially in its rising, as did the Comet observed by Haly Rodoan.[1]

Eighth. A comet acts strongly on those places on Earth which it is directly above. And therefore, the wider the zone of the *Caelum* that it passes through from south to north, the greater the portion of the Earth lying under that zone that it will affect with great changes. From which the reason is evident why the great and terrible Comet of 1618,[2] which began with a southern declination of 17 degrees and left off in a northern declination of 80 degrees, with a retrograde motion and a long tail, principally portended the invasion of the Chinese empire by the Tartars[3]; for the whole of China suffered from that region or zone of the *Caelum*. I say *principally*, for even though through the whole circumference of the Earth subject to that zone it made great changes; nevertheless, the invasion of China by the Tartars with the horrendous massacre of men was the principal effect of it, having begun at the time that the Comet appeared.

Ninth. The presages of comets selected in their appearance and progress taken from the nature of the signs, according as they are

---

[1] Haly Rodoan or Haly Abenrudian was ʿAlî ibn Riḍwân (988-1061 or 1067), an Egyptian astrologer, who was the author of *Tractatus de cometarum significationibus per xii signa zodiaci* 'A Treatise on the Significations of Comets in the 12 Signs of the Zodiac' (Nürnberg, 1563). The comet in question was observed in 1006; Haly's chart of its appearance (set for the lunation of 30 Apr 1006) is given by Cardan, *Commentary*, p. 213.

[2] There were two comets in the year 1618. Morin refers to the second one, now known as Comet 1618 II. According to calculations made from the orbit in Brian G. Marsden's *Catalogue of Cometary Orbits* (Hillside, N.J.: Enslow Publishers, 1983), its Declination was 17° South on or about 25 November, and its motion was retrograde. Thereafter, the Declination rapidly increased in the northerly direction, reaching 75° North on or about 22 January 1619.

[3] Morin apparently refers to the invasion of Chinese territory in 1618 by the Manchu under Nurhaci (1559-1626), who began the overthrow of the Ming Dynasty, which was completed by his successors with the establishment of the Ch'ing Dynasty in 1644.

commonly said to be human, wild beasts, bicorporeal, etc.; then from the forms of the constellations Aries (Ram), Taurus (Bull), Pisces (Fishes), Serpentarius (Serpent-holder), Delphinus (Dolphin), Hydra (Water-snake), etc. are groundless and only founded upon fables and fictions, but not presages taken from the proper natures of the fixed stars and constellations.

Tenth. Judgment must be made of a Comet in any particular sign as of a Planet analogous by nature to it in that same sign.

Eleventh. Comets oriental to the Sun are said to produce their own effects more quickly than those that are occidental to the Sun.

Twelfth. Regions of the World from which Comets begin to emerge and move must be noted. For the place from which a Comet emerges indicates that something evil will be produced from there, and that it will affect places to which that Comet moves by its own motion, namely to the east, west, north. or south.

And these things said about the general effects of Comets, traced through the whole World which they traverse, should be sufficient.

But in their types, in so far as they are considered in celestial charts, a two-fold observation occurs. The **First** is with regard to general charts, namely the Annual Revolution of the Sun and the lunations, either with or without an eclipse. for it is said in the last Aphorism of the *Centiloquy* that it must be observed whether Comets oriental to the Sun within the distance of one sign appear in the angles, or in the succedent places, or in the cadents, which must be understood to refer to the figure of the Annual Revolution of the Sun or the synod of the Moon that immediately precedes the appearance of the Comet, as I have explained in my *Astrological Notes*,[1] in which the true doctrine of the whole *Centiloquy* is handed down.

---

[1] His *Remarques astrologiques*, mentioned in a previous note, contains an extensive commentary on all 100 Aphorisms of the *Centiloquy*.

And it will have to be judged from that about the effects of a particular Comet in the region to which that figure pertains; certainly, considering the house of the figure in which the comet falls in its appearance, and its determination, and its connection with the rulers of that figure, noting also its transits through the principal places of the figure, and then its celestial state.

The **Second** is with regard to natal horoscopes. For similarly, it must be observed in what house of the figure the appearing Comet falls, and then what is its celestial state. For if it is badly disposed, and it has fallen into the 1st house, by being especially for life, with an unlucky radical direction and a similar Revolution of the Sun or the Moon, death will have to be feared. If it is well disposed and it falls into the 10th, it will be lucky for undertakings and dignities with a current radical direction, and a similar revolution of the Sun or the Moon, it will also signify something great in undertakings and honors; and so with the rest [of the houses].

But those ones who are born at the time of the appearance of a comet are very powerfully affected by it, according to the determination of that Comet and the celestial state of the Comet; and for them, something great is signified if the Comet is in the ASC or the MC of the natal figure. But those who are born after the appearance of the Comet are not otherwise affected by it except as the Comet pertains to the lunation that immediately preceded the nativity, if it had appeared during the lunation.

Whoever wants to see more things about Comets that are less true, indeed alien to reason, may read the ample collections of Junctinus on this subject.[1]

Chapter 16. *How the Daily Effects of the Stars on these Sublunar Things should be Predicted.*

The daily effects of the stars on these sublunar things depend on the universal constitutions, which have been sufficiently discussed

---

[1] Namely in Junctinus's famous *Speculum Astronomiae* 'Mirror of Astrology' (Lyons: Symphorien Beraud, 1583. 2nd ed.).

previously. For if a universal constitution of the year and the month presages rain, the daily constitution of the *Caelum* presaging rain (such as an application of the Moon to Saturn) will give rain, but not however if the universal constitution has signified dryness. Moreover, there are effects of the universal constitutions in at least seven different ways—namely, heat or cold, dryness or humidity, wind or calm, lightning flashes, thunder, lightning, fertility or sterility, sickness or health, and peace or war; of which, individual instances are signified by their own genuine causes that are powerful in those universal constitutions, as was said above. And 6 ways are given for predicting the daily effects of the stars on these sublunar things, which must be called a daily or particular constitution, and which will now be discussed individually.

First. By the doctrine of Offusius, the imperfection of which we disclosed in Section II, Chapter 1. Add that, by it only hot and cold can be predicted, then dryness and humidity in the air; for the Sun above the horizon anywhere or any time heats; but [it cannot predict] winds, thunder, lightning flashes, storms, and such like, or what is going to happen presently; and in this [method] no account is taken of the elemental nature of the signs.

Second. It is by Kepler's doctrine, which tries to provide a reason for all meteorology by the syzygies of the Planets, viewed simply and unrestrictedly, which is rightly rejected by us in that same Section II, Chapter 1, on account of the reasons set forth there.

Third. It is by the directions of the Lights or the angles in a universal constitution, or of the Planets ruling that constitution, to conformable promissors, which are those same Planets and their aspects, or powerful fixed stars that are in that constitution. For if the Sun in an Annual Constitution or the Moon in a monthly one, are directed to Saturn ruler of the constitution, which is retrograde in a humid sign; and the quarter of the year is especially spring or winter, rains will happen from such a direction, especially if the universal constitution and especially if the monthly one has signified rains.

But if at the same time directions differing in virtue occur, judgment will have to be made from the more effective one, taking into account the quarter of the year, and the place, and the monthly constitution. And for each promissor, the nature and the celestial and terrestrial state will have to be looked at, both in the figure of the constitution and on the day of the completed direction. And these things must be observed for each direction.

Fourth. It is by the applications of the Planets, with regard to which no small difficulties occur. For [the task] for us is not about predicting the daily effects for the places on Earth lying hid under our horizon, but only for those that pertain to our horizon, for which the figures of the universal constitutions are erected. But now, when one Planet applies to another, both can be above the horizon or both below, or one above and the other below, or one or both on the horizon. If they are both above the horizon or on the horizon, there is no doubt that that application would be very powerful in the place of the figure; if only one, it will be of moderate virtue; but if both should be below the Earth, there will either be no or little virtue in that place. And this will be especially apparent in the *Opening of the Gates*.[1]

Moreover, this reason seems to me to be because since the daily changes of the air are very powerful elementals, and they therefore principally depend upon the elemental qualities of the stars, it is especially found that to produce those things, the stars themselves should be above the horizon, or at least both of them should not be below the Earth, as is plain from the Sun, which in our air does not pour on its heat when is located below the Earth. But I have seen nothing about this shown by the ancients; and therefore the experiences of their successors may be trusted.

Another minor difficulty occurs. For although Kepler by *syzygies* only understood them to be partile, as is plain from the daily effects that he attributes to a partile syzygy of Saturn and Ju-

---

[1] That is, in the case of a very heavy deluge.

piter or Mars. Nevertheless, it is certain and accepted by astrologers that every total syzygy comprises three principal moments of time—namely, the application, properly said, when the swifter Planet by its own orb of virtue touches the center of the slower Planet; the partile syzygy; and the separation, when the swifter Planet departs by the virtue of its own orb from the center of the slower Planet.

And when astrologers speak of the effects of those stars from their applications, they do not exclude the partile syzygy and the separation. But now the *center* is that which the total syzygies of Saturn and Jupiter may last through several months; those of Jupiter and Mars for more than a month; but the total syzygies of the Sun, Venus, and Mercury with Saturn, Jupiter, and Mars among themselves may last for several days. Therefore, from these individually and looked at simply, one cannot make a daily prognosis for the constitutions of the air for any particular place on earth.

However, the Moon, on account of her swift motion of course in rousing up daily storms through her syzygies with the Planets, is the most appropriate and the most powerful; but because during the total [time] of her syzygy, she goes around the whole circumference of the Earth, therefore from her total syzygy, looked at individually, one cannot predict even the daily effects in any particular place on earth, although astrologers acknowledge that the effects occur from an application properly said, occasionally from a partile syzygy, and never from a separation.

And although it squares with reason that they should be from the first application, when the sublunar disposition is mature, from the partile syzygy, when it is still incomplete, and from the separation when it is more incomplete, either by reason of the place, or by reason of the quarter of the year (which maturity or incompletion is not known to us sufficiently for prediction).

However, it is certain that in the same place on Earth, and in the same quarter of the year, it does not rain as many times as the

Moon applies to or is partilely joined to Saturn in a humid sign, or separates from him. And consequently, there is still something required, either on the part of Saturn, or on the part of the Moon, or on the part of both; namely, that they may be powers in the preceding universal constitution, that they are at least not both below the Earth, and that they are posited in a conformable place with respect to the horizon, namely in the ASC, MC, or DSC, or with fixed stars conformable to the effect.

And if all of this should have occurred (which Kepler never thought about), the Planets would act, even at their first application, on the air and the Terrestrial Globe, and not here in themselves, as Kepler dreamed; or they would act at a partile syzygy, or in their separation, according as at whichever moments the Planets and the fixed stars were disposed more concordantly to the horizon. And, by the common consensus of astrologers, the effects will be especially in accord with the nature of the Planet to which the Moon applies, and its state. And from other applications of the Planets, it will have to be predicted similarly.

About which, there are many more Aphorisms in the old astrologers referring to this rule—that the stars produce their own effects, not promiscuously, but according to certain laws. Moreover, how the planets through the mixture of their rays produce, rains, winds, calms, heat, cold, storms, etc. is very difficult to define. For it is not, as by the collision of two stones the sparks of fire are cast out; and so, by the coming together of two Planets, conspicuous meteors are cast out into the air; but the elemental mixed qualities rising up are producers of those meteors.[1]

The **Fifth** motion is through the rising and setting of the stars or constellations, which is two-fold, namely absolutely and respectively. The absolute rising is the ascension of a Planet or a star above the horizon without respect to anything. But the respective [motion] of that Planet is by the common consensus of astrologers

---

[1] In Morin's time meteors, like comets, were thought by some to be generated by the Planets.

either the ascension of the star above the horizon with respect to something else, that is the Sun. And the same thing must be said about the setting.

Furthermore, a star rises respectively to the Sun, or it sets in two ways, namely *truly* and *apparently*. The *true* rising and setting is with both the Sun and the star rising or setting at the same time located on the horizon. And such a rising and setting are again two-fold, that is either with the Sun or in its opposition. A star rising with the Sun rising is said to be *matutine* or arising *cosmically*, and one setting with the Sun setting is said to be *vespertine* or setting *acronychally*.[1] But one rising when the Sun is setting is called *vespertine* or rising *acronychally*.

Similarly, an apparent rising or setting (which is also commonly called *heliacal*) is two-fold, [meaning] of course, a little before Sun rise and a little after Sun set; and both of these again are two-fold, namely *matutine rising* and *vespertine rising*.

Matutine rising is heliacal, when the star before the rising of the Sun, at first not visible, first comes into sight through the elongation of the Sun from a star that is slower or retrograde; it is appropriate for the fixed stars and all the Planets, except the Moon. But the vespertine rising is heliacal, when the star after the setting of the Sun at first not visible, first comes into sight through its elongation from the slower Sun; and this is appropriate only for Venus and Mercury, and especially for the Moon.

The matutine setting is heliacal, when the star seen in the morning before Sun rise, first disappears through its approach to the Sun. And this is appropriate for Venus, Mercury, and especially for the Moon, which by their own motion are faster than the Sun. And fi-

---

[1] The words *matutine* and *vespertine* here mean *morning star* and *evening star* respectively, referring to the appearance of a star before the Sun rises or after the Sun sets. The Greek word *acronychal* (lit. 'point of night') refers to something that is sighted when the Sun touches the western horizon and then sinks below it. An *acronychal rising* is a star that is opposed to the Sun, so that it rises as the Sun sets. Astronomers would call this *in opposition*.

nally, the vespertine setting is heliacal, when the star, first seen in the evening after the setting of the Sun, first disappears through the approach of the Sun to a slower or retrograde star; and this is appropriate for the fixed stars and all the Planets, except the Moon.

From these previous statements, it must be known that the above said risings and settings of both the Planets and the fixed stars are powerful for arousing daily changes in the air, but especially the vespertine risings and settings, both the true and the apparent ones; and then especially when those stars have some rulership in the preceding universal constitution. For they do not change the air through the whole circumference of the Earth, although through the whole circumference they are rising and setting. And among those stars or constellations that are thought to be stormy, the famous ones are Arcturus, Orion, the Pleiades, the Hyades, the Eye of Taurus,[1] Praesepe, the Aselli,[2] Lucida,[3] Librae, the Heart of Scorpio,[4] the Heart and Tail of Leo,[5] Canis Major and Minor,[6] Castor & Pollux, The Head of Hercules,[7] Aquila, Delphinus, and many others; concerning which, consult the astrologers and experience. For one must not entirely trust the writings of the astrologers, nor their tables of the rising and setting of the fixed stars, both because some are accommodated to the Julian calendar, others to the Gregorian calendar; and then because error is also discovered in them with regard to the true rising or setting with respect to the Sun; and this from some supporters of astrology can hardly be noticed.

And therefore, it will be safer to look at the risings and settings of the fixed stars on a celestial globe, and then to inquire about

---

[1] Aldebaran or α Tauri.
[2] The little stars λ and 6 Cancri, which are usually called Aselli or the Little Asses.
[3] Lucida means 'the bright one'. Probably, Schedir or αá Cassiopeiae.
[4] Antares or α Scorpii.
[5] Regulus or α Leonis and Denebola or β Leonis.
[6] Sirius or α Canis Majoris and Procyon or α Canis Minoris.
[7] Ras Algethi or α Herculis.

their presages; or, look at them in Origanus, Part 3, Chapter 6, or in the *Dianoia Astrologica* of Wolfgang Satler,[1] Chapters 28 & 29, or in [the books of] others who have written about these.[2] For to discuss and expound them here would be too tiresome; and it is sufficient for us to show a natural way, to set forth general rules, to solve difficulties, and to warn about avoiding errors. Those things that seem to be lacking here, we shall perhaps supply in our *Predictive Astrology*, if God the Best and Greatest bestows [a longer] life [on us].[3]

But it must be noted that the true risings and settings of the fixed stars must not only be noted with respect to the Sun or the Moon, but also the other Planets, and also those claiming for themselves the rulership of a universal constitution. For those risings and settings are scarcely less important in strength than the respective risings and settings of the Lights.

And finally, the **Sixth** way is through the phenomena seen in the *Caelum*, the air, the water, or on Earth, which is the common astrology of farmers and native people. For from those close and perceptible causes impending in the air, they are accustomed to predict changes in a marvelous fashion, and from those to look after themselves and their property if they need to, and if it can be done, lest in this matter they should seem to be of a worse condition than a brute animal.

Incidentally, Ptolemy speaks of this in the last chapter of [*Tetrabiblos*], Book 2, but the most fully and best of all, Mizauld[1]

---

[1] The reference is to the *Dianoia Astrologica...* 'Astrological Thought...' (Montisbelgardi, 1605) of Wolfgang Satler of Basel, Switzerland. See Lynn Thorndike, *History of Magic and Experimental Science* (New York: Columbia University Press, 1923-1958. 8 vols.), vol. 6, pp. 143-144.

[2] A modern work is *Mundane Tables of Fixed Stars in Astrology* by Perceval and Fox (Blackwood terrace, N.J.: Quick Specs, 1980).

[3] Alas, that did not happen. Morin refers to his intention to write a book specifically dedicated to making predictions using the methods that he explained in the *Astrologia Gallica*. But he died not long after making his final revisions to the AG, which was published five years after his death through the generosity of Queen Marie Louise of Poland (1611-1667), a grateful former client.

in his *Aeromantia* or *Astrologia Meteorologica*, which [you should] open up and learn through experience. For this knowledge is not only very useful on land and sea for agriculture, seamanship, medicine, hunting, military matters, etc., but it also affords notable honor to one skilled in its practice. And whoever has excelled in it and has lived at court, in addition to admiration, will also procure the favor of Kings and Princes for himself. Especially if he possesses the practical knowledge of the 3rd, 4th, and 5th ways, which embraces the knowledge of universal constitutions. But all of these things previously said are sufficient for the theory of astrology, and for the honor and glory of the Omnipotent Creator of Heaven and Earth, for Whom let there be praise and the giving of thanks eternally.

Amen.

End of the Twenty-Fifth Book.

---

[1] Antoine Mizauld (1510?-1578) was a very prolific author. I am uncertain which of his books Morin refers to—possibly to his *Le Mireur de l'air . . . de touts changements de temps* 'The Mirror of the Air . . . of all the Changes in the Weather' (Paris: R. & C. Chaudière, 1547. 94 ff. 8vo.).

Appendix I.
The Method of Offusius as Revised by Morin.[1]

This method, of which Morin speaks on several occasions, permits one to determine some coefficients for each planet, expressing numerically at a given moment, the acting force of the constituent elements of that planet. Offusius puts first, for each planet, two coefficients corresponding to the power of its elements when it is found on the horizon and at its minimum distance from the earth (at its perigee).

	Hot	Cold	Dry	Humid
SUN	24		48	
MARS	1		12	
SATURN		96	12	
JUPITER	1.5			6
VENUS	1.5			6
MERCURY		6	12	
MOON		12		121
	27	114	84	133

To know the value of these coefficients at a particular instant, it is necessary to multiply the figures from the tables:

1. By the cube or the square of the ratio of the apparent actual diameter of the star to its apparent diameter at perigee (cube for the hot, square for the other three elements).

2. By the cube or the square of a coefficient depending upon the altitude of the planet above the horizon,[2] cube for the hot, square for the other elements. This coefficient is given by the formula

$1 + N / 30$, where N represents the planet's altitude in degrees above the horizon.

---
[1] Translated from Jean Hieroz, *L'Astrologie mondiale* (Paris: Éditions Leymarie, 1946), pp. 163-165.
[2] Do not forget that the elementary action is zero below the horizon.

3. By the cube or the square of a coefficient (cube for the hot, square for the others) depending upon the number of hours elapsed since the rising of the star. This coefficient is given by the formula

$1 + N / 8$, where N represents the number of hours.

Thus, for the Moon's humidity at its perigee at 65 degrees above the horizon and having risen seven hours previously, one must multiply 121, the figure from the table, by 1 for its distance to the Earth, by the square of $1 + 65 / 30$, that is by 10, for the altitude, and by the square of $1 + 2$, that is 9, for the time elapsed since its rising; then one has:

$$121 \times 1 \times 10 \times 9 = 10980$$

Morin does not accept either the initial coefficients or those of the variation. He proposes the following method:

With the thermometer, one will measure exactly, during four or five hours, the increase of heat due of the Sun, the hourly increases being noted, and that on some sphere, but especially on the right sphere,[1] the day of the Equinox; this observation will serve as a base for the oblique and parallel spheres, as is said further along.

As for the influence of the altitude of the Sun at the time elapsed since its rising and of the length of its diurnal arc, one will note that two observations being made, either in places of the same latitude or in places of different latitudes, if the altitudes and the times elapsed are the same, the diurnal arcs are identical; if the altitudes are the same, but the times elapsed (or the reverse), the diurnal arcs are different; finally, if the diurnal arcs are identical and the elapsed times are different, the altitudes are different, because if two of these elements have not varied, the third must remain identical.

---

[1] One calls the *right sphere* the sphere that is local to the Equator; the *parallel sphere*, the sphere local at the Pole; and finally, the *oblique sphere*, the sphere that is local to a particular latitude.

That much said, one will observe at the Equator on the day of the equinox, from the first to the third hour after its rising; the first altitude will be 15 degrees and the second 45 degrees, and as the diurnal arc is the same for the two observations, the differences of heat can only come from the altitude and from the time elapsed. If the productions of heat were proportional to the altitude and to the time, they would be in the ratio of 15° in an hour, that is 15° in the first case and at 45° in three hours, that is 135° in the second case. Consequently, if the increase registered by the thermometer had been in the first case 2/3 of a degree, it must be (2/3) X (135/15), that is 6 degrees in the second case, which is effectively registered by the thermometer. Likewise, the increase for 90 degrees of altitude in six hours would have to be 24 degrees.

If on different spheres one has at the same instant the same altitude of the Sun, it is certain that the elapsed times and the diurnal arcs differ. One will note that these proportions of heat will be presented just as the ratio of the time elapsed to the diurnal arc of a sphere relative to the same ratio of the other sphere is presented. Thus, if the Sun is elevated by 15° on the right sphere and on the parallel sphere, the elapsed time will be one hour for a semi-arc of six hours on the right sphere, and consequently the ratio between the time elapsed and the semi-arc will be 1/6. On the parallel sphere, the time elapsed will be forty-one days for a semi-arc of 93 days, and the ratio envisaged will be 41/93. If the increase of heat on the right sphere has been 2/3 of a degree, it will be on the parallel sphere:

$$(2/3) \times (6/1) \times (41/93) = 1° \, 71/93$$

If one supposes the Sun to be elevated on the two spheres by 23°30' (which is the maximum on the parallel sphere), the elapsed time on the right sphere will be 1:34, and as the semi-arc is, as we have already said, 6 hours, the ratio will be 47/180; on the parallel sphere, the time elapsed will be 93 days for a semi-arc of the same value; the ratio there will then be 1. If the elevation of the heat has been on the right sphere at 122/75 degrees, it will be on the parallel sphere

(122/75) X (180/47) X 1 or 6° 162/705

The elevation is then definitely more elevated at the Pole than at the Equator, but not exorbitantly, in view of the difference in the elapsed times, and it does not seem contrary to experience.

If one had considered the method recommended by Offusius, the increase of the parallel sphere would have been more than 2,000 degrees for the same elevation of 122/75 degrees at the Equator, which is absolutely contrary to material possibilities.

What we have said about the heat of the Sun can be applied to the cold of the Moon and Saturn, to the dryness and the humidity, by utilizing the following table of the elementary qualities of the planets as proposed by Morin:

	Hot	Cold	Dry	Humid
SUN	5.5		2	
MOON		5		6
SATURN		3.5	3	
JUPITER	1.5		1	
MARS	2.5		3	
VENUS	0.5			4
MERCURY		1.5	1	
	10	10	10	10

Appendix II.
World War II Charts drawn by Jean Hieroz[1]

Astrologers have often been criticized for not having known how to announce the war of 1939 in advance; but is the insufficiency of their science the only cause of this? Personally, having wanted to predict in July 1938 the mobilization of some classes [of the military], which took place the next month, the management of *L'Avenir du Plateau Central* (in which, at that time, I was publishing my monthly predictions) refused my article under the pretext that it was likely to provoke panic. I was asked (very simply) to change my predictions. This request, which I of course refused, brought about the end of my collaboration with that periodical. I must admit that, when the fact was accomplished, *L'Avenir* made honorable amends and inserted the rejected article preceded by an explanatory caption;[2] however, the Editor-in-chief was careful to request of me the resumption of my collaboration. And here are the reasons that, to my great regret, restrained me from making known to the public the analysis that was going to appear in the *Constitutions du Ciel* of 1939. All of its merit, moreover, must go back to the Master whose methods I utilize and not to myself, his modest disciple:

> The entry of the Sun into Aries (Fig. 8)[3] occurs at Paris the 21st of March at 12:29; that which puts the MC at 8 Aries and the ASC at 0 degrees of Leo. Mars, ruler of the Primordial Point [P.P.], is exalted in Capricorn; its ruler, Saturn, is situated in Aries, that is to say in mutual reception by sign rulership with Mars. Such a case was for-

---
[1]Translated from Jean Hieroz, *L'Astrologie mondiale* (Paris: Éditions Leymarie, 1946), pp. 166-170.
[2]In the issue of 16 November 1938.
[3]Translator's Note. The following charts are drawn in a French style that puts the cuspal numbers inside the wheel and the positions of the planets outside the wheel.

mally foreseen by Morin (the 4th paragraph of Chapter 3, Section II). [Thus,] Saturn and Mars share the rulership of the Primordial Point. Since Mars is also the ruler of the MC, the following angle, to which Saturn is conjoined, it is obvious that the rulership of the year is divided between the two malefics. Moreover, that would be very inauspicious, for Saturn is in exile and the ruler of the 7th house, the house of WAR, and Mars is in the 6th in exact square with the Sun. The first aphorism of Chapter 14, Section II, informs us that *the malefic planets dominating at the Primordial Point and badly disposed presage some evils. Those will be still more grave if the said planets occupy or govern the angles of the figure (here, Mars is ruler of the MC, and Saturn conjoins the MC) and extremely grave if they are determined to evil by the places that they occupy or govern, for example if they are in the 4th, 6th, 7th, 8th, or 12th house* (here, Saturn is ruler of the 7th, and Mars is in the 6th). Grave evils being obviously probable, it remains to determine the epoch and if possible the exact date. In order to do that, we are going to consider the subordinate charts according to the 4th aphorism of Chapter 13, Section II, which teaches us that *several simultaneous universal charts, for example a Mundane Revolution of the Sun and a New Moon, produce the greatest effects, especially if the charts have the same ASC or the same ruler of the Primordial Point!*

Precisely, the second quarter of the year, the solar ingress into Cancer (Fig. 9) has its ASC in Leo like the Aries Ingress. Furthermore, in it Mars is also the ruler of the MC and is also found to be governed by Saturn. The latter planet is not only still conjoined to the MC, but this time it is in partile conjunction with it.

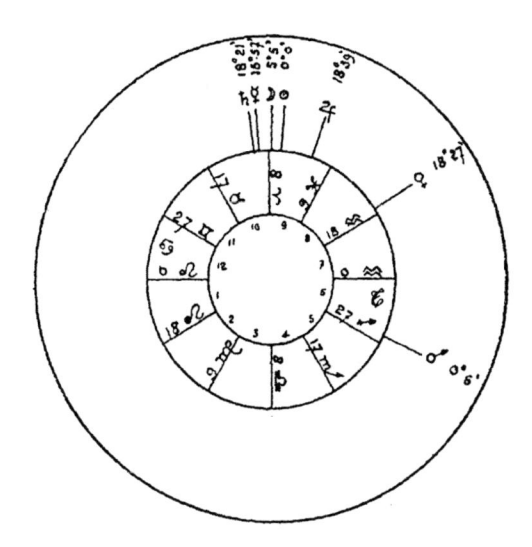

Fig. 8

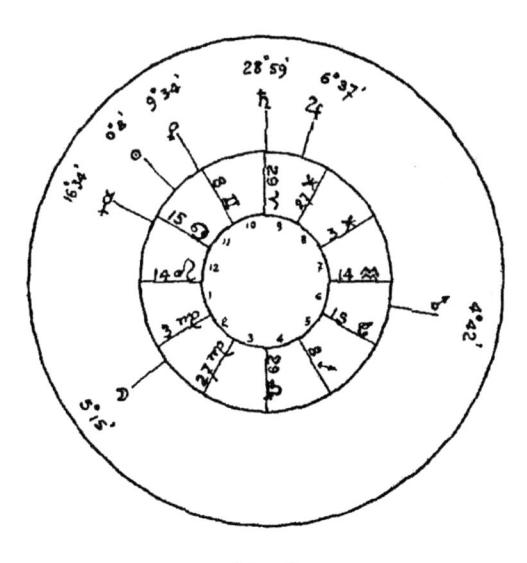

Fig. 9

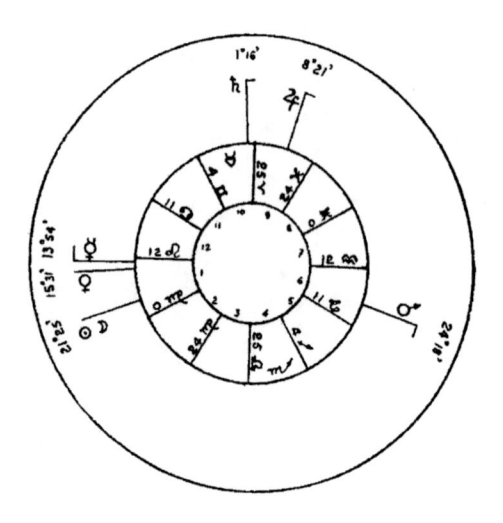

Fig. 10

Precisely also, the lunation of 14 August (Fig. 10) presents the same characteristics: ASC in Leo, Mars in the 6th, ruler of the MC; Saturn in the 10th, ruler of the 7th.

We have, therefore, in 1939 not only two but even three simultaneous charts, all three of which have the same ASC, the same ruler of the MC, the same ruler of the 7th in the MC, and the same malefic in the 6th. *Since the first constitution and the one of superior order realizes its effects powerfully in the posterior and subordinate charts if the latter have some significations similar to [those of] the first* (Aphorism 3, Chapter 13, Section II), it is exceedingly probable that it is in the course of the second quarter, and more exactly in the course of the lunation commencing on the 14th of August, that the first chart, the Aries Ingress, will realize its "extremely grave effects."

Aphorism 3 of Chapter 12 of the first Section indicates to us how to determine more precisely the date of the event by means of directions and transits.

1. By directions. We read there in effect: *They (the effects) are produced by the fact of the directions of the luminaries or of the angles, especially of the ASC, towards some congruent promittors, as well as towards some of the rulers of the universal chart.* In the course of the lunation from the 15th of August to the 13th of September, we were able to calculate three directions of this kind:

MC square Mars on 11 September
Sun opposite Saturn, about the 3rd of September
Moon opposite Saturn about the 8th of September,

2. By transits. We read further in the same aphorism: The effects are born... when the luminaries apply by body or by aspect to the rulers of the charts; and we know on the other hand (Chapter IX, Section I) that *in the syzygies, the swiftest planet is the only one to be examined*; we must then, in the lunation of the 14th of August take note of the transits of the Moon to Mars and Saturn. We find:

Moon conjunct Mars on 26 August at 10:04
Moon conjunct Saturn on 3 September at 12:33

We state definitely that a unique date calls itself to our attention, at the same time by directions and by transits. This date is:

the THIRD OF SEPTEMBER 1939

It is then very probable that it is on this day that the inauspicious effects of this deplorable Ingress of 21 March 1939 will manifest themselves.

Was this study actually written before the outburst of the catastrophe? I would have a good chance of pretending that it was, while protecting myself behind the ostracism of my former editor-in-chief and resting upon the success of my previous prognostications that appeared in the same periodical:

> On 7 December 1937, I announced for the following spring "a government accepted by all the sound elements of the nation." It is known that the

225

Ministry of Édouard Daladier [1884-1970], established on 10 April 1938, was considered by the sound elements as the downfall of the Popular Front.[1]

On 4 March 1938 I announced the fall of the Chautemps[2] cabinet for the 13th or the 27th of the same month. The second Blum cabinet was established on 13 March.

On 2 April I announced the imminent fall of Blum. This happened the 9th of that same month, following an unexpected vote of the Senate.

On 20 July I announced an approaching mobilization of some [military] classes (which occurred on 24 September).[4] Furthermore, I pointed out "the moderating role of Paris and Rome in the Prague-Berlin dispute"[5] (the article, however, only appeared on 16 November).

But I owe it to the truth to acknowledge that although I had clearly noticed, from the beginning of 1939, the similarity of the three charts and announced to all my entourage some grave events for that lunation, [yet] the calculation of the directions and the investigation of the transits fixing the date of 3 September were made after the fact, at the time of the translation of the present book, in order to verify the excellence of Morin's methods.

---

[1]Translator's Note. The socialist government under Premier Léon Blum (1872-1950) which had been voted into office at the general election in the spring of 1936.

[2]Translator's Note. Camille Chautemps (1885-1963).

[3]Translator's Note. Léon Blum's Popular Front government was overthrown by a vote of 214 to 47 in the French Senate. Édouard Daladier (1884-1970) was chosen to replace Blum.

[4]Translator's Note. Billboards were posted throughout France the night of 23/24 September calling up roughly a million reservists to report for active duty in the armed forces.

[5]Translator's Note. This was the demand Hitler made on Czechoslovakia that it yield one of its provinces, the Sudetenland, to Germany.

Appendix 3
World War Charts

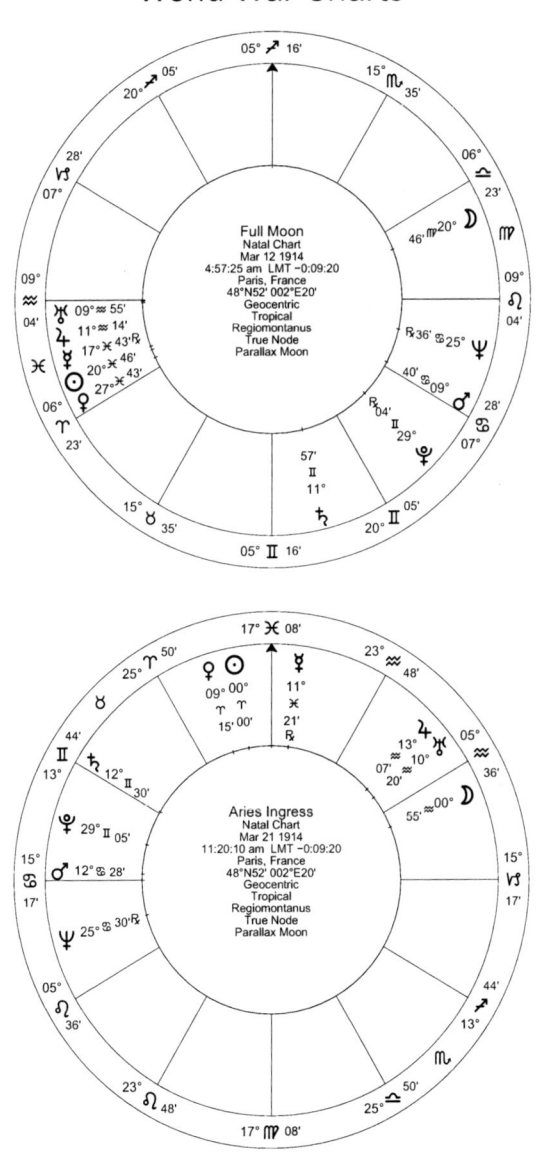

227

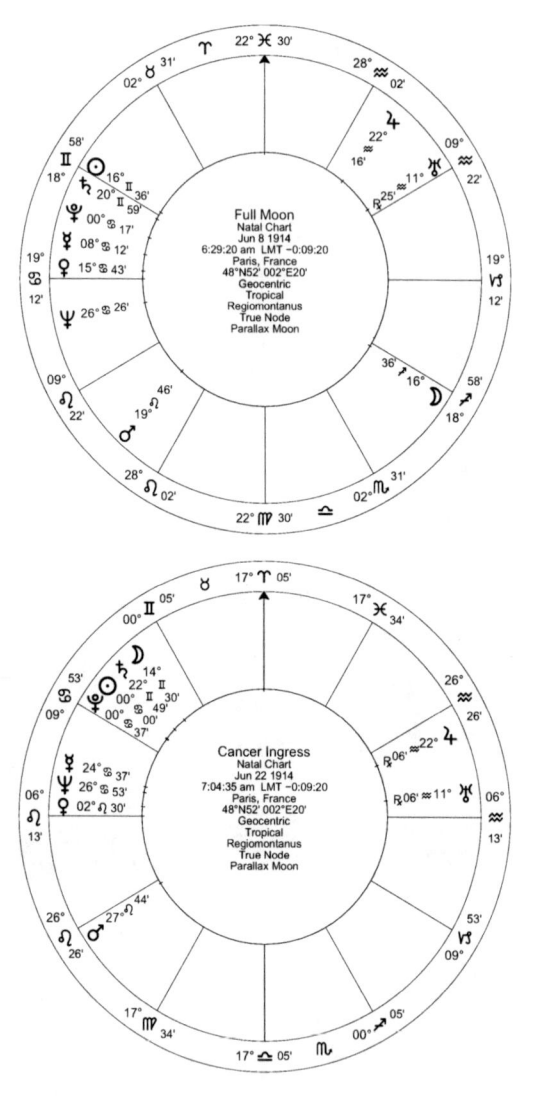

These charts are drawn for Paris, France, 48N52, LMT, with Regiomontanus cusps and the Moon affected by parallax (which Morin recommended but did not use). (The charts for Brussels would be rotated 2 degrees.) The War began with the invasion of Belgium at 8:02 AM on 4 August 1914.

Appendix 4.

The time used in all of the charts in AG Book 25 is Local Apparent Time (LAT). To assist the reader who may want to recalculate some of the charts, I have prepared a table of the Equation of Time for the year 1625. That year is approximately in the middle of the time period spanned by the charts. The Equation of Time changes slowly from year to year, but the table shown below is sufficiently accurate for dates within 75 years or more before or after 1625.

The argument of the table is the true longitude of the Sun. To find the value of the Equation of Time, locate the solar longitude that is just before the longitude of the Sun and the one just after; these are at 5 degree intervals. Interpolate these two values to get the value for an intermediate longitude. Once found, the Equation of Time can be rounded off to the nearest whole minute.

Table of the Equation of Time for the Year 1625

Sun	Eq.T	Sun	Eq.T	Sun	Eq.T	Sun	Eq.T
0	+7.7	90	+0.9	180	-7.7	270	-0.9
5	+6.1	95	+2.0	185	-9.4	275	+1.6
10	+4.5	100	+3.0	190	-11.0	280	+4.0
15	+2.9	105	+4.0	195	-12.4	285	+6.3
20	+1.4	110	+4.8	200	-13.7	290	+8.4
25	-0.0	115	+5.3	205	-14.7	295	+10.2
30	-1.3	120	+5.6	210	-15.4	300	+11.8
35	-2.3	125	+5.7	215	-15.9	305	+13.1
40	-3.2	130	+5.5	220	-16.1	310	+14.1
45	-3.8	135	+5.0	225	-15.9	315	+14.7
50	-4.2	140	+4.3	230	-15.4	320	+15.0
55	-4.3	145	+3.3	235	-14.5	325	+14.9
60	-4.1	150	+2.1	240	-13.3	330	+14.6
65	-3.7	155	+0.7	245	-11.8	335	+13.9
70	-3.1	160	-0.8	250	-10.0	340	+13.0
75	-2.3	165	-2.5	255	-7.9	345	+11.9
80	-1.3	170	-4.2	260	-5.7	350	+10.6
85	-0.2	175	-5.9	265	-3.3	355	+9.2
90	+0.9	180	-7.7	270	-0.9	360	+7.7

LMT = LAT + Equation of Time
LMT = LAT - Equation of Time

Suppose for example that the Sun in a chart is in 23°19′ of Scorpio. This is equivalent to 233°19′ or 233.3′ to the nearest tenth of a degree. Looking in the table, we find for 230° that the Equation of Time has the value -15.4, and for 235° the value is -14.5. The difference is 0.9 and it is decreasing. We want 3.3/5 or 0.67 of that difference; it will be 0.67 X 0.9 or 0.6., so we subtract that amount from the figure for 230°, and we have -15.4 reduced by 0.6 or -14.8. That is the value in minutes and tenths of a minute. We can round it off, and we will say that the approximate value of the Equation of Time is -15 minutes. Then, if the stated time was 6:05 AM LAT, the equivalent LMT will be 6:05 AM -0:15 or 5:50 AM LMT.

Appendix 5
The Mansions of the Moon for the Year 2000

Table of the Mansions of the Moon.

1	a little dry	3 ♉ 58	15	wet	3 ♏ 58
2	temperate	16 ♉ 49	16	cold & wet	16 ♏ 49
3	wet	29 ♉ 41	17	wet	29 ♏ 41
4	cold & wet	12 ♊ 32	18	dry	12 ♐ 32
5	dry	25 ♊ 24	19	wet	25 ♐ 24
6	temperate	8 ♋ 15	20	temperate	8 ♑ 15
7	wet	21 ♋ 07	21	wet	21 ♑ 07
8	a little wet	3 ♌ 58	22	temperate	3 ♒ 58
9	dry	16 ♌ 49	23	wet	16 ♒ 49
10	wet	29 ♌ 41	24	a little cold	29 ♒ 41
11	a little cold	12 ♍ 32	25	dry	12 ♓ 32
12	wet	25 ♍ 24	26	a little dry	25 ♓ 24
13	temperate	8 ♎ 15	27	wet	8 ♈ 15
14	a little wet	21 ♎ 07	28	temperate	21 ♈ 07

Index of Persons

Achilles, *Homeric hero* 20
Albohazen Haly (ʿAlî ibn abî al-Rijâl), *astrologer* 140
Albumasar (Abû Maʿshar), *astrologer* 14,21n.2,22,155,157
Alexander the Great 20
Al-Kindî, *science writer* 140,155,167
Ancients, 67,69,177,199,209
Arabs 14n.1,19n.1,109,132,140
Aristotle, *philosopher* 8,20,92
Astrologers, xiv,3,5,13,14,18,21n.2,22,24-26,37,43-44,53,55, 57-64,68,84,85,87,90-91,97n.1,104,108-109,112-114,116-117, 127,130-133,137-139,141,145-147,152-157,168-169,175,182, 189,203n.2,210-213,221
Astronomers xiv,5-6,8,30,55,64,97n.2,174n.1,185n.1,212n.1
Bajazet (Bayazid), Sultan of Turkey 198
Baldwin, Richard S., *translator* vii n.3
Blum, Léon, *prime minister* 226
Brahe, Tycho, *astronomer* 30, 34,50-51,53,121,140n.4,152-153
Cardan, Jerome, *astrologer* 4,11,19,25,36,53,57,68-69,71,73, 81-83,85,96-97,99,127,135-167,141,169,170,172,176-178,194-1 96,203,205
Chautemps, Camille, *prime minister* 226
Claudianus, Claudius, *poet* 203n.1
Commanders of armies, 133
Daladier, Édouard, *prime minister* 226
Dukes 137
Emperors 134,198
Eudoxus of Cnidus 174
Firmicus Maternus, Julius, *astrologer* 20,21n.1,132,138n.2, 139n.1

Firminius (Firmin de Bauval), 139
Gassendi, Pierre, *astronomer* 60,121
God 3,8-9,11n.3,75,132,134,141,178,185,203,214
Haly, *astrologer* 19,127,139,168-169,188
Haly Abenragel (ʿAlî ibn abî al-Rigâl) 140,188n.1
Haly Rodoan (ʿAlî ibn Riḍwân) 205
Haly Abenrudian (ʿAlî ibn Riḍwân) 19n.1,188n.1
Holden, James Herschel, *translator* x n.2,15n.1,131n.1,203n.2
Homer, *poet* 20
Kepler, Johann, *astronomer* xiv,5,8,9n.1,30-33,36n.1,51,110-112,140n.4,145,153n.1,175,208-209,211
Kings 9,18,84,128,133-134,187,189,196,207,215
Ignorant astrologers 111
LaBruzza, Anthony Louis, *translator* x n.4
Langsberg (Lansberge, Philip van), *astronomer* 31n.1
Little, Lucy, *translator* x n.1
Llacer, Pepita Sanchis, *translator* x n.4
Magnates 134,160
Marie Louise, Queen of Poland ix
Mason, Zoltan, *astrologer & publisher* x n.1
Ministers 29,198
Morin, Jean Baptiste, *passim*
Offusius, Jean François, *astrologer* 110,112,125-126,208,217-220
Old astrologers, 3,5,14,18,21n.2,22,26,30,37,38,43,53-54,57-59, 68,84-85,87,91,104,109,112-114,117,137-138,141-142,145-146, 152,155,157,169,189
Origanus, David, *mathematician & astrologer* 6,50-51,53,56,63, 132-133,168,174,214
Paris Alexander, Prince of Troy 21n.1
Philip III, King of Spain 196
Philip IV, King of Spain 196

Pontano, Giovanni, *humanist scholar* 132
Popes 134,153n.2
Princes 32,44,70,71,73,75,103,107,108,110,117
Ptolemy, Claudius, *science writer* 4,18,20,25,27,29,34,44,53, 58-59,68-69,73,80-81,83-91,93,96,99,100,112,127,130,131n.1, 132-141,152,,169,172,174,176-178,194-196,203,214
Queens ix,73,108,116n.9
Royer, J., *publisher* 61n.1
Satler, Wolfgang, *writer on astrology* 116
Sauk, Jonas, *publisher* 15n.4
Selva, Henri, *translator* ix n.1
Tamerlane (Timur-i-leng), *Tartar conqueror* 108
Villennes, Nicolas Bourdin, Marquess of, *astrologer* 111

Bibliography

Albohazen Haly (ʿAlî ibn abî al-Rijâl)
De iudiciis astrorum.
[The Judgments of the Stars,
with the Liber novem iudicum at the end]
Basel: Liechtenstein, 1571.

Cardan, Jerome
In Quadripartitum Ptolomei.
[the Quadripartite with Cardan's Commentary]
Basel: , 1578. repr of 1552 ed.
repr. in vol. 5 of the Opera Omnia edition, pp. 93-368, as
Claudii Ptolemaei Pelusiensis Libri Quatuor
De astrorum iudiciis cum expositione Hieronymi Cardani.
Lyons: Huguetan and Ravaud, 1663. 10 vols.
New York and London: Johnson Reprint Corp., 1967. 10 vols.
facsimile reprint

Firmin de Beauval
Repertorium pronosticum de mutatione aeris.
[A Treatise on Changes in the Air]
Paris: Iacobus Kerver, 1539.

Holden, James Herschel
A History of Horoscopic Astrology.
Tempe, Az.: A.F.A., Inc., 1996. paper xv, 359 pp. diagrs
Tempe, Az.: A.F.A., Inc., 2006. 2nd ed. rev. paper xviii, 378 pp. diagrs

Kepler, Johann
Tabulae Rudolphinae...
Ulm: Jonas Sauk, 1627.

Tabulae Rudolphinae…
supputatae a Joanne Baptista Morino…
ad accuratum et facile compendium redactae.
[The Rudolphine Tables…
calculated by Jean Baptise Morin…
and reduced to an accurate and easy compendium]
Paris: J. LeBrun, 1650.

Tables Rudolphines…
trans. into French by Jean Peyroux
with facsimiles of the Latin original
Paris: A. Blanchard, 1986.

Morin, Jean Baptise
Astrologia Gallica.
The Hague: A. Vlacq, 1661. folio

Morin, Jean Baptiste
La Théorie des Déterminations Astrologiques
de Morin De Villefranche.
[Astrologia Gallica, Book 21]
trans. by Henri Selva
Paris: Bodin, 1897.
Paris: Bodin, 1902. repr.
Paris: Éditions Traditionelles, 1976.repr in facsimile
Paris: Éditions Traditionelles, 1991. repr. of the 1976 ed.

Astrosynthesis.
[Astrologia Gallica, Book 21]
trans. from Selva's French version by Lucy Little
New York: Zoltan Mason, 1974. 192 pp.

Astrologia Gallica/Books 13-15 & 19
trans. by James Herschel Holden
Tempe, Az.: A.F.A., Inc., 2007. paper

The Morinus System of Horoscope Interpretation/
Astrologia Gallica, Book Twenty-One.
trans. by Richard S. Baldwin
Washington: A.F.A., Inc., 1974. paper 109 pp.
Tempe, Az.: A.F.A., Inc., 2008. paper repr. viii, 144 pp.

Astrologia Gallica/Book Twenty-Two/Directions.
trans. by James Herschel Holden
Tempe, Az.: A.F.A., Inc., 1994. paper xv, 292 pp. diagrs

Astrologia Gallica/Book Twenty-Three/Revolutions.
trans. by James Herschel Holden
Tempe, Az.: A.F.A., Inc., 2002.
Tempe, Az.: A.F.A., Inc.,2004. 2nd ed. revised paper xi, 112 pp. diagrs

Astrologia Gallica/ Book Twenty-Four/
Progressions and Transits.
trans. by James Herschel Holden
Tempe, Az.: A.F.A., Inc., 2004.

L'astrologie mondiale/ et météorologique/
de Morin de Villefranche.
[The Mundane and Meteorological Astrology
of Morin De Villefranche.]
[Astrologia Gallica, Book 25.]
trans. into French by Jean Hieroz
with a Summary and Appendices
Paris: Les Éditions Leymarie,1946. paper 176 pp. diagrs tables

The Mundane and Meteorological Astrology
of Morin De Villefranche.
[Astrologia Gallica, Book 25, with a Summary
and Appendices by Jean Hieroz]
trans. from the French by James Herschel Holden
(never published) x, 128 pp.

Hieroz, Jean
La doctrine des élections de Morin
[part of Astrologia Gallica, Book 26]
trans. into French by Jean Hieroz
Nice: Les Cahiers Astrologiques, 1941.

Offusius, JoFrancus
De divina astrorum facultate in larvatam astrologiam
'On the divine Power of the Stars against a bewitched Astrology'
Paris: J. Royer, 1570.

Origanus, David
Ephemerides.
Frankfurt on the Oder: Andreas Eichhorn, 1609. 3 vols.

Origen
Peri Archôn 'On First Principles'
trans. by Trannius Rufinus into Latin as
De Principiis 'On the Principles'
trans. into English as 'On the First Principles'
by G. W. Butterworth
New York" Harper & Row, 1966.

Perceval and Fox
Mundane Tables of the Fixed Stars.
Blackwood terrace, N.J.: Quick Specs, 1980. 3rd ed.

Ptolemy, Claudius
Ptolemy's Tetrabiblos/ or Quadrpartite...
trans. by J. M. Ashmand from the Greek
Paraphrase by Proclus
London: W. Foulsham & Co., 1917. repr. xxxiii,242 pp. 8vo.
Ptolemy/ Tetrabiblos. [Loeb Classical Library series]
ed. and trans. by F.E. Robbins
London: William Heinemann, 1940. xxiv,466 pp.

Note: The chapter numbers in the Latin translation[1] of the *Tetrabiblos* used by Jerome Cardan do not always agree with the chapter numbers of the two translations above, nor do either of the latter agree exactly with the latest edition of the Greek text by Wolfgang Hübner, *Claudii Ptolemaei/ Opera quae exstant omnia* Volumen III I ΑΠΟΤΕΛΕΣΜΑΤΙΚΑ (Stuttgart and Leipzig: B.G. Teubner, 1998). If the references given in the present translation of Book 25 do not indicate the appropriate chapter in whichever text the reader is using, he should look at the chapters immediately preceding or following the one mentioned.

Schöner, Johann
Tabulae astronomicae...
[Astronomical Tables...]
Nürnberg: Johann Petreius, 1536.

---

[1] According to F.E. Robbins, it was made by Antonio Gogava directly from the Greek text (presumably that of Camerarius published in 1535) and first published at Louvain in 1543; it was subsequently reprinted several times.

Printed in the United States
128352LV00001B/1-99/P